Tory and Anna

Praying that Th...
you closer together
of us as an elder...
the Lord in leading Terra Nova Troy.

The Power of
PRAYER™
to ENRICH
YOUR
Marriage

STORMIE
OMARTIAN

Grateful to serve alongside you!

Pastor Heidi

H

HARVEST HOUSE PUBLISHERS
EUGENE, OREGON

Unless otherwise indicated, all Scripture quotations are taken from the New King James Version®. Copyright © 1982 by Thomas Nelson, Inc. Used by permission. All rights reserved.

Verses marked NCV are taken from the New Century Version®. Copyright © 2005 by Thomas Nelson, Inc. Used by permission. All rights reserved.

Verses marked NIV are taken from the Holy Bible, New International Version®, NIV®. Copyright © 1973, 1978, 1984, 2011 by Biblica, Inc.® Used by permission. All rights reserved worldwide.

Verses marked MSG are taken from THE MESSAGE, copyright © 1993, 2002, 2018 by Eugene H. Peterson. Used by permission of NavPress. All rights reserved. Represented by Tyndale House Publishers, Inc.

THE POWER OF PRAYER is a trademark of The Hawkins Children's LLC. Harvest House Publishers, Inc., is the exclusive licensee of the trademark THE POWER OF PRAYER.

Cover by Bryce Williamson

Cover photo (c) mikkipat, Boonyachoat / gettyimages

Back cover author photo © Michael Gomez

Interior design by Chad Dougherty

Italics in quoted Scriptures indicates emphasis added by the author.

For bulk, special sales, or ministry purchases, please call 1-800-547-8979. Email: Customerservice@hhpbooks.com

The Power of Prayer™ to Enrich Your Marriage

Previously published as *The Power of Prayer™ to Change Your Marriage*, now with extensive revisions and new material
Copyright © 2007, 2021 by Stormie Omartian
Published by Harvest House Publishers
Eugene, Oregon 97408
www.harvesthousepublishers.com
ISBN 978-0-7369-8241-2 (pbk.)
ISBN 978-0-7369-8242-9 (eBook)

Library of Congress Cataloging-in-Publication Data
    Omartian, Stormie.
    [Praying through the deeper issues of marriage]
    The power of prayer to change your marriage / Stormie Omartian.
        p. cm.
    Originally published: Praying through the deeper issues of marriage. c2007
    ISBN-13: 978-0-7369-2515-0 (pbk.)
    1. Spouses—Religious life. 2. Prayer—Christianity. 3. Marriage—Religious aspects—Christianity. I. Title.
    BV4596.M3O43 2009
    248.8'44—dc22
                                                                      2008017307

All rights reserved. No part of this publication may be reproduced, stored in a retrieval system, or transmitted in any form or by any means—electronic, mechanical, digital, photocopy, recording, or any other—except for brief quotations in printed reviews, without the prior permission of the publisher.

Printed in the United States of America

22 23 24 25 26 27 28 29 / BP-CD / 10 9 8 7 6 5 4 3 2

Contents

With God's power working in us,
God can do much, much more than
anything we can ask or imagine.

EPHESIANS 3:20 NCV

What You Need to Know About the Power of Prayer to Enrich Your Marriage

*R*ecent statistics suggest that soon nearly half of all marriages will end in divorce. Does this mean, then, that every marriage has only a fifty-fifty chance of making it? That can't be right. There must be exceptions to this. I'm sure there are some couples who have never had a problem and their marriage has always been perfect. I have never met any of them, but they must be out there. And surely there are newly married couples for whom the glow has not worn off and reality has not set in, and they have not yet experienced the stresses, losses, and trials of life that can put a strain on any marriage.

Thanks to the thousands of letters, emails, phone calls, and contacts on my website and social media—including the many who have approached me to talk after a speaking engagement or a book signing—countless people have told me about the problems they are facing in their marriages. I kept a record of their stories (not their names), and in this book I included the 14 most common reasons given for their marital problems. I believe in the power of prayer to *affect* these in a life-changing way.

I wrote this book for everyone who is married—or planning to *be* married—and I hope it will be used not only to *prevent* possible struggles from developing into anything serious, but also for praying *through* current struggles to find healing, restoration, and enrichment in your marriage relationship. The good news is that when change is needed in a marriage, the power of God working through us as we pray can change everything—even the problems we face that seem to be insurmountable and unchangeable. Can it be that our prayers could produce *divorce-proof* marriages? It's definitely worth making a consistent and faith-filled effort to pray fervently about them.

The truth is, God has more for us in our marriages than just avoiding divorce. He wants us to be happy and fulfilled in them too. He is not glorified when we are married and miserable. He also has a great purpose for each marriage, but His purpose cannot be fully realized if the people in them are living in strife and discouragement.

You might be surprised if you knew how many people there are who *appear* to have perfect marriages and yet are struggling with serious problems. Even the friends and family around them don't suspect they are having difficulties because of their ability to cover them up and present an amazingly strong front. Many people believe they can gut it out and live with the situation, but too often that proves unbearable. This is especially true as people get older and realize that nothing is changing in their marriage, and they know they can't live as they have been for the rest of their lives.

I am thoroughly convinced that all of these problems could be avoided if we would truly understand what God wants for our marriages and how the enemy of our soul will always try to thwart that. And we can, too often, play right into his hand. But there is a way to hasten the demise of the enemy's plans and see God's plans for our lives and our marriages prevail.

It's called heartfelt prayer.

Of course, you can't change someone's will, but your prayers for your spouse can help him (her) to better hear from God. Whether he (she) chooses to *listen* to the prompting of the Lord to his (her) heart is within that person's will to make the choice.

Nearly every marriage has its challenges. So if your marriage has already been challenged in any number of ways, don't think you are failing. You are normal. The good news is that God has a plan to restore your marriage to the way He intended it to be. And He wants you to partner with Him in order to see that happen. The way you do that is to live close to God and be fervently in prayer every day for your spouse and your marriage.

I know this works because my husband and I have at one time or another struggled with most of these problems ourselves. We have had times of communication breakdown between us that were so bad we didn't speak to each other for days, and then we only spoke what was absolutely necessary and nothing that bordered on real communication for months. We were both so broken by situations in each of our pasts, and my husband's anger and my supersensitive reaction to it nearly caused our marriage to be one of the 50 percent that didn't make it. We've had our times of unforgiveness, and we've both struggled with negative emotions such as depression, anxiety, and fear that permeated the atmosphere of our home.

There have also been seasons when my husband and I were so occupied with raising children that we neglected *us*. We've had times of financial difficulty and disagreements over it. We've experienced a hardening of our hearts toward one another, and occasions when we each felt as though we were very low on the other's priority list. We have actually used the "D" word, threatening to get a divorce, even though neither of us really wanted that. I have personally felt at times that all hope was lost and we needed a miracle. And it was true, because outside of a miracle of God, there was *no hope*.

Actually, it did take a miracle of God to turn things around. I saw God miraculously change our hearts and teach us to move into the wholeness He has for us. But it didn't happen by doing nothing. It happened as a result of consistent *prayer* and *faith* in God to *hear* our prayers and *answer* in *His way* and *His timing*. It happened because of God's grace and His power to do what seemed impossible to us. It happened because in each situation, we chose to give up *our own way* and live *God's way*, according to His Word.

How Your Past Can Affect Your Marriage

The reason I was so sensitive to my husband's anger was because I was raised by a mentally ill mother who was angry about everything.

She was angry because she thought her father—my grandfather—loved her older and younger sisters more than he loved her. She thought this because when she was 11, *her* mother died suddenly and tragically in childbirth and her father wasn't able to care for his three daughters. My mother was sent to live with other family members, and she felt rejected because of it. All this happened during the Depression when times were hard and money was scarce. People were just trying to cope with their own problems and didn't have the time, resources, or knowledge necessary to help a young child cope with hers.

When my mother was 19, she had rheumatic fever, and her mental illness manifested with anger and delusions after that. She became angry at people she thought were following her and trying to kill her. She could seem normal one minute and crazy the next. She was adept at hiding her dark side when she needed to, but she couldn't keep up the facade for long. Her mental instability always came out, usually when someone powerless and vulnerable was alone with her.

My dad told me that when he married her, he thought she was normal. That is, until they were driving to their honeymoon destination and she made him bypass the hotel where they were supposed to stay because she thought people were following her there to kill her. After driving to and fleeing from two more hotels in the same manner, my dad finally put his foot down. Upon arriving at the fourth hotel, he said, "This is enough. We're staying here." He was in love with her, and it seemed as though he was willing to put up with anything to be married to her.

My mother was beautiful. Everyone said she looked like Vivian Leigh in *Gone with the Wind.* I looked like my dad. In fact, when people would say, "Your mother looks like Vivian Leigh and you look like your dad," I felt hurt. I took it to mean that I resembled a guy instead of a girl. Once I became an adult and my friends had daughters who looked like their fathers, I realized it didn't mean that at all. It meant that they—or I should say *we*—looked like a female version of our father. That's not a bad thing. So I suffered over that for years for nothing. Anyway, I inherited my mother's good eyesight and teeth, and for that I am very grateful.

My mother was always angry at my dad because he could never *do* enough, *be* enough, or *give* enough to suit her. And she took all this anger out on him, and then me when he was gone. We lived on an isolated ranch in Wyoming, miles from town and the nearest neighbor. My dad was gone a lot out in the fields rounding up and feeding cattle; mending fences; planting, irrigating, and harvesting crops; and working at a distant logging mill in the off season for extra money. Life on a ranch with no one to help is beyond a full-time job. It is a combination of many hard and burdensome jobs—especially in chilly winters with too many below-zero days.

When he was gone, my mother kept me locked in a small closet underneath the stairs where the basket of laundry was kept. I was safe in the closet from her physical abuse for a while, but other terrors lurked there. It was pitch-black inside except for a tiny ray of light coming from underneath the door. I always sat in the basket and kept my legs pulled up so that any rats or mice claiming this closet as their home would not be able to touch me. I had once discovered a big rattlesnake coiled up in the house, and that memory never left me. My dad killed the snake, but meeting that snake's mother in the closet was always an imminent possibility in my mind. I was terrified.

Once we moved from that ranch I was not locked in the closet anymore, but my mother became more and more physically and verbally abusive. I never knew when she would slap me hard across the face. That was her favorite thing to do, and it seemed to give her joy and satisfaction. I feel now that every time she did it, she was getting even with the mother and father who she felt abandoned her, the family she lived with who she thought didn't want her, and the God who never rescued her from the people she believed were trying to kill her.

By the time I was in my teens I knew she was mentally ill, but I often wondered to myself, *What if she is really telling the truth? What if Frank Sinatra and the pope had actually hired the mob to kill her like she said?* For a while I watched carefully to see if I could identify any of the shadowy figures she said were behind her everywhere she went, but as hard as I tried I never did see even one suspicious thing. When she started using very foul language at the people she thought were watching her through the mirrors and TV, I could no longer even give her the benefit of the doubt. Many times when she was out in public—at the grocery store, for example—she would suddenly turn on some innocent person and verbally attack them, saying loudly that she knew what they were up to, she knew they were following her and trying to kill her, and she was going to report this to the police. When I was with her at those times, I quickly walked the other way and pretended I didn't know her. I didn't dare look at the faces of the people she was attacking to see how they were taking it. I can only imagine their fright as she could become quite scary.

As a result of living with her, I grew up with fear, anxiety, depression, hopelessness, loneliness, and a deep sadness in my heart that never went away. That's because she told me every day how I had ruined her life, and I was worthless and would never amount to anything. As I grew older I never felt as though I were a part of anything or anyone. I needed acceptance and love, and I sought both wherever and however I could find them. Once I left home after high school, I tried everything to get rid of the pain I felt inside. I became involved with Eastern religions and occult practices, always attempting to discover some kind of purpose and meaning for my life. I looked for love in all the wrong faces and became more and more depressed with the failure of each relationship. I worked hard to put myself through college so I wouldn't have any debt because I didn't see how I could ever pay it back.

After my junior year at UCLA, I found great work in television as a singer/dancer/actress. Drugs and alcohol were everywhere, but I only took them when I wasn't working because I was too professional to do anything stupid enough to jeopardize my jobs. However, a few times I took too many drugs trying to numb my emotional pain, and I came dangerously close to accidentally killing myself.

When I was 28, my friend Terry, with whom I had been working on recording sessions and television shows, took me to meet her pastor. He talked to me about Jesus in a way I had never heard before. He told me God had a purpose for my life, but I would never fully realize that purpose outside of receiving Jesus as my Lord. He had the power to change me from the inside out. He gave me three books to take home and read, one of which was the Gospel of John in a small book form. I read them all in the days following our meeting. When Terry took me back to see her pastor again the following week, I received the Lord in his office. That's when I began to sense that God had a plan for my life, and my years of purposelessness finally came to an end.

During a week of recording sessions that Terry had called me to sing on with her, I met a young man named Michael Omartian before I became a believer. A couple years later, we ended up at the same church and dated about a year before we were married. During that dating time I prayed and prayed for God to show me if Michael was the one I should marry, and every time I did that I felt the peace of God assuring me that this was His will. I kept releasing Michael to the Lord, saying, "God, take him out of my life and close the door if we are not to be together." And I would have let him go if God had showed me to do so because I was well aware of how I had ruined my life doing things my own way. I wasn't going to trust *my* judgment now; I wanted only what God wanted. By the time we did get married, I was convinced it was the right thing to do. Because of that certainty, when Michael and I had problems in the years to come, I always remembered the assurance from God that we were supposed to be together. That's why it is important to pray—alone and together—with your future mate before you get married. But if you did not do that, don't worry. God will still work powerfully through your prayers now because He is a redeemer and a healer.

It's Never Too Soon to Pray for Your Marriage

The greatest problem I saw in our marriage was my husband's anger. It was explosive, unpredictable, and always directed at me. Because of my past I was way too sensitive and fragile to take it or deal with it. At first I thought it was all my fault. I thought, *I must be a terrible person to make him so angry at me all the time.* I was trying the best I could, but it wasn't enough. I was already too broken and hurting to be able to stand up to it, or better yet to understand where he was coming from.

After we were married less than a year, I went through major deliverance from fear, depression, and anxiety with the help of a gifted pastor's wife named Mary Anne, who prayed powerfully for me. And that helped in miraculous ways. Also, my husband and I went to Christian marriage counselors, and they showed me that Michael's anger was *his* problem, not mine. In fact, one of the marriage counselors we went to at the time said to me, "Michael would have this anger no matter whom he was married to. If he had married someone else, he would have directed his anger at her."

That knowledge helped me to not feel like a failure, but I still couldn't get on top of how beat up I felt when he would attack me with angry words. It was as though my mother were slapping me in the face all over again. It made me feel the same way—small, helpless, and without value. His anger was like a snake hidden from sight, always coiled and ready to strike when I least expected it. It would become a deep problem that nearly destroyed our marriage.

For a long time I was mad at God for letting me marry someone who was like my mother in any way. I saw no signs whatsoever of Michael's anger before we were married, and I questioned why it was never revealed to me. I did see him battle with depression and feelings of failure, but I had those issues too. I thought I could help him through them because I understood those feelings so well. I thought we would be there for each other. I mistakenly believed that because God had called us to be together that there wouldn't be any problems when we got married.

In Michael's defense, I believe now that his anger came from having dyslexia back in the days when people didn't know what that was. His mother told me she was very hard on him because he struggled so much in school and she thought he was being rebellious. Having been blessed with a dyslexic child myself, I came to understand the frustration of the person who has it and the deep feelings of failure they have because they can't learn the same way everyone else does.

I also understand it from a parent's perspective. Before the problem is diagnosed, you can't figure out why your child isn't doing as well as they should be doing in school. You know how bright the child is, how creative and gifted, and how amazing their memory is, but when it comes to reading they seem to shut off. They appear rebellious because it seems that they are refusing to do the work, but the truth is they can't. So while I definitely sympathized with what Michael's mother went through, I also felt sorry for Michael. He suffered tremendously with overwhelming feelings of failure and depression because of it.

I believe now that's where his anger came from. He was angry over the frustration of being a creative dyslexic in a rigid and uncreative educational system. He was angry at his mother for often being angry at him for something he couldn't do anything about. And he took his anger out on me.

I'm going to tell you more of our story later in the book, but I want to reveal to you now that it has a good ending. Our marriage has gone through many tough times, but we have been married for more than 48 years and, God willing, will celebrate our fiftieth wedding anniversary together. The only reason we wouldn't celebrate it together will *not* be because of divorce.

My husband and I have changed remarkably for the better, and I will be sharing with you how that happened. I'm not saying we are perfect. Far from it. But we are living proof that if you *want* to, you can change. Or I should say, if you are willing to allow God to change you and pray for your husband (wife) to allow God to make changes in him (her), God will do it. And if you hang in there and keep praying, you will see things turn around. So if you want to protect your marriage from the things that can destroy it, or you long to restore the damage that has already been done, read on and see how best to do it. You can find the success you desire in your marriage if you do things God's way and refuse to give up.

It's Never Too Late to Pray for Change

We are told over and over, "Don't even try to change your husband (wife) because he (she) will never change." Hearing those dire predictions repeatedly can make you feel hopeless. If your marriage is miserable because of something intolerable your spouse does, and you're told he (she) will never change, then what hope do you have for your future together? The truth is, both he (she) and you *can* change. It's just that *you can't* make it happen. Only *God can* make effective changes.

Below are five important truths about change from God's perspective.

1. *The truth is, everyone needs to change.* God says so. In fact, it's His will for our lives that we change because He wants each one of us to become more like Him. And that is a never-ending project, for we all fall far short of the glory of God (see Romans 3:21-23). We will always need to submit to the Lord and not think so highly of ourselves that we feel we don't need to change. God is in the business of changing people. That's why, through our prayers and the power of the Holy Spirit, there is always hope for change—not only for ourselves, but for our spouse as well.

2. *The truth is, every person can change.* *You* can change. And *your spouse* can change. Don't let anyone tell you otherwise. It's not that a person *can't* change; but not changing is usually because of the following reasons:

- They aren't aware they *need* to.
- They don't believe they *have* to.
- They *don't want* to.
- They don't know *how* to.
- They won't ask God what *He* wants.
- They don't feel they are *able* to.
- They are happy with the *way* they *are*.

3. *The truth is, being married creates the perfect opportunity for change.* When you are married, you find out how much you need to improve yourself. It is prideful and selfish for anyone to get married and think they are so perfect they don't need to change in any way. Each one of us always needs to change in many ways—some more than others—but God will start with the one who is *willing*. And the good news is, this is where His blessings will be directed first as well. Remember that both you and your husband (wife) *can* be changed. God is waiting for you to invite Him to do that. Marriage always inspires change.

4. *The truth is, people cannot make someone else change.* Never is that more true than in a marriage. A wife can't change her husband.

A husband can't change his wife. But *God* can change both. We have to learn that it's not *our* job to change our spouse. It's the work of the Holy Spirit. No amount of criticizing and nagging will accomplish it, no matter how hard we try. God made each of us in *His* image, and He doesn't want us to try to make our spouse over into *our* image. Our job is to accept our spouse as he (she) is and pray for the Lord to make the necessary changes in him (her). Meanwhile, as He is working on your spouse's heart, God will also be working in yours. In the process of praying for changes in *him* (*her*), God will change *you* first if you are willing to let Him do so.

5. The truth is, only God can work changes in us that last. Only God has the power to transform us. We just have to be willing to say, "Lord, I recognize that I am far from perfect, and I realize I need to be changed in order to become more like You. I know I can't change myself in any lasting way, but *You can.* Lord, change me into the person You want me to be and show me what I need to do. I praise You and thank You for the transformation You are working in me."

Remember only God can:

- Make someone aware they *need* to change.
- Help someone see they *have* to change.
- Encourage someone to *want* to change.
- Show someone *how* to change.
- Enable someone to *make* a change.

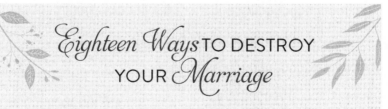

Eighteen Ways TO DESTROY YOUR Marriage

1. Stop communicating openly and honestly.
2. Be consistently angry, selfish, rude, and abusive.

3. Refuse to forgive your spouse for any offense, no matter how small.

4. Stay depressed and negative as much as possible.

5. Convince your spouse that your children are more important than he (she) is.

6. Be consistently lazy and refuse to do much around the house or on your job.

7. Spend money foolishly and continually run up great debt.

8. Give place to annoying habits and defend your right to have them.

9. Don't care about what your spouse needs as long as you get what you want.

10. Habitually look at films, TV, magazines, or advertising and compare your husband (wife) to the glorified images you see there.

11. Allow your heart to grow hard toward your husband (wife) and refuse to ever say "I'm sorry," "Forgive me," or "I love you."

12. Make something other than God and your spouse your top priority.

13. Threaten to get a divorce every time something comes up between you that needs to be worked out.

14. Entertain an obsession of the heart over someone other than your husband (wife).

15. Allow grief over a loss to ruin the rest of your life.

16. Refuse to compromise and agree on anything.

17. Don't try to reconcile your differences.

18. Give up and refuse to believe that God is a God of miracles who can restore love and hope.

No One Is Immune to Problems

Each of the above 18 ways to destroy a marriage can start as something small and turn into something big overnight, even in the best of relationships. You may have an idyllic marriage with the most perfect of mates and you may be close to perfection yourself, but so were Adam and Eve, and look what happened to them.

Don't buy into the dangerous belief that you are immune to problems in your marriage. Too many people have thought that and ended in divorce court. Or equally as bad, they have allowed their marriage to be filled with so much strife and unforgiveness that it became miserable, lifeless, and dead. They lost sight of the purpose God had for them in being married in the first place. And make no mistake, He does have a great purpose for your marriage.

Today there is an epidemic of despair, hopelessness, and pain because of marriages in crisis. There is no greater torment, outside of the death of a loved one, than that which is suffered when a marriage relationship has broken down. The sense of failure, guilt, sadness, and heartbreak over a divorce is unbearable. And staying in a miserable marriage is intolerable. Either choice is heartbreaking.

However, just like the *problem* can happen to *anyone,* so can the *solution* to it. The solutions I have written about in this book are *doable.* And not just for the deeply spiritual and highly disciplined. They are doable for *everyone.* If *I* can do them, *you* can do them. *The reason they are doable* is because they are part of God's will and way for your marriage, and He will help you accomplish them if your heart is willing. *The reason they are not easy,* however, is because of one thing—*the condition of our own heart has to be right,* and changing that can often seem impossible. It's hard to take our blinders off when we've grown so used to them that we don't even know they are there. Marital problems develop in someone's *heart* first, so that is where we have to go to find the root of the problem, and that is where healing begins.

Understand the Authority God Has Given You

God has sovereignly declared that He is not going to just fix things for us without any input on our part. He wants to teach us to have great faith in Him and move in the authority He has given us in prayer. Without us praying, He *won't* do it. Without His help and power, we *can't* do it.

Let's get some basic facts straight. If you believe Jesus Christ is the Son of God and you have invited Him into your life to rule there, then you are a child of God. You are a child of God, but you have no relationship with Him if you have not received Jesus, who gave His life for you so you can have life with Him forever. Receiving the Lord makes you the son or daughter of a King. You were born again into royalty. And you are destined to reign over the forces of evil. God has "delivered us from the power of darkness and conveyed us into the kingdom of the Son of His love" (Colossians 1:13).

Knowing Jesus and being God's child is where our authority in prayer begins. Praying is putting our authority into action. Satan has the power to destroy us, but we have been given authority over him. "Behold, I give you the authority to trample on *serpents* and *scorpions*, and over *all the power of the enemy*, and nothing shall by any means hurt you" (Luke 10:19).

As I mentioned earlier, I was raised in the wild lands of Wyoming, and I have had way more experience with snakes than I ever wanted. When I think of how many times I came close to rattlesnakes coiled and ready to strike—I have been just inches away a few times—it's a miracle I have never been bitten by one. Snakes slither silently in, and you don't realize they are there until you are upon them and they startle you. Scorpions are known for their sudden, painful, and venomous sting. If you would think of all the threats to your marriage as being like snakes and scorpions, it will help you to see their potential for pain and destruction.

Whether it's something dangerous that sneaks silently into your marriage unnoticed at first, or something small but deadly that rises up and stabs you when you least expect it, leaving you wounded and poisoned, God will work His power through you so you can exercise your authority over all that opposes you through prayer in Jesus' name.

God has given us *free choice* concerning who we will allow to have authority in our lives. Will we respect *God's* authority, or will we bow to the influence of others? When we choose Jesus, He gives us authority over all situations in our lives. But if we don't submit to Him in obedience to His ways, and in reverence for who He is and what He accomplished on the cross, we will not be able to move in the authority He paid for with His life. The only way to move into all God has for us is to be totally submitted to the authority of Jesus in our lives. God has given us *authority* over the enemy because of what Jesus did on the cross. When we learn to use the power God has given us—meaning *His* power—and the authority over the power of the enemy—meaning the right to exert it in Jesus' name—incredible things can happen in our lives and in our marriages.

Taking Authority over the Enemy's Plans in Prayer

The best place to start taking authority over your life is by praying regularly for your husband (wife) and your marriage. Your prayers for your husband (wife) have great power in the spirit realm. The same enemy of your soul who wants to see *you* destroyed also wants to see *your marriage* destroyed. If you don't realize that, you will end up thinking that your spouse is the enemy and your fight is with him (her). While it may be true he (she) is *acting* like the devil sometimes, he (she) is not the enemy. Jesus won the victory over death and hell, so if you are living in hell in your marriage relationship, you have not yet moved into the victory God has for you.

Whenever you find yourself in a tough situation in your life or in your marriage, take authority over it with prayer in Jesus' name. That doesn't mean you are trying to control your spouse. It means you are inviting *God* to be in control of your life and your marriage and surrendering both to Him.

When you pray with God-given authority, it releases the power of God to work in both of your lives. You can't necessarily change the strong will of your spouse, but when you pray for him (her), you invite God to create an atmosphere in the spirit realm around him (her) that helps him (her) to better hear the truth. After you pray, praise God for the victory He has already won on your behalf. Thank Him that He has a way out of any situation, even when it appears hopeless.

God never said we won't have problems.

Actually, God said we *will* have problems and trials. We can count on it. And when you are married, you will not only have *your* problems; you will have your spouse's problems as well. But the good news is, Jesus overcame all that for us. When we align ourselves with Him in prayer and obedience, He will help us to either rise above our problems or walk through them successfully. He will give you the power to be more than a conqueror (Romans 8:37). That's because Jesus has already conquered death and hell and has secured the victory over the enemy for us. We have to learn to walk with God in that victory. We do that when we pray.

Jesus has enabled you to not only conquer the territory God has for you, but to also experience His miracle of peace in the process.

Praying with Urgency and Power

I don't want to just talk to you *about* praying for yourself, your husband (wife), and your marriage, I want to help you learn *how* to pray in power. I want to inspire you with great hope that things can change. I'm not talking about being religious, saying "church" words, speaking "Christianese," or quoting "catchy phrases" without any power accompanying them. I am talking about praying in a way that will bring results.

I can tell you how to swim, I can describe the water, and I can teach you all the correct moves, but at some point you are going to have to get in the water. Once you get into the stream of God leading you as you pray, you are going to find yourself not only staying afloat, but also rising to the top of each wave of life that might normally overwhelm you.

One of God's greatest promises says that "all things work together for good to those who love God, to those who are the called according to His purpose" (Romans 8:28). But if you read the verses *before* that promise, you will see that the Bible is talking about prayer. In other words, can it be that all things work together for good if we are *praying*? It sounds like that to me. Things are not promised to work out for good automatically. If there have been things in your life you feel did not work out for good, it's possible that somewhere, sometime, the people who should have been praying for you or your situation, actually weren't.

You have the power to control your own destiny. You can choose heaven or hell as your eternal home. You can choose to give God control of your life and let Him move you into the purpose for which He created you. You can choose either to give up on your marriage or stay and fight for it in prayer and whatever else God shows you to do. You can choose to enrich your marriage by praying for your husband (wife) and yourself in a way that can *prevent* bad things from creeping in, or to *heal* those negative things that have already gained ground in your marriage.

What Jesus accomplished at the cross seems baffling and foolish to someone who has never been born again and had their spiritual blinders removed. But to us who believe, it is the greatest manifestation of God's power. "The message of the cross is foolishness to those who are perishing, but to us who are being saved it is the power of God" (1 Corinthians 1:18). When you invite Jesus into your life, that same power that resurrected Him will manifest and resurrect all the dead areas of your life—including your marriage.

God knows we need that. He knows we can't come up with a foolproof plan that will keep our marriages together. We are way too selfish and blind. We are lacking in wisdom and the spirit of self-sacrifice. "The LORD knows the thoughts of man, that they are futile" (Psalm 94:11). He wants *us* to realize that too. He wants *us* to understand that we can't do it without *Him*. He wants us to believe that He is greater than any hurricane, flood, or tsunami of circumstances and emotions that would threaten to wash over your relationship.

God is even greater than you or your spouse's anger, depression, or inability to communicate. He is more powerful than the unforgiveness or hardness of heart in either of you. God is stronger than bad debt, bad habits, and weak willpower. He made you to be victorious over all that and more, but you cannot proceed "having a form of godliness but denying its power" (2 Timothy 3:5). You have to run to the cross with gratefulness for His sacrifice on your behalf and acknowledge God's power in your life.

God had a plan for your life before you were even born. He says it is He "who has saved us and *called us with a holy calling,* not according to our works, but *according to His own purpose* and *grace* which was given to us in Christ Jesus before time began" (2 Timothy 1:9). He called you and your husband (wife) for a purpose, but He still gives you a choice. You can choose *His* destiny for your life, or you can try to make your own.

Let me give you a tip about this that will save you a lot of time and effort: The life you try to make happen will never be as good as the one you let God make happen.

One of the questions I have been asked countless times is "What if I am the only one praying in my marriage?" While it is the best situation if a husband and wife pray together, I want to assure you that your prayers for your marriage have power even when you are the only one praying. That's because the two of you are one in the eyes of God, and your prayers have power.

Of course, the power is even greater when the two of you pray together, but I don't want to belabor that point. If you have a husband (wife) who will pray with you, consider yourself blessed. Many people don't have that. But don't lose heart. God hears your prayers according to His will, and He will answer in surprising ways.

What if you are the only person in the marriage who is a believer? Or you only are living God's way? Or you are the only one willing to submit to God's perfecting process? Or you are the only one really willing to work on the relationship? What if you understand the enemy's attack on your marriage and your spouse doesn't get it? Can *your* prayers alone save the marriage?

Yes, they can. That scenario is much more common than you might think. In fact, I have heard of great miracles in that regard. I believe it is well worth trying for.

Can Prayer Really Prevent Bad Things from Happening?

Of course, it would be best to pray about possible problems *before* any of them ever developed. Or better yet would be to pray about them *before* you walk down the aisle. However, even though it would be wonderful to have all these things resolved *before* you get married, I believe it is actually impossible. That's because you and your spouse have never before lived together as man and wife. And this is true even if you have lived together before marriage. No man or woman truly understands their own limits and capabilities before they have made that public declaration and have entered into this legally binding life-time commitment. When you do that, you are forced to deal with things in yourself and in your spouse as they affect your lives together.

We all put our best foot forward when we are dating, but it's impossible to do that every day for the rest of our lives. Everyone has good days and bad days, weaknesses and strengths, times of patience and times of not so much. Everyone has moments when they let words slip out of their mouth that shouldn't have been spoken, and also times they should have said or done something and didn't. But marriage provides an opportunity to give one another the security you need to come face-to-face with who you really are and have the freedom to be set free to heal and grow. That's why praying in advance of these things happening doesn't mean that difficult things won't ever happen, but if something does, you will be able to survive these times successfully, knowing God is using them to perfect both of you.

The thing you have to remember is that God has more for you than you can imagine. I know this is hard to comprehend because we can imagine some amazing things. We can dream big. But even considering your greatest dream for yourself, what God has for you is far greater. The Bible says: "Eye has not seen, nor ear heard, nor have entered into the heart of man the things which God has prepared for those who love Him" (1 Corinthians 2:9). It can be as a married couple too. You may have trouble imagining your marriage being better than your greatest dream for it, but it can be. The reason I know this is true is because it is God's will for your life. It's what He wants for you. I have seen God do miracles in my own marriage and in the lives of countless married couples whom I have prayed with and heard from over the years. I'm not saying our marriage is perfect, but it's a lot better than I thought it could ever be at this point. And I know it's because of the power of God working through our prayers. It was hard work, but it was worth it.

Are you ready to pray for the purpose of preventing common problems in your marriage? Are you ready to do what it takes to pray for a needed change? Are you ready to protect your marriage relationship so it will last a lifetime?

If so, read on to find out how.

1

Pray to Keep Communication Open Between You

The most difficult thing about a marriage is that there are *two* people in it. And we all know that the problem is usually with the other person. If we were just trying to work things out by ourselves, we could certainly do a good job of it, but we have to fit our dreams, desires, hopes, abilities, mind-sets, assumptions, needs, and habits in with those of our spouse. And that takes three things: communication, communication, and communication.

Verbally, emotionally, and physically.

The foundation of a good marriage that will last a lifetime has to be built on communication. It is the way intimacy is established. Anytime communication is shut off, intimacy suffers. And a marriage without intimacy is dying. You and your spouse must each be able to have a sense of closeness in your marriage—an assurance you are on the same team. Without good communication, it will be very hard to achieve that.

The closest relationship you will ever have is with your spouse because you share everything. Not being able to communicate with him (her)—or he (she) not being able to communicate with you— paves the way for an intolerable existence. Not knowing what your spouse is thinking or feeling makes building a life together difficult, if not impossible. If neither of you know what the other's internal plans and visions are for the future, how will you know if you are moving into it together?

How can you show your commitment to the relationship if you never share that with your spouse? How do you get the sense that you are always going to be there for each other if you don't periodically tell or show each other that? If you don't express your fears and inner turmoil, how can you receive the encouragement you need? Without good verbal communication, the depth of your physical intimacy is limited as well. That intimate part of your life together will then become an act without feeling.

Communication needs to be prayed about every day—preferably in advance of any communication breakdown. But if communication between you is already suffering, pray for the breakthrough you both need in order to change that.

Pray That You Both Will Always Be Willing to Change

If *one* of you believes that the communication is not good in your relationship, then some changes have to be made.

God is a God of change. Although *He* is unchanging—*He* is the same yesterday, today, and forever—He doesn't want *us* to be like that. That's because *He* doesn't *need* to change. *We do. He* is *perfect. We're not.* He wants us to always be changing because He desires that we become more and more like Him. If we are resistant to being changed, then we are resistant to God because God is all about changing *us*.

If one or both people in a marriage are resistant to the changing, transforming, and perfecting work of the Holy Spirit in their life, then there are certain to be bad habits that develop. Our flesh is like that—it's always headed toward the destructive if we are not careful and prayerful. The longer these bad habits go on, the more entrenched they become. But the good news is that any stronghold of bad habits can be broken in an instant by the power of God, no matter how long they have been there. Even bad habits with regard to communication in your marriage can be completely eliminated. Anyone can learn to communicate better if they are willing to make the effort. We have to pray that our marriage partner is always open to good communication.

Have you ever felt as though your life is stuck in one place? That you cannot move beyond where you are? Things can become that way in a marriage too. You can get into a rut. You can feel stuck in a relationship that isn't growing, isn't getting better, and isn't going anywhere. And only one of you—or perhaps neither of you—is willing to change anything in order to make it better.

Marriage is not something we enter into to see what we can get *out* of it. It's something we ask ourselves every day what we can put *into* it. Marriage is a covenant relationship, which means it is supposed to be a commitment until death parts us. Unfortunately, too often a *marriage* dies before the *people* in it do.

Getting married is just the very beginning of your relationship. *Being* married frees you to feel secure enough to let your true self show—for better or for worse—for the purpose of seeing where you need God's healing, transformation, and restoration. *Staying* married depends on you both being able to communicate well with one another, and to care for one another unselfishly.

The only way to keep growing together and not apart is by good communication. What other way can love and respect be shown? How else can you really be on the same team? What would happen in a football game if the quarterback never communicated with the rest of the team? It would be a disaster. They would never reach their goal. They would never experience victory. It's the same in a marriage. That's why it is entirely selfish and destructive to refuse to communicate with your spouse for whatever reason. You have to pray for good communication in your marriage as soon as you are aware of the need to do so.

Right from the Start

In the beginning God had the marriage relationship in mind. Even though Adam was able to communicate with God every day, God saw that this wasn't enough. God said, "It is not good that man should be alone; I will make him a helper comparable to him" (Genesis 2:18). That means the woman He created for him wasn't merely an airhead with a great body. She *complemented* him. She *helped* him. And he needed her *companionship* and *support.* He needed someone to *communicate* with him on his level. If Adam could have done it all by himself, he wouldn't have needed Eve. She wasn't just an afterthought. She *completed* him.

God made Eve from the rib He took out of Adam (Genesis 2:21-22). That means a man will always feel something missing without his wife. And, likewise, a woman has a natural sense of belonging at her husband's side as his support. I've known a number of single men and women for years who are now in their sixties and have never married, and no matter how many friends they had in their life, they still suffered with periodic bouts of loneliness. And this only increased with age. I know there are exceptions to that, such as the men and women who have devoted their lives to God's service and because of His grace didn't suffer with that kind of loneliness. But from the start God recognized a husband's and a wife's deep need to communicate with one another.

I Know Personally How Important Good Communication Is

If you have already experienced divorce, you know the horrible pain of it and don't want to ever go through it again. You also know that when you are contemplating a divorce, you make a list in your mind of all the things that will change, and you ask yourself, *Is it worth it? Do the gains balance out the losses?* If communication is bad—or if the only communication is negative—you end up thinking you don't have much to lose and everything to gain.

I was married before I became a believer, and there was no communication in our relationship at all. Not only were we not on the same page, we weren't even in the same book. I came to the point where I felt as though I were living in hell, and I was ready to give up anything in order to feel hope, relief, and some degree of peace again. I wanted out so badly that I walked away from everything, taking only the possessions I brought into the marriage in the first place, even though I worked for nearly two years to support him while he stayed home and watched TV. I didn't want to live another day in that slow death, and I saw no way whatsoever that life could ever be any different.

In his culture, men did not lift a finger to help around the house—or anywhere else, for that matter. Nor did they work, apparently. I found that I could not physically work 10- to 12-hour days and then come home to do *all* the cooking and *all* the cleaning because that was what he demanded. He daily evaluated my performance and recited the ways I had not lived up to the standards of his mother. He wanted me to be her and I just couldn't. He spent hours every day at her house while I worked, and he would still be there when I came home at night. It was like living alone again, except not as much fun. And I wasn't strong enough to take the constant criticism without any encouragement or sense of being loved. In his defense, he was probably trying to make me into the wife he wanted, and I was not a whole enough person at that time to be able to be all that.

He wasn't a believer, and he became extremely angry when he found out I had become one. After we had been married less than a year, I started going to church by myself every Sunday, which he thought was a waste of time when I could be cleaning or working another job to support him. One Sunday afternoon I came home from church feeling especially uplifted in my spirit, and I tried to talk to him about the Lord. He became irate and told me in a loud and threatening voice that I was forbidden to ever speak the name of Jesus in *his* house or his presence again and never as long as I was with *him*. It was the final straw that broke the back of my thinly spined marriage. I had been hanging on to the edge of a cliff by a delicate branch and had finally found hope and a reason to live, and now he was going to chop off the branch. It was like cutting off the air I breathed. That meant, of course, I had to leave *his* house and his presence. After I left him I felt free to not only breathe, but to speak the name of Jesus whenever I wanted. It was liberating.

Some time later I got married again, but this time it was different. The most important difference being that my second husband, Michael, was a believer. We went to church together. We prayed together. We went to Christian marriage counselors together. So there was always hope for change in both of us. And I believed that any problems we had could be easily fixed.

However, we each came into the marriage with deep insecurities. He felt like a failure because he couldn't live up to his mother's expectations. I felt like a failure because my mentally ill mother had no good expectations of me whatsoever. When she told me repeatedly that I was worthless and would never amount to anything, I had no reason to doubt her, even though I desperately looked for one. So my husband was *angry* and depressed. I was *anxious* and depressed. Because we were two damaged people, hurting each other was easy. Although we communicated well in the beginning, there would be lapses where he would lash out in anger and I thought he was being cruel, so I would withdraw out of hurt, causing him to believe I didn't care. Communication became more and more difficult as time went on, and we were miserable. At this point I did not know how to pray for him, and I certainly knew nothing about praying to prevent a lack of communication from happening.

When our marriage came to the ultimate crisis point after years like this, I wanted to leave. But in prayer about it one day, the Lord showed me that if I would pray for my husband every day the way God wanted me to, He would use me as an instrument of healing and deliverance for our marriage. I said yes to that and quickly learned to pray the way the Lord was showing me. As I did, I began to see changes—especially in our communication. It wasn't an overnight transformation. It was more like a day by day moving into the territory God had for us to conquer, and not giving up when there were times of setback.

The suffering that happens in an unhappy marriage is horrendous because there is no escape. Unless you get a divorce and dissolve the relationship completely, you are stuck there and have to work it out. If your spouse isn't willing to do anything to make it better, it is a nightmare. That's why praying about having good communication is so important right from the start—before you are married if possible. If not, then as soon as you realize how crucial this is.

It's also very good to be reading the Word of God and attending church together where there is good Bible teaching. But I've seen too many marriages in the church end in divorce. I've even seen too many people who were great Bible teachers leave their husbands or wives. I've also seen marriages between people who never go to church or read the Bible last a lifetime. So there has to be more to saving a marriage than any kind of pat answer like "read the Word and stay in church." Even though I believe these two things are a must, you still have to do more. You have to pray, and pray specifically about your communication, because without that your marriage doesn't have a chance.

If This Has Already Happened to You

I took a survey of women before I wrote *The Power of a Praying Husband,* and the most important thing women wanted was that their husbands would talk to them more. This is a very big issue in a marriage. You may have been married 30 years to a poor communicator— or you may be one yourself—but God can change both of you. We *all* can learn to communicate better.

I know a couple who spend more time in silence than they do talking. They argue so much when they talk that they have chosen to not communicate at all. This is an unnatural way to live. If you have that kind of situation, then you are not fulfilling the plan God has for your marriage. Communication is more about *serving God's will* than it is your own. It's more about doing *what's right* than it is deciding *who's right.* If you want to glorify God in your marriage, pray that the two of you will have good communication. That takes two hearts caring enough about one another to refuse to be selfish.

If you and your husband (wife) are already experiencing a lack of good communication and your spouse doesn't want to change right now, then be glad that God can change *you first* while you pray for the Holy Spirit to work on *him* (*her*). God can help *you* to not be so easily hurt by your spouse's poor communication skills. The Lord can give *you* such joy and excitement about *your* life in Him that you don't feel rejected when your husband (wife) is silent. If *you* are the one who has trouble communicating, ask God to give you a heart for your spouse that desires to express your love and thoughts openly.

You and your spouse became one in God's eyes the day you were married (Ephesians 5:31), but there is still a process of becoming one in your everyday lives together from then on. The day-to-day living out of this concept of total unity doesn't just happen; it takes time and effort. *Both* husband and wife have to compromise in order to do it. When one person stops putting forth any effort to talk things out or make the marriage better, it becomes a nightmare for the other. If only one is communicating and the other is not, the marriage is headed for serious problems. One person trying to carry the entire weight of a marriage relationship will work for only so long.

I want to share specifically some ways I learned to pray about having good communication that make a big difference when it comes to greatly enriching your relationship.

Pray That You and Your Husband (Wife) Are Always Kind to Each Other

How many marriages could be saved if both the husband and wife would just be nice to one another? It's called common decency. The Bible says, "Love edifies" (1 Corinthians 8:1). That means love builds up and makes stronger. Love doesn't speak mean-spirited and sarcastic words that tear down. *What* we say and the *manner* in which we say it can either communicate love or total disregard. Loveless words of criticism destroy a marriage relationship, so we have to ask ourselves if the satisfaction derived from saying them is really worth the hurt and destruction they cause. God doesn't think so. He says that real love "does not behave rudely, does not seek its own, is not provoked, thinks no evil" (1 Corinthians 13:5). There is no reason to treat your spouse badly. If you want to improve and enrich your marriage, just being nice is a good place to start.

When a person is not treated well by their spouse, it keeps them from feeling safe enough to share their deepest thoughts and emotions, and this shuts off an important part of their relationship. If you have already fallen into bad habits of critical and insensitive speech toward your spouse, repent of that now and ask God to change your heart. If your husband (wife) frequently directs negative and critical speech toward *you,* pray for an awakening in him (her). Pray that the grave consequences of such careless words will be revealed to his (her) understanding. I know it may seem pointless to do anything if *you* are the only one making the effort and your spouse seems to be doing nothing, but I have found that when *you* do the right thing, even when your spouse doesn't, God blesses *you.* And that makes a big difference.

Have you seen couples who are married but seem like strangers? I used to know a couple who must have memorized the old saying, "If you can't say something nice, then don't say anything" because they never said anything. At least not to each other. Theirs was a lifeless marriage. When one spouse is emotionally distant or noncommunicative, it forces the other to have to endure all struggles alone. When there is no compatibility, there is no one with whom to share life. And when some people realize that they cannot rely on their spouse to come through with friendship and emotional support, it becomes easy to turn to another person who will. If one of you can't be nice, then you can't be friends, and your marriage will be an endurance test.

Friends enjoy being with one another. They don't act like strangers. They don't say words to bring the other down and destroy any hope or joy. If you and your husband (wife) have not been good in the friendship department, ask God to help you change your ways. If you have been good friends all along, ask God to show you how to be better friends than you have ever been in the past. Ask God to keep you both from falling into bad habits and mind-sets concerning this.

God says our words have power. If "death and life are in the power of the tongue," then we must choose our words carefully (Proverbs 18:21). Pray that God will help you and your spouse to always speak words to each other that are kind, loving, positive, good, uplifting, encouraging, and life-giving. Ask God to be in charge of your marriage, and tell Him you'll do whatever it takes to see that it becomes all He intended it to be. Even if it means being nice when you don't feel like it.

Pray That You and Your Husband (Wife) Will Always Be Truthful and Honest

A marriage absolutely must be based on trust. If you can't trust each other, then who can you trust? That's why lying to your spouse is one of the worst things you can do to damage your relationship. The Bible says clearly, "Do not lie to one another, since you have put off the old man with his deeds" (Colossians 3:9). Every lie has dangerous and far-reaching consequences. "A false witness will not go unpunished, and he who speaks lies will not escape" (Proverbs 19:5). The worst consequence is that lying distances you from God. "He who tells lies shall not continue in my presence" (Psalm 101:7). Lying also distances you from one another and stops the flow of good communication.

In a marriage, it's important to be both *truthful* and *honest*. And there is a difference between the two. When you tell a lie, you are not truthful, but it is possible to tell the truth and still not be honest. That happens when you are not forthcoming with the *whole* truth. You may not have actually told a lie, but you didn't reveal everything you needed to reveal. Now, you don't need to reveal every single thought to every person you see, because then no one would want to be around you. But you do need to be forthcoming with your spouse, because you hope he (she) will be with you for the rest of your life.

You know if you have told a lie or not, but sometimes you can inadvertently be less than honest about your true feelings because you don't know how to express them fully. You are not entirely honest if you haven't shared your feelings and thoughts. *A person who never communicates with their spouse cannot be completely honest because total honesty requires good communication.* Of course, it's not good to be expressing every thought you have every moment you have one, even with your spouse, because then he (she) won't want to be around you either. But God will give you discernment about that too if you ask Him for it.

Here are some things to remember about being honest:

1. *Be honest about how you feel regarding the things your spouse does.* You have to express your feelings when something seriously bothers you about your spouse's actions. If you are not honest with him (her) about this, nothing will ever change. Then bitterness and anger can build up in your heart and lead to resentment and unforgiveness. You not only have to know *what* to say, but *when* and *how* to say it. And God will always be the best judge of that. So anytime you need to say something important to your husband (wife) that may be hard to hear, ask God to show you the right time and right way to say it. Ask Him to prepare your spouse's heart to receive it and give you the perfect words to say so you can speak "the truth in love" (Ephesians 4:15). The Bible says that there is "a time to keep silence, and a time to speak"

(Ecclesiastes 3:7). Ask God to help you know the difference between the two. Timing is everything.

2. *Be honest about the way you see things.* It's important for each of you to share your thoughts, plans, fears, concerns, hopes, and dreams for the future. You have to get these things out of your heart and into the open. Job said, "I will speak, that I may find relief" (Job 32:20). And that's exactly what you will find too. If your husband (wife) is the kind of person with whom it's difficult to communicate, ask God to break down that barrier in his (her) heart. Outside of going to a counselor who will be able to help you both open up and talk, you need a move of the Holy Spirit to do that, so pray for one. A husband and wife are constantly adjusting to each other in their marriage because no two people *are* the same or *stay* the same. (Even though at times it may seem as though nothing ever changes.) But they can never adjust properly to each other if they don't know what adjustments to make. If one of you is not honest with the other about these things, you can both easily make wrong assumptions and cause wrong adjustments.

3. *Be honest about your past.* When I first realized that Michael and I were getting serious, I knew I couldn't go any further in my relationship with him without being completely forthcoming about my past. But before I told him everything, I prayed that God would prepare his heart to receive it and give me the right words and time to say it.

He already knew about my mother, even though he didn't fully comprehend the seriousness of her mental illness until after we were married and we went to visit my parents for a weekend. But there were other things I had to tell him, and I didn't know whether he would totally reject me because of them. But he was completely accepting of what I told him and said it didn't change his mind about me at all. It was a great relief to get it out in the open and off my shoulders.

I've known other people who had secrets from their past that they never revealed to their spouse until well after they were married, and this late revelation shook the level of trust that had been established early on. Being totally honest about your past helps you to live more successfully in the present. It helps you to better move into the future God has for you. You don't want to always be looking over your shoulder to see if something is coming back to haunt you. The sooner you are forthcoming, the better.

4. *Be honest about everything you are doing.* I know a man who is constantly lying to his wife about the things he does. They don't have a close relationship, and his dishonesty could very well lead to a divorce in the future. Every lie breaks down trust. And when a husband or wife loses trust, the foundation of their marriage crumbles. Of course, trust can be restored again when the one who is lying confesses and truly repents. If anyone has to lie to their spouse about what they are doing, then that person's priorities are completely out of order. They are definitely not putting God first above all else.

Ten Things THAT ARE TRUE ABOUT *Telling The Truth*

1. ***Truth is what you choose to think about.*** "Finally, brethren, whatever things are true…meditate on these things" (Philippians 4:8).

2. ***Truth is a decision you make about the words you speak.*** "My mouth will speak truth; wickedness is an abomination to my lips" (Proverbs 8:7).

3. ***Truth is the way you choose to walk.*** "I have chosen the way of truth; Your judgments I have laid before me" (Psalm 119:30).

4. ***Truth liberates you.*** "You shall know the truth, and the truth shall make you free" (John 8:32).

5. ***Truth protects you.*** "Stand therefore, having girded your waist with truth, having put on the breastplate of righteousness" (Ephesians 6:14).

6. ***Truth purifies your soul.*** "Since you have purified your

souls in obeying the truth through the Spirit in sincere love of the brethren, love one another fervently with a pure heart" (1 Peter 1:22).

7. *Truth pleases God.* "I have no greater joy than to hear that my children walk in truth" (3 John 1:4).

8. *Truth can be branded in your heart.* "Let not mercy and truth forsake you; bind them around your neck, write them on the tablet of your heart" (Proverbs 3:3).

9. *Truth brings you into God's light.* "He who does the truth comes to the light, that his deeds may be clearly seen, that they have been done in God" (John 3:21).

10. *Truth in your heart invites a greater sense of God's presence when you pray.* "The LORD is near to all who call upon Him, to all who call upon Him in truth" (Psalm 145:18).

Pray That Your Heart Will Be Filled with God's Love

The best way to have good communication with your spouse is to first be in good communication with God. If it's true that "out of the abundance of the heart the mouth speaks" (Matthew 12:34), then you have to ask God to fill your heart abundantly with His love every day so that the words you speak are loving. The Bible says that "no man can tame the tongue. It is an unruly evil, full of deadly poison" (James 3:8). Left to ourselves, we will naturally say hurtful and destructive words. The Bible also says, "The preparations of the heart belong to man, but the answer of the tongue is from the LORD" (Proverbs 16:1). You can prepare your heart by being in the presence of God in prayer, in worship, and by reading His Word. Then His love will overflow in your words.

When truth is hard to hear in a marriage, ask God for a greater portion of His love with which to communicate it. Whenever you speak from a bad attitude or a loveless heart, it cuts off your spouse's ability to hear what you're saying. Ask God to give you wisdom to say the right things the right way. "The heart of the wise teaches his mouth, and adds learning to his lips" (Proverbs 16:23). When you make an effort to speak words that communicate love, it pays off. It pleases God, and there is always great reward in that.

Don't let animosity swell up and become a flood pouring over your relationship. Dam up arguments with honest communication and loving words. "The beginning of strife is like releasing water; therefore stop contention before a quarrel starts" (Proverbs 17:14). Ask God to make your heart so filled with His love that your words will be like healing waters of encouragement and restoration instead of an open floodgate that produces serious water damage.

Pray That You Can Understand His (Her) Body Language

We had a little white long-haired Chihuahua. He was actually my daughter's dog, but she wasn't able to take him with her when she moved out because of her work and travel schedule. I guess that made him our grand-dog. His name was Wrigley, but Michael and I called him "The Great I Want." That's because unless he was sleeping, Wrigley always wanted something. Wrigley communicated his wants by sitting up on his hind legs and putting his paws together as though he was praying, and he waved them up and down while relentlessly squeaking. He could balance that way for longer than you ever dreamed possible. You could ignore the sitting up and the praying paws, but there is no way you were going to ignore the squeaking. It would drive us crazy. The only way to get him to stop was to ask him simple questions about all the things he usually wanted and see how many times his paws went up and down. Because he always wanted *everything*, his paws would go up and down at least one or two times for anything you said. There were key words we had to speak, such as "Outside?" "Dinner?" "Hold you?" "Bed?" "Blanket?" "Bone?" "Biscuit?" "Toy?" "Walk?" "Ride?" He understood all of these perfectly.

Do you want to go *outside?* Do you want *dinner?* Do you want me to *hold you?* Do you want a *biscuit?* Do you want your *bone?* Do you want to go for a *ride?* Actually, we learned not to say "ride" unless we were committed to taking him on one. Because no matter how much he needed to go "outside" or how hungry he was for "dinner," a "ride" took precedence over everything. And once you had said the "R" word, if you didn't follow through you would be squeaked to death.

When you asked Wrigley these questions, you had to be very discerning as to how many times his praying paws went up and down. One time for "bone," two times for "dinner," two times for "hold you." And so on through the entire cycle because all his wants were relative. The word that got the greatest up and down movement of the praying paws indicated what he wanted most. The only word he never responded to was "bath." I tried throwing that word in a couple times, and Wrigley was frozen in silence with a look on his face that said *Don't see me. Don't see me.* One time when he desperately had to go outside, he waved his paws at least six times in the space of two seconds and we knew it was an emergency.

The thing is, the expression on Wrigley's face never changed when he was doing his praying paws, so you could not tell by looking at his face what he wanted. And his squeaks all had the same intensity. It was the subtle signals in his body language that we had to take into consideration in order to discern what he was after. We learned a lot from Wrigley.

The point in all this is that sometimes we have to look very carefully at the body language of our spouse in order to figure out what he (she) truly wants and what is going on inside him (her). We have to ask the right questions and be able to discern his (her) reaction to them. We have to read between the lines. Ask God to enable you to recognize these subtle signs in your husband (wife) in order to know what he (she) is thinking. Ask God to help *you* communicate so clearly that your husband (wife) doesn't have to search for helpful signs in your body language in order to understand you. Pray that God will reveal to you all you need to see in order to better understand him (her).

Pray That the Two of You Will Always Find Things You Like to Do Together

What do you and your husband (wife) like to do together? If you can think of something, that's good. But if you are struggling to think of even one thing, then this is a problem for your relationship. In order to have good communication you must have things you enjoy doing together, even if it's something as simple as sitting together watching the sunset or reading books or taking walks or going out to eat. If you work together, you still need something you enjoy doing together outside of work.

My husband and I tried golfing together for a short period of time. We tried tennis too. But my husband's goal was to win at all costs and mine was to just have fun. I didn't like risking my life trying to have fun. So we gave that up.

At this stage in our lives, due to a miraculous answer to my husband's prayers, we both like football. (Watching, not playing.) He bought me a book called *Football for Dummies* (I didn't get offended), took me to games, and was willing to explain the same thing over and over and over until I got it. Not an easy task for an impatient type A, but this was important to him and so he persevered. And it paid off because now I love the game. We watch football games together on TV and attend them in person when our team is in town. If you knew how much I used to think that this was the biggest waste of time, you would realize how miraculous this is. Michael and I had *both* been praying that we would have something we like to do together. And *he* won. I still have to shop alone.

Pray That God Will Help You to Honor One Another

Don't you hate it when you are with another couple and one of them says something critical, demeaning, or dishonoring about the other? Nothing causes people to feel more uncomfortable than a husband or wife making unkind jabs at one another in front of them. And it can force *you* into the awkward position of having to possibly take sides in the matter, which you really can't because no one knows the inner workings of someone else's marriage. Sometimes the one who appears to be the charming and wonderful person is actually the offending person who is nice to everyone but their spouse. And the spouse who appears bitter or nasty has actually been pushed to the edge of what she (he) can take.

Husbands are especially exhorted to give honor to their wives, and the consequence of failing to do so is not having their prayers answered. "Husbands, likewise, dwell with them with understanding, giving *honor* to the wife, as to the weaker vessel, and as being heirs together of the grace of life, *that your prayers may not be hindered*" (1 Peter 3:7). This consequence is about as serious as it can get and should not be taken lightly.

Husbands are also admonished to *love* their wives, and wives are to *respect* their husbands and *submit* to them (Ephesians 5:22-33). For wives, godly submission is something you willingly do. It's not something your husband forces you to do. That's slavery. Submission is communicated in a godly way by showing respect to your husband. But a wife finds submitting to her husband far *easier* if he is submitted to God, which is the way God wants it. She finds it *harder* to do if he is not submitted to God or if he has disrespected her in any way. Ask God to help you and your husband (wife) to unfailingly show honor, respect, appreciation, and love to one another—*especially* in front of other people.

Ten Things TO REMEMBER ABOUT THE *Words You Speak*

1. ***Choose your words carefully.*** "Let no corrupt word proceed out of your mouth, but what is good for necessary edification, that it may impart grace to the hearers" (Ephesians 4:29).

2. ***Gentle words have more power than harsh words.*** "A gentle tongue breaks a bone" (Proverbs 25:15).

3. ***You must think before you speak.*** "The heart of the righteous studies how to answer, but the mouth of the wicked pours forth evil" (Proverbs 15:28).

4. ***Don't talk too much.*** "In the multitude of words sin is

not lacking, but he who restrains his lips is wise" (Proverbs 10:19).

5. ***Your words can cause you to stumble.*** "We all stumble in many things. If anyone does not stumble in word, he is a perfect man, able also to bridle the whole body" (James 3:2).

6. ***Kind words are life-giving.*** "Pleasant words are like a honeycomb, sweetness to the soul and health to the bones" (Proverbs 16:24).

7. ***Your words can bring about great destruction.*** "The tongue is a little member and boasts great things. See how great a forest a little fire kindles!" (James 3:5).

8. ***If you want a good life, watch what you say.*** "He who would love life and see good days, let him refrain his tongue from evil, and his lips from speaking deceit" (1 Peter 3:10).

9. ***Your words can be inspired by the enemy.*** "The tongue is a fire, a world of iniquity. The tongue is so set among our members that it defiles the whole body, and sets on fire the course of nature; and it is set on fire by hell" (James 3:6).

10. ***Your unkind words hurt you more than they hurt your spouse.*** "By your words you will be justified, and by your words you will be condemned" (Matthew 12:37).

Pray That You Both Listen Well

A big part of communicating is learning to listen. That means not doing all the talking. It means asking God to give you ears to hear and a heart that is willing to receive what your spouse is saying. Often you can "bear one another's burdens, and so fulfill the law of Christ" by simply *listening* to your spouse talk about what his (her) burdens are (Galatians 6:2). If you are married to someone who is too distracted to listen, or refuses to listen because it might give the appearance of not knowing everything, or not being in control, or doesn't value what you have to say, pray that God will give him (her) ears to hear. Believe me, there is a greater impact when God convicts someone of not listening than there is when *you* try to do it.

Sometimes we *think* we know what the other person is saying, but God says not to answer too soon before you fully listen. "He who answers a matter before he hears it, it is folly and shame to him" (Proverbs 18:13). Listening means not talking while the other talks. How can you "rejoice with those who rejoice, and weep with those who weep" if you don't listen well enough to know if they're weeping or rejoicing? (Romans 12:15). If it seems your husband (wife) doesn't listen to you— or if he (she) mentions that *you* don't listen to him (her)—ask God to give you both a heart to hear. He loves answering that prayer.

Have you ever had something come between you and your spouse— just when everything seems to be going well—and break down the lines of communication so that you suddenly find yourselves completely missing each other? There may be some confusion, or an argument, or a distortion of what is being said, and you can't even understand the reason for it. Disrupting the lines of communication between a husband and wife is one of the enemy's most common tactics. Always keep in mind that the enemy of your soul is also the enemy of your marriage, and therefore the enemy of your communication. This disruption can happen in even the best of marriages, and in such subtle ways that you think it's you.

Ask God to keep you both aware of the enemy's hand trying to stir up strife and misunderstandings between you. Don't allow it to happen. Pray that the enemy's plan to disrupt communication will not succeed. If you see that it already has, declare that because *God* is *for* you, no one can be against you—not even the two of you.

PRAYERS *for* MY MARRIAGE

Prayer for Good Communication in My Marriage

Lord, I pray You would help my husband (wife) and me to be able to share our thoughts and feelings and refuse to be people who don't really talk to each other. Teach us to trust one another enough to talk about our deepest hopes, dreams, fears, and struggles. Teach us to spend time communicating with *You* every day so that our communication with each other will always be good.

Enable us to openly express love for one another each day, refusing to speak words that tear down, but only words that build up (Ephesians 4:29). Help us to be totally honest and open about everything. Teach us to listen carefully so we recognize the signs that give us greater understanding of one another. Show us how to find things we enjoy doing together so that we will always grow closer and never apart. Enable us to communicate kindness, appreciation, and honor to each other at all times.

Teach us to recognize the enemy's plan to steal, rob, and destroy our marriage. Enable us to understand his methods and recognize his attempts to stir up strife and miscommunication between us. Teach us to take instant authority over any attack he brings against us—especially in the area of communication. Help us to settle all matters of disagreement between us in a loving, compromising, and considerate manner. In Jesus' name I pray.

Prayer for Me to Communicate Well with My Husband (Wife)

Lord, I invite You to change me in the ways I need to be changed. Reveal any times where I have not said the right words or communicated the right thoughts to my husband (wife), and I will confess it before You, for I know I fall far short of Your glory (Romans 3:23). Teach me how to communicate openly and honestly so I will speak excellent, right, and truthful words (Proverbs 8:6-9). I know I cannot live in Your presence if I don't speak the truth (Psalm 15:1-3). Take away any deceit in my heart and mind so that evil will be far from me (Proverbs 17:20).

I pray that Your love will be so strong in my heart and mind that it comes out in everything I say. Give me the right words for every situation. Help me to remember to show appreciation to my husband (wife) for the good things he (she) does. Open my eyes if I am not seeing all of them. Give me ears to really hear what my husband (wife) is saying so that I can bear some of his (her) burdens by simply listening. Make me quick to hear and slow to speak (James 1:19). Give me the wisdom to have a good sense of timing.

Lord, You are greater than anything I face and stronger than all that opposes me and our marriage. Thank You that You have given me authority over the enemy. I pray I will always recognize his hand in our lives so that I will not allow any of his evil intentions to disrupt our relationship. I pray that "my mouth shall speak wisdom, and the meditation of my heart shall give understanding" (Psalm 49:3). I thank You in advance for the answers to my prayers. In Jesus' name I pray.

Prayer for My Husband (Wife) to Communicate Well with Me

Lord, I thank You for my husband (wife) and pray that You would open his (her) heart to all that You have for him (her) and for our marriage together. Help him (her) to know You better, to understand Your ways, and to see things from Your perspective. Show him (her) how to view the two of us the way You do. Make changes in him (her) that need to be made so that nothing will hinder him (her) from fulfilling the purpose and destiny You have for his (her) life and our lives together.

Lord, open my husband's (wife's) heart and fill it with Your love so that it overflows in the words he (she) speaks. Help him (her) to understand the consequences for any careless or hurtful words. Teach us both to be more discerning about what wounds the heart of the other. Speak through us so that our words to each other will be *Your* words. Enable us to be instruments of Your peace and grace every time we speak to each other. Convict my husband's (wife's) heart of the times he (she) has said words that have hurt me and did not glorify You. Enable him (her) to speak words of life and not death, words that build up and not tear down. Increase his (her) knowledge of Your ways so that he (she) will communicate openly, and never allow a cold silence to exist between us.

Lord, help my husband (wife) to be honest about everything. Convict his (her) heart about any times he (she) has not been. Break down any belief in him (her) that deceit is acceptable. Strengthen him (her) to resist the father of all lies (John 8:44). May he (she) refuse to be snared by his (her) own words (Proverbs 6:2). Halt any division between us, and cause us to be of the same mind and have the same good judgment (1 Corinthians 1:10). Where he (she) has had trouble communicating well, enable him (her) to do so now. Thank You that You are our rock and our Redeemer, and You can redeem all things (Psalm 78:35). In Jesus' name I pray.

TRUTH *to* STAND ON

Let the words of my mouth and the meditation of my heart
be acceptable in Your sight, O LORD, my strength
and my Redeemer.

PSALM 19:14

Though I speak with the tongues of men
and of angels, but have not love,
I have become sounding brass or a clanging cymbal.

1 CORINTHIANS 13:1

We all stumble in many things.
If anyone does not stumble in word,
he is a perfect man, able also to bridle the whole body.

JAMES 3:2

Husbands ought to love their own wives as their own bodies;
he who loves his wife loves himself...
and let the wife see that she respects her husband.

EPHESIANS 5:28,33

Wives, submit to your own husbands, as to the Lord...
Husbands love your wives, just as Christ also loved
the church and gave Himself for her.

EPHESIANS 5:22,25

PRACTICAL STEPS *to* GOING DEEPER

1. Read Hebrews 10:35-36 in your Bible. These verses speak of *not losing heart* when you go through trials, but instead to *have confidence*. This doesn't mean confidence in ourselves, but rather *confidence in God and His power to sustain us*. Write out a prayer asking God for those qualities shown here in italics so you can stand strong and see God do miracles in you and your spouse and your marriage.

2. What do you think is the best quality about your own communication skills? How would you like to improve the way you communicate with your spouse? What do you appreciate most about your spouse's communications skills? What would you most like to see improved about your spouse's ability to communicate well with you? In light of your answers, write out a prayer asking God to help you and your husband (wife) to either keep up the good work or improve your ability to communicate in the ways you would like to see happen.

3. Read Proverbs 3:3 in your Bible. The New King James Version says, "Let not mercy and truth forsake you...write them on the tablet of your heart." Write out a prayer asking God to help you and your spouse make *mercy* and *truth* to be so much a part of you that you never even consider doing anything less than what is merciful and truthful, especially toward each other.

2

Pray to Keep Anger from Hurting Your Relationship

The quickest way to put a halt to all meaningful and constructive communication in a marriage is for one spouse to allow anger to be aimed at the other. Anger is often accompanied by rudeness and verbal abuse, which not only damages the soul of the one who is on the receiving end of it, but also that of the angry person. That never works out well. It's best to pray ongoingly about this so that even moments of infrequent anger become obsolete in your marriage.

Arguments happen in every marriage. Every one of us can become angry about something at some point. But it is possible to argue without venting anger at one another. And it is worth praying to prevent that from happening. It's possible to express anger in a civilized and godly manner and not attack and hurt a spouse or children. If you frequently see anger rising up in either you or your spouse, it's a sign of trouble ahead. Anger always turns off communication, so if one or both of you can't get control of your anger, then the distance between you is bound to grow.

What the Bible Says About Anger

One of the most common complaints I hear from women struggling in their marriages is a problem with anger in their husbands. I occasionally hear it from men as a complaint about their wives, but it seems that more women suffer because of their husbands' anger. I have never seen any good come from one spouse venting their anger on the other, but I have seen a whole lot of devastation. That's why God has plenty to say about anger in His Word.

The Bible says that "he who troubles his own house will inherit the wind" (Proverbs 11:29). That means a person who constantly stirs up strife in his own family will never find all the success and blessing the Lord has for him. It means even if that person does get anything, it will blow through his fingers like the wind, and he won't be able to hold on to it.

Anything a person does that upsets their spouse and children troubles their house. Using anger to control their spouse troubles their house. Raising their voice in explosive, loud, demeaning words troubles their house. Being rude and abusive troubles their house. The consequences for entertaining anger are quite serious.

The anger I am talking about can drive a person to go beyond what is acceptable behavior. That kind of anger directed at a spouse is always selfish, and it will cause deep resentment. No one wants to be ruled by someone's anger—especially not from a husband (wife). Every angry outburst directed at a family member kills something in that person. It will eventually kill love, erode hope, and destroy the relationship.

We can be angry about something that happened. Anger's good when it's in response to such things as a violation of human rights, social injustice, or irreverence for the things of God. It is not good when communicating with your husband (wife). We can have temporary anger toward someone we think is an offender, but we cannot sin in the process. The Bible says, "'Be angry, and do not sin': do not let the sun go down on your wrath, nor give place to the devil" (Ephesians 4:26-27). That means no attacking, or hurting, or holding a grudge and waiting for payback time.

When angry words and actions beat up the soul of a family member, even if their body is untouched, it destroys their sense of who God made them to be. It hurts them in a grievous way and sucks love out of their heart. The Bible says, "Put off all these: anger, wrath, malice, blasphemy, filthy language out of your mouth" (Colossians 3:8). This is worth praying about to *prevent*. And it's crucial to pray about in order to *restore* the love and trust that has been eroded by angry outbursts. Pray that neither you nor your spouse will ever trouble your family with anger.

Seek the One Whose Love Is Unfailing

The first commandment says that the *most important thing* you can do is *love God.* The second commandment says that the *next most important thing* you can do is *love others* as you love yourself (Matthew 22:37-39). And the *most important person* to love above all others is your *spouse.*

A husband is supposed to love his wife (Ephesians 5:25), and a wife her husband (Titus 2:4). Loving your spouse is one of the ways you love and serve the Lord. God wants you as a married couple to love each other the way He loves you. But who can love the way Jesus loves *us*? He laid down His life for us. Who can love like that every day? When you get up every morning. When you see each other after a hard day. When one or both of you are definitely not at your best. *The only way you can truly love each other as God intended—and Jesus demonstrated—is to ask God to fill you each day with His love.* Selfless love, which is a fruit of the Spirit, comes by having the Spirit of love poured into you.

Christ demonstrated His love for the church by sacrificing Himself for her. (The "church" in the Bible refers to all of us who are believers in Jesus, not to a building.) He didn't get angry and yell at the church or be mean to the church or criticize and put down the church. He loved the church and gave Himself for her. This is the kind of love God wants us to have for our spouse. But this kind of love cannot be conjured up in the flesh. It takes the Lord of love filling your heart to overflowing with *His* love.

Regardless of how you are feeling in your life or your marriage, God will always fill your heart afresh with His love if you ask Him to. And as you spend time in God's presence in praise, worship, prayer, and in His Word, you will be infused with His love. When you have love because God has filled your heart with *His* love, it's far better than trying to conjure up a feeling of love in the flesh that you don't naturally have at the moment. By being filled with *God's* love—which is far greater than *human* love—you will have the ability to love your husband (wife) the way God wants you to, no matter what is happening.

Feelings of love in a marriage can rise and fall. Human love can ebb and flow. It changes because of emotions, circumstances, and seasons. But the love God wants us to have for our spouse is something that stays steady. It is a constant stream that pours from heaven into our human soul and overflows to those around us. But we can't love that way without *God's* help. That's why we have to stay connected to the Lord and tap into that love every day by spending time with *Him*. The only way you can always be patient, kind, loving, and *not easily angered* is if you are plugged into God's love. The only way for God's love to consistently flow out of you toward your spouse is to be filled to overflowing with it.

God's love is the fountainhead from which a good marriage flows. *Loving your husband or wife is the most important thing you can do next to loving God, because you have to become more like God to do it well.* The love of God will keep someone from being selfish, demanding, critical, angry, rude, or abusive. When God's love is in your heart, you will want to be patient and kind, and you won't want to insist on having your own way. You will be happy to say you're sorry, and you won't care about keeping a record of wrongs. In the flesh this is not possible, but with God it is.

If you want to stay in love with your spouse, stay in love with the Lord. And pray that your husband (wife) can do the same, because the flow of love found in Christ will touch you both and create an atmosphere of love, peace, and harmony within you that will greatly touch and enrich your relationship.

Anyone Can Get Free of Destructive Anger if They Want To

Everyone gets angry sometimes. Some people get angry *all* the time. Those people can't hold their anger in. A person like that always has anger bubbling just under the surface, waiting for some perceived imperfection in someone or some situation to summon it forth. It can explode in a moment of weakness on those around them. To be able to communicate without anger takes someone who can control his own spirit and not be controlled by their flesh. It takes a person of mercy instead of a person of wrath. "The merciful man does good for his own soul, but he who is cruel troubles his own flesh" (Proverbs 11:17).

It's not that a married couple can never get angry at one another. But if it happens often and in a hurtful way, there must be genuine repentance on the angry person's part—that means sincerely apologizing before God and before the person hurt by it—and have the clear intention of never doing that again. And there must be complete forgiveness from the spouse to whom the anger was directed. If those two things do not happen, the damage from that anger will be as if a hole was shot through the fabric of your relationship. Enough holes like that, and they will weaken the relationship so badly that only a miracle of God can keep it from ripping apart. We can only escape the consequences of our anger—which is sin—by the forgiveness of God and the power of the Holy Spirit.

The reason an angry person *can* get free of his own anger is because God sent His Son, Jesus, to save us from the consequences of our sins (Romans 8:2). When we receive Jesus, the Holy Spirit enables us to "not walk according to the flesh but according to the Spirit" (Romans 8:4). In other words, because of God's Spirit in us, we have the power to reject all works of the flesh. But we have to *want* to do that, because if we don't, we will be led by our desires for constant fleshly gratification. We must desire to be led by the Spirit of God.

Abusive Anger Is Never Acceptable

There is never a time when anger directed at a spouse will please God. It will always be fleshly minded and God hates it. "To be carnally minded is death, but to be spiritually minded is life and peace. Because the carnal mind is enmity against God; for it is not subject to the law of God, nor indeed can be. So then, those who are in the flesh cannot please God" (Romans 8:6-8). No one who has any sense of who God is—who He *really* is—wants to be in the position of not pleasing Him.

If you or your husband (wife) repeatedly commit a *sin,* you invite the spirit associated with that sin to have a *place* in your *heart.* For example, if you tell enough lies, you invite a lying spirit to operate in your life. Then you start lying even when you have no reason to, and lying becomes a habit you can't break. In the same way, if you allow yourself to frequently give place to feelings of anger at your spouse or your children, you will end up with an angry spirit that can surface and attack at any time.

When you or your husband (wife) do not control your anger, anger will control *you.* Only the power of God's Holy Spirit can set you free from a fleshly spirit of anger. But no one can be set free from something they don't even recognize they have invited into their life. That's why it is best to pray in advance of this happening if possible. But if it is already happening, you have the power and authority in Jesus' name to resist it in your marriage by praying for your spouse—or yourself—to be set free of it.

If we live according to our flesh—that means giving the flesh what it wants when it wants it—we reap death. The death of our relationships and the death of the future God has for us. If we want to see our marriages succeed, we have to put to death the constant gratifying of our flesh. If we want to see our purpose and future fulfilled, we have to live according to the Spirit and not the flesh. "If you live according to the flesh you will die; but if by the Spirit you put to death the deeds of the body, you will live. For as many as are led by the Spirit of God, these are sons of God" (Romans 8:13-14).

We don't have to be a slave to our flesh by giving place to anger. When we are led by God's Spirit, we are truly children of God, and we will inherit the blessings God has for us.

Seven Things THAT ARE TRUE ABOUT *Anger*

1. ***You are able to stop being angry.*** "Cease from anger, and forsake wrath; do not fret—it only causes harm" (Psalm 37:8).

2. ***Anger stirs up strife and causes you to sin.*** "An angry man stirs up strife, and a furious man abounds in transgression" (Proverbs 29:22).

3. ***Taking control of anger makes you stronger.*** "He who is slow to anger is better than the mighty, and he who rules his spirit than he who takes a city" (Proverbs 16:32).

4. ***It is to your benefit to let some things go instead of getting angry.*** "The discretion of a man makes him slow to anger, and his glory is to overlook a transgression" (Proverbs 19:11).

5. ***Only fools are quick to get angry.*** "Do not hasten in your spirit to be angry, for anger rests in the bosom of fools" (Ecclesiastes 7:9).

6. ***Angry people are never good to be around.*** "Make no friendship with an angry man, and with a furious man do not go" (Proverbs 22:24).

7. ***Angry words inspire more anger.*** "A soft answer turns away wrath, but a harsh word stirs up anger" (Proverbs 15:1).

If You Are Often Angry

There is an epidemic of anger in marriages today. If anger is expressed frequently without repentance and forgiveness, it erodes all that has been established in the relationship and builds a wall between a husband and wife that will eventually become insurmountable. Anger has consequences, and they are never more apparent than in a marriage.

If you are the one with anger, you can make a sound-minded decision to not be ruled by it. The hurt you inflict on the soul of someone God has given you to love will bring consequences you won't want to experience. Don't allow yourself to direct anger at your spouse. Direct it instead at the enemy of your soul and marriage. No matter what happens in your life, take it to God first. Ask God if displaying your anger will be glorifying to Him. He will put the answer to that in your heart.

As with all negative emotions, anger begins in the mind. What you do and say comes out of what takes root in your mind. So fill your mind with the right thoughts. Paul said it beautifully: "Summing it all up, friends, I'd say you'll do best by filling your minds and meditating on things true, noble, reputable, authentic, compelling, gracious—the best, not the worst; the beautiful, not the ugly; things to praise, not things to curse...Do that, and God, who makes everything work together, will work you into His most excellent harmonies" (Philippians 4:8-9 MSG).

Don't let anger control you. Control *it* instead. When you let anger control you, you constantly blame your spouse for the things that upset you. Anger can make you blind to the feelings of other people. It can cause you to hurt people you love. When you are angry, it is hard to see anything except your own feelings. That's why most angry people have no clue as to how hurtful their anger is and what it's doing to their spouse and children.

If your husband (wife) makes you angry, ask God to reveal to you if this is truly something you should be angry about. If not, ask God to take your anger away. Ask God to give you a calm spirit, the right words, and perfect timing so you can confront your spouse in a godly manner about what has angered you. Then, with the leading of the Holy Spirit, calmly express your feelings without attacking your husband (wife). Write out your feelings *first* so you can delete any words you might regret.

Try to remember that both of you are on the same side and have a common enemy, so be angry at the enemy. Don't ever take revenge. It will only make *you* sick. Let *God* punish the offender if it's necessary. God says, "Vengeance is Mine" and He means it (Deuteronomy 32:35). Lashing out at your spouse with the desire to hurt will only punish you.

If Your Husband (Wife) Is Often Angry

Common courtesy is required in a marriage. Why should a person be polite, considerate, and kind to everyone else, and rude, inconsiderate, and mean to the family they are supposed to love most? If your spouse treats a stranger with more courtesy than he (she) does you, then he (she) is committing a sin that grieves the Holy Spirit. This is not a good position to be in. If you are the one being treated that way, know that God does not want you to deal with your spouse's angry spirit. If you have been hurt and deeply wounded as a result of your spouse's anger, turn to God to save, heal, and deliver you from any resentment and give you peace.

Most people with an anger problem don't see themselves as angry; they see themselves as right. They feel completely justified in what they say and do because they think they have a right to be angry. And the more self-centered they are, the more they feed off their own anger.

If there is an anger problem in your spouse, take it to God immediately. Ask Him to give you *His* perspective on it. If it is minor and a rare occurrence and you should just overlook it, ask God to help you do so. If it is a problem, ask God to show you how to talk to your husband (wife) about it. Letting any issue go unresolved is dangerous—this is especially true of anger. Pray for your husband (wife) to be completely free of it. One of the greatest things you can give your spouse is your commitment to pray for him (her). Your prayers are a gift that will help him (her) get his (her) anger under control. "A gift in secret pacifies anger" (Proverbs 21:14).

If This Has Already Happened to You

If hurtful anger has already manifested in your marriage, keep in mind that it matters to God how a person treats their spouse. A husband or wife will be called to account if it is not good. Knowing that should make us all watch what we do and say, and help us to be more careful about this.

The way I reacted to my husband's anger directed at me was to withdraw from him. But that meant while Michael would get all of his anger out of *his* system, it would still be stuck in *mine*. Eventually, when I was finally able to see the ultimate consequences for not treating your spouse with love and kindness, I began to feel sorrier for him than I did for myself. I saw that as long as I repented of any resentment I had, I could be free. There would be consequences in *his* life, but not *mine*. I prayed for him to see the truth about his anger—how it displeased the

Lord—and how he would bear the consequences for it. Even though it still hurt me every time he was angry, I loved him enough to not want to see him suffer because of it.

If you are married to someone who is often angry and who takes his (her) anger out on you, or your children, know that this kind of behavior is hurting him (her) more than it is you. It may hurt you now, but it will hurt him (her) for a lifetime if it does not stop. It will shut off the blessings God wants to bring into his (her) life. He (she) can delay his (her) destiny because of anger. "Do not let your mouth cause your flesh to sin, nor say before the messenger of God that it was an error. Why should God be angry at your excuse and destroy the work of your hands?" (Ecclesiastes 5:6).

Do you ever see something that resides deep within yourself or your spouse that seems to have a life of its own? Does it fester and churn and appear to maintain a readiness to surge and strike at any moment, for any reason? And does the manifestation of anger seem way out of proportion to the offense? If you said yes to any of these questions, that indicates there is a problem. If some little thing can trigger anger, and suddenly rage comes forth when least expected over what seems to be a nonissue, this requires serious intervention in prayer and counseling. That kind of anger looks for a reason and a way to attack and hurt, and there seems to be great satisfaction in it. There appears to be little if any recognition in the angry person of what their anger does to those toward whom it is directed. In the angry person's mind anger is always justified because he (she) deserves to be angry for whatever reason.

A person's frequent anger can be explained, but it is never justified. I am not talking about an incident happening that would make anyone angry. I am talking about someone who has an angry spirit inside of them that they frequently give place to because it gives them the opportunity to be in control and get their way. It forces their spouse and children to walk on eggshells because they are always afraid that it is going to erupt again. This is no way to live—especially not in a marriage where there is no escape.

Pray for your husband (wife) not to be controlled by anger. If it already has become a problem, pray for him (her) to see what harm it is causing to himself (herself), as well as to everyone around him (her) who sees it and is affected by it. Pray he (she) will see how foolish he (she) is acting and will want to be set free of all anger.

Seven Things THAT ARE TRUE ABOUT *Being a Fool*

1. ***A fool thinks he is always right.*** "The way of a fool is right in his own eyes, but he who heeds counsel is wise" (Proverbs 12:15).

2. ***A fool cares only about himself.*** "A fool has no delight in understanding, but in expressing his own heart" (Proverbs 18:2).

3. ***A fool finds it easy to quarrel.*** "It is honorable for a man to stop striving, since any fool can start a quarrel" (Proverbs 20:3).

4. ***A fool trusts himself completely.*** "He who trusts in his own heart is a fool, but whoever walks wisely will be delivered" (Proverbs 28:26).

5. ***A fool vents all his feelings.*** "A fool vents all his feelings, but a wise man holds them back" (Proverbs 29:11).

6. ***A fool's words will do him harm.*** "The words of a wise man's mouth are gracious, but the lips of a fool shall swallow him up" (Ecclesiastes 10:12).

7. ***A fool destroys himself.*** "Fools are undone by their big mouths; their souls are crushed by their words" (Proverbs 18:7 MSG).

If Anger Becomes Abusive

If a person gives *place* to anger and goes with it wherever it takes them, and if they say and do whatever feels good at the moment as they release that anger toward their spouse, it is abuse. There is a difference between simply getting angry about something, and letting anger become a weapon that crushes a spouse or child's heart, beats down their spirit, or hurts their physical body. Someone who will allow their anger to go that far has a mental and emotional disorder and needs professional help. In order to be free of that kind of anger, they also need the power of the Holy Spirit to cleanse their heart and deliver them from this selfish work of the flesh.

Abusive people love their anger to the point of actually looking for ways to be angry. Anger empowers them and fuels the fire they love to fan into flame. It gives them what they perceive as control. But actually, anger illustrates their utter lack of control. Lashing out and yelling at someone God has given you to love is sin.

Any words spoken in explosive anger can be abusive. A loudly raised voice and poor choice of words can cut like a knife into a person's soul. Angry outbursts are loveless and full of the desire to hurt. The verbal abuser doesn't try to see it from the perspective of the person they are abusing. They don't care to know how badly their anger makes the recipient of their anger feel because all they care about is how *they* feel themselves. If there are ever times when your spouse's angry outburst has killed something in you, that's abuse. Or if there are times when your own angry words have destroyed something in your spouse or your children, that is abuse. Abuse destroys lives.

If you ever find your husband (wife) beating you down with his (her) words and you feel threatened, ask God to show you what to do. *I'm not telling any wife to stay in her marriage if her mental or physical health is in danger, and especially not if her life is being threatened in any way whatsoever.*

Abuse of any kind goes against all that God is and all that He has for you. No one is required to take it.

If you are afraid of what your spouse might do to harm you or your children, make plans to get free right away. Secretly find a place to go and people to help you move out. I have known of too many people who waited too long and suffered devastating consequences. Don't be one of those statistics.

If your husband is physically abusing you, call a domestic violence hotline or emergency services. Ask someone to help you do what you need to do.

Find someone who understands the situation and can help you make the right decisions as to what to do about it. If you need to leave home for your own safety or the safety of your children, they will help you do that. Even if you don't end up leaving immediately, it is good to have a plan. You need a safe place to go, a way to get there, someone to help, money you can have access to, and the legal papers and possessions you need to take with you.

Physical abuse doesn't go away on its own. It only gets worse. If you don't want to help yourself, then think about helping your husband by leaving and not returning until he gets help and is cured. Being destroyed by someone who has an emotional disorder such as uncontrolled anger is not the kind of self-sacrifice or martyrdom God is looking for. Don't enable your husband to suffer the consequences of his own sin of abuse. Help him get the healing needed to become a whole person. You can pray for him from afar. Ask God to deliver your husband (wife) from the evil spirit troubling him (her) (see 1 Samuel 16:14-23).

There is no excuse for abuse. It is never justified.

A man who physically or emotionally abuses his wife is emotionally sick and has a serious problem. Of all emotional disorders, anger can be by far the most destructive. It is more destructive than depression, anxiety, or fear because it is usually directed at the spouse in some abusive and destructive way. Don't fool around with this; it's too dangerous. He (she) needs professional help and fast. A man who beats his wife and children in any way should be removed from them completely. Even if the abuse is only verbal, it is still extremely damaging. Scars happen internally as well as externally. Anger and abuse is the problem of the person who has it and not the fault of the one abused. No possible action or words of yours deserve violent, angry outbursts. Do not blame yourself.

You are not saved by your husband (wife) or your marriage. You are saved by Jesus Christ. While I am not advocating divorce, you should still know that you will not lose your salvation if you end up getting divorced. In an abusive situation, you may lose your life if you don't.

Don't Underestimate the Value of Good Christian Counseling

If you or your spouse has an anger problem, even if it has not progressed to abuse, seek counseling together or apart as soon as possible. If nothing else, you may need a referee. If your spouse refuses to go, seek it for yourself. Don't ignore signs that suggest something is broken and needs to be fixed. Find a good Christian counselor who does not believe "the abused person asked for it," or that "you have to stay in an abusive relationship because God said to submit to your husband." Both of these views are not only unbelievably out of touch with reality, but are cruel, wrong, ungodly, and dangerous. Find a counselor who truly knows God's ways and values you and your children's individual lives as God does.

If you have not seen any anger manifested in either you or your husband (wife), thank God for that and pray you never will. If you have experienced it, take all the advice I shared in this chapter seriously. Don't do nothing.

PRAYERS *for* MY MARRIAGE

Prayer to Keep Anger from Hurting Our Relationship

Dear Lord, help me and my husband (wife) to be "slaves of righteousness" so we will always do the right thing and never allow anger to control our lives in any way (Romans 6:19). Keep us from ever using anger as a weapon to hurt one another so that it drives a wedge between us. Fill our hearts full of Your love and peace so there is no room for anger, rudeness, or any kind of abuse. Teach us to pray about everything and make all of our needs known to You, knowing that when we do You have promised in Your Word to give us Your peace (see Philippians 4:6-7).

Enable us to always see the best in one another and not the worst. Teach us to find reasons to praise and not complain about each other so that we can be brought into harmony with You (see Philippians 4:8-9). Help us to always "pursue the things which make for peace" and the things by which we may edify one another (Romans 14:19). Enable us to exhibit the fruit of the Spirit—which is "love, joy, peace, longsuffering, kindness, goodness, faithfulness, gentleness, self-control"—and not a harvest of the flesh (Galatians 5:22-23). Take all anger from us and teach us to love each other from a pure heart and a good conscience (1 Timothy 1:5-6). In Jesus' name I pray.

Prayer to Keep Anger from Ruling Me

Lord, help me to dwell on the good and the positive in my life and in my husband (wife). I know that it is You who "looks deep inside people and searches through their thoughts" (Proverbs 20:27 NCV). Search the inner depths of my heart and expose anything that is not of You so I can be set free of it.

Lord, where I have directed anger toward my husband (wife) or held anger inside of me, I confess that as sin and ask You to forgive me and take all anger away. Heal any wounds that I have inflicted in him (her) with my words. Help me to speak good words to my husband (wife), for I know that pleases You (Proverbs 15:23). Where I have shown anger toward any other family member, I confess it to You as sin. Bring Your restoration to every situation where it is needed.

Thank You, Lord, that You will redeem my soul in peace from the battle that is against me (Psalm 55:18). I believe that You, the God of peace, "will crush Satan" under my feet shortly (Romans 16:20). Help me to live righteously because I know there is a connection between obedience to Your ways and peace (Psalm 85:10). Help me to "depart from evil and do good; seek peace and pursue it" (Psalm 34:14). Thank You that You will take away all anger in me, and any rudeness or abusive behavior I have exhibited at any time toward my husband (wife) or children. Keep me in perfect peace, because my mind is fixed on You (Isaiah 26:3). In Jesus' name I pray.

Prayer to Keep Anger from Ruling My Husband (Wife)

Lord, I don't want to ever feel that "my soul has dwelt too long with one who hates peace" (Psalm 120:6). Deliver my husband (wife) from any anger, rudeness, or abusive behavior. Your Word says, "A wholesome tongue is a tree of life, but perverseness in it breaks the spirit" (Proverbs 15:4). Where I have ever felt that an angry spirit in my husband (wife) has hurt me or broken my spirit, I pray You would heal those wounds and take away any resentment I have because of it.

I pray You would set my husband (wife) free from anger. Help him (her) to recognize a spirit of anger rising up in him (her) and reject it completely. Strengthen him (her) to be able to control his (her) mind and emotions and help him (her) to remember that "we do not wrestle against flesh and blood, but against principalities, against powers," and the rulers of darkness and wickedness (Ephesians 6:12). Teach him (her) to be slow to anger the way You are (James 1:19). Help him (her) to understand that anger never produces spiritual fruit (James 1:20). I pray that all anger, rudeness, or abusive behavior in my husband (wife) will be evaporated by the power of Your Holy Spirit, and that he (she) will have a strong desire to reject his (her) carnal side and become spiritually minded. Let there be no reason for me to fear his (her) anger. But if there is, give me wisdom about what I should do and help me to do it.

Direct his (her) heart "into the love of God and into the patience of Christ" (2 Thessalonians 3:5). Help him (her) to flee anger and pursue righteousness, godliness, faith, love, patience, and gentleness (1 Timothy 6:11). Help me to "lie down in peace, and sleep; for You alone, O LORD, make me dwell in safety" (Psalm 4:8). In Jesus' name I pray.

TRUTH *to* STAND ON

Be angry, and do not sin.
Meditate within your heart on your bed, and be still.

PSALM 4:4

So then, my beloved brethren,
let every man be swift to hear, slow to speak, slow to wrath;
for the wrath of man does not produce the righteousness of
God.

JAMES 1:19-20

Beloved, let us love one another, for love is of God;
and everyone who loves is born of God and knows God...
In this is love, not that we loved God,
but that He loved us and sent His Son
to be the propitiation for our sins.
Beloved, if God so loved us,
we also ought to love one another.

1 JOHN 4:7,10-11

Above all things have fervent love for one another,
for love will cover a multitude of sins.

1 PETER 4:8

If you abide in Me, and My words abide in you,
you will ask what you desire, and it shall be done for you.

JOHN 15:7

PRACTICAL STEPS *to* GOING DEEPER

1. Read Ephesians 4:26-27 in your Bible. Do you or your spouse ever
have anger that results in hurtful words or actions? If so, how would

you like to see any kind of anger better resolved? Write out a prayer telling God about any anger situation between you and your spouse and how you would like to see it resolved. If you never have any anger problems toward each other, write out a prayer asking God to help you both always keep it that way.

2. Read John 15:10-12 in your Bible. What is the promise of the Lord in these verses? What is the benefit of living God's way? What should be the guiding force behind how you and your spouse relate to one another? Do you feel there has been enough love expressed between you and your spouse, or do you think that could be improved? Write out your answers in a prayer to God. If you feel your love for one another is expressed perfectly, write out a prayer thanking God for that and praying it will always be that way.

3. Read 1 Peter 4:8 in your Bible. What does your husband (wife) need from you above all else? What does having deep love for one another do for your marriage? Write out a prayer asking God to help you and your spouse to be so in love with the Lord that you never fall out of love for each other. If you feel in any way that your expression of love for one another has already diminished from what you would like it to be, ask God to ignite *His* love within you both and restore your love for one another in greater dimensions than you have ever had before.

3

Pray to Keep Forgiveness Flowing Freely

*I*t is crucial in any marriage that you be able to forgive each other the way Jesus has forgiven you (Ephesians 4:32). Jesus forgave you completely. No looking back. No remembering. That means you should not keep a list of the ways you have been wronged by others. It means refusing to carry bitterness and resentment about anything. It means not allowing yourself to be an injustice collector who keeps one foot in the past, always brooding over what happened there. It means living each day free of bad memories and looking to the future with hope. True forgiveness means completely letting go of an offense and refusing to hold it against the offender. That kind of forgiveness is impossible for any length of time without the Lord's help. We need God helping us to forgive every day. That's why it is so important to pray about this as early as possible in your marriage—as soon as you realize the need for it—and preferably as a preventative right from the start.

Sometimes Forgiveness Has Layers

Forgiveness is a decision we make, and we certainly *know* if we made that decision or not. We don't accidentally forgive someone without realizing it. But it *is* possible to *not forgive* someone without realizing it. We can think we've let go of something when we haven't. Not totally. That's because if the offenses have been repeated over a period of time, they build up in layers inside of us. Forgiveness can be a process in that case, and we have to work through the layers. The deepest and most painful layers can come at the end, which can make you feel like you're not getting anywhere. But it's not true. It's just that you are getting down to the deeper layers that are more hurtful because they have been stuffed down and covered over by an extreme effort to move on. It is a survival tactic.

Mary Anne was the Christian counselor I had seen who asked me to confess my unforgiveness toward my mother. Months after that she called me into her office and told me she felt God had revealed to her that I had unforgiveness toward my dad as well. I told her I didn't think that was right because my dad was not abusive to me. I thought, *Why would I need to forgive him?* She said, "Just ask God about it and see what He reveals."

On my drive home from her office, I prayed about this and said, "Lord, do I have any unforgiveness in me toward my dad?"

I fully expected God to say, "Definitely not, My good and faithful servant." But instantly I was struck through the heart by the truth. God clearly impressed upon me that I had truly not forgiven my father. In that moment I saw the deep unforgiveness I had toward my dad for all those years of not protecting me from my mother. And he was the only one who could. He was never abusive to me, so I didn't think there was any reason to forgive him. But when my eyes were opened to the truth, I saw how my father had never rescued me from my mother's insanity—he never rescued me from the closet where I was sent by my mother—and I had held this deep hurt against him without even realizing it.

I broke down and sobbed so hard I had to pull my car over to the side of the freeway. I confessed my unforgiveness toward my dad and asked God to forgive me. When I did that, I felt a release in my spirit that I had never felt before. Looking back now, I believe that if I had not *asked* God specifically to reveal any unforgiveness in my heart, I doubt if I could have ever seen this on my own. We can't always see our own unforgiving attitudes, but God will show us the truth if we ask Him to.

Make the Right Choice

Forgiveness is a choice we have to make every day. We must choose to *live* in forgiveness. And never is that truer than when you are married. Besides *loving* your husband (wife), the next most important thing you can do in your marriage is *forgive* him (her) for whatever he (she) has done to upset you.

Even in the best of marriages, forgiveness is always necessary. For two completely different humans to live together in harmony, there are bound to be disappointments, misunderstandings, and hurts. We have to continually be "bearing with one another, and forgiving one another" (Colossians 3:13). We can't wait until our spouse deserves it or asks for it. Not forgiving kills your relationship. It also kills your health. It kills your joy. And it upsets your close walk with God.

When Jesus was asked by His disciples if we need to forgive others as many as *seven times,* He said that *"seventy times seven"* was more like it (Matthew 18:21-22). I did the math and that's 490 times. The point is, we need to forgive as often as necessary. You might be living with someone you have to forgive 490 times a day, but you will still have to forgive as often as it takes for your heart to be free.

In the prayer that Jesus taught us to pray, He said to *ask* God to forgive us, just as we forgive *others* (Matthew 6:12). That means if we ask God for forgiveness for things we've done, while at the same time refusing to forgive our spouse, then we are not going to enjoy the full benefits of God's forgiveness to us. In other words, if we don't release others by forgiving them, we ourselves will not find the release we need to move on in our lives (Mark 11:25). Not forgiving will always hold us back. Although we may try hard, we won't be able to move beyond where we are to where we're supposed to be.

If you have ever been emotionally devastated by something your husband (wife) has said or done—or something he (she) did *not* say or do—sometimes the hurt is so great that you feel you can't get over it enough to forgive. The unforgiveness and bitterness can become so deeply rooted that it takes a major work of God to make you even *want* to forgive. When that happens, ask God to help you. Say, "God, help me to want to forgive my husband (wife). Help me to forgive him (her) completely." You have to do this "lest any root of bitterness springing up cause trouble, and by this many become defiled" (Hebrews 12:15). Bitterness is hard to get rid of, and it does the most damage to *you*.

Not only is it important to forgive your spouse, but it is also important for you to forgive everyone else in your life. If you have any unforgiveness toward a family member, neighbor, friend, acquaintance, or coworker, it will take its toll on you personally. It will cause you to become bitter, and it will show on your face and be revealed in your voice when you speak. It will come out in your body in the form of sickness or disease of some sort. Our bodies, minds, and souls were not designed to live in unforgiveness. It destroys us from the inside out, because it is a poison for which there is no antidote except total forgiveness. And it will affect your marriage whether you realize it or not, because unforgiveness comes out in your personality and people sense it, even if they don't know what it is.

Decide to Be a Forgiving Person

I have learned that the best way to live is to decide in *advance* to be a person who forgives. It takes the pressure off because you don't have to try to make that decision every time something bad happens and you're reeling from disappointment, hurt, or your own anger.

Once I was finally and fully convinced that not forgiving destroys us and forgiveness sets us free, I decided to be a forgiving person all the time. Of course, once I made that decision, I was put to the test. But the next time my husband became angry, instead of reacting to him in my normal negative way, I caught myself and remembered that I had made the decision to forgive him even for the future times when he gets that way. I had already come to understand that I had not done anything deserving of this anger to my knowledge, so instead of withdrawing in hurt the way I usually would have, I pressed him for why he was so angry and upset. As it turned out, it was something that had happened at work. When he told me about it, I could totally understand why he felt the way he did. I would have been upset too. What I did not understand was why he felt he had the right to take it out on me. I called him on it every time it happened and prayed he would start recognizing it was wrong on his own. He eventually did and apologized each time it happened.

The truth is every person has a story in their past that has made them who they are. And only God knows the whole story. Every angry and cruel person has had some kind of mistreatment, pain, and tragedy in their past—sometimes a hurt so deep they can't even express or understand it—and they sometimes do terrible things to the very people they are supposed to love because of it. Their need to express it outweighs their sense of decency and compassion. It's as if a spirit of revenge takes over for them, and they vent their pain and frustration through their anger without even considering what it does to the heart and soul of the person on the receiving end. The fact that there is an explanation as to why an angry person acts inappropriately to their spouse in *no way justifies cruel* or *rude behavior.*

No matter how cruel or mean a person has been to you, releasing them with your forgiveness frees *you.* It releases you from them so you can move on without that bad memory keeping you stuck in the past. That doesn't mean you allow that person to continue hurting you.

Once I decided *in advance* of it ever happening again, that I was going to forgive my husband for his anger, I felt sad for Michael when he became angry. I knew he was hurting himself by cutting off what God wanted to bring into his life and that he would be the loser because of it. I felt sorry for the little boy who was made to feel like a failure for something he didn't understand and couldn't help. I regret that I wasn't healed, whole, and mature enough sooner so I would not have taken his misdirected anger so personally. Even though it was directed at me, it had a history back before I ever knew him. Only after God had worked complete forgiveness in my heart was I able to see all that.

Remember What God Has Following You

Because God is a God of mercy and His mercy endures forever, you can trust that He will have mercy on you (1 Chronicles 17:13). *King David said, "Surely goodness and mercy shall follow me all the days of my life; and I will dwell in the house of the* LORD *forever"* (Psalm 23:6). That means if God's goodness and mercy are following you, they are covering your back. When you see God's goodness and mercy in your rearview mirror, that makes it easier for you to show goodness and mercy to others. Jesus said, "Blessed are the merciful, for they shall obtain mercy" (Matthew 5:7). If you want to always be the beneficiary of God's mercy, you must extend it to others. One way you show mercy to your husband (wife) is by forgiving him (her) whenever he (she) does or says something that hurts or disturbs you.

God's mercy is far-reaching. "As the heavens are high above the earth, so great is His mercy toward those who fear Him; as far as the east is from the west, so far has He removed our transgressions from us" (Psalm 103:11-12). That is about as far-reaching as it gets. We will always have trouble extending that much mercy without God's help. In other words, if on our own we can't find the mercy in us to be able to forgive completely, God will help us when we ask Him to. There are times when something in us wants to punish, get even, or hurt back instead of being merciful and forgiving. But when we do that we get locked up inside, just as if we are in a physical prison. Forgiveness is the only key to unlock that prison door and get free. And it starts with having a heart of mercy.

Seven Things THAT ARE TRUE ABOUT *God's Mercy*

1. **God's mercy is great.** "Great is Your mercy toward me, and You have delivered my soul from the depths of Sheol" (Psalm 86:13).

2. **God's mercy is abundant toward you.** "The Lord is merciful and gracious, slow to anger, and abounding in mercy" (Psalm 103:8).

3. **When you have mercy the way God does, you find**

life. "He who follows righteousness and mercy finds life, righteousness and honor" (Proverbs 21:21).

4. *Forgiveness is an act of mercy.* "I desire mercy and not sacrifice, and the knowledge of God more than burnt offerings" (Hosea 6:6).

5. *God's mercy covers all your concerns.* "The LORD will perfect that which concerns me; Your mercy, O LORD, endures forever; do not forsake the works of Your hands" (Psalm 138:8).

6. *When you don't have mercy, you are not shown mercy.* "Judgment is without mercy to the one who has shown no mercy. Mercy triumphs over judgment" (James 2:13).

7. *God's mercy never ends.* "The LORD is good; His mercy is everlasting, and His truth endures to all generations" (Psalm 100:5).

First Things First

The first thing the disciples did after Jesus was resurrected and they received the Holy Spirit was to forgive others (John 20:21-23). It is also the first thing we need to do as we come before God each day. Say, "Lord, show me where I have unforgiveness, and I will confess it to You as sin so I can be free from it." If you already know that you have unforgiveness in your heart, confess it to the Lord. It's not that He doesn't know about it. It's that He wants you to say it. Confession is for *you.* Then say, "Lord, take this burden of unforgiveness off my shoulders and help me to let go of it completely so I can walk free."

What's even harder is that God asks us to *bless* those who hurt us (Matthew 5:43-44). Sometimes it feels as though not killing them should be enough. But God wants more than restraint. He wants us to actually want good things for them. He want us to show mercy to someone we think doesn't deserve it, just as He showed mercy to us when *we* didn't deserve it. The thing is, forgiving your spouse does not depend on him (her) asking you for forgiveness or showing any repentance. If we wait for that, we could wait a lifetime for something that may never happen.

Though horrible things were done to Joseph in the Bible, he was amazingly forgiving. He was sold into slavery by his jealous brothers, but he still found favor wherever he went. He ended up in prison after being falsely accused, but was eventually appointed second in command to Pharaoh. Through it all, Joseph knew that what others intended for evil, God was using for good. He eventually said that very thing to his brothers who had betrayed him (Genesis 50:20). When we have that kind of amazing willingness to forgive, God will use our very act of forgiveness to turn things around in our marriage. He can even restore a marriage that is dying if the people in it extend total forgiveness to one another.

Seven Things THAT ARE TRUE ABOUT *Forgiving*

1. ***Forgiving brings blessings to you.*** "Finally, all of you be of one mind, having compassion for one another; love as brothers, be tenderhearted, be courteous; not returning evil for evil or reviling for reviling, but on the contrary blessing, knowing that you were called to this, that you may inherit a blessing" (1 Peter 3:8-9).

2. ***Forgiving others paves the way for you to be forgiven.*** "Judge not, and you shall not be judged. Condemn not, and you shall not be condemned. Forgive, and you will be forgiven" (Luke 6:37).

3. ***Forgiving allows you to forget and move forward.*** "One thing I do, forgetting those things which are behind and reaching forward to those things which are ahead, I press

toward the goal for the prize of the upward call of God in Christ Jesus" (Philippians 3:13-14).

4. *Forgiving frees you to worship God with your whole heart.* "Therefore if you bring your gift to the altar, and there remember that your brother has something against you, leave your gift there before the altar, and go your way. First be reconciled to your brother, and then come and offer your gift" (Matthew 5:23-24).

5. *Forgiving proves that you are kind and tenderhearted.* "And be kind to one another, tenderhearted, forgiving one another, just as God in Christ forgave you" (Ephesians 4:32).

6. *Forgiving makes you Christlike.* "Even as Christ forgave you, so you also must do" (Colossians 3:13).

7. *Forgiving is the way you pursue peace and keep from becoming bitter.* "Pursue peace with all people, and holiness, without which no one will see the Lord: looking carefully lest anyone fall short of the grace of God; lest any root of bitterness springing up cause trouble, and by this many become defiled" (Hebrews 12:14-15).

If This Has Already Happened to You

In the beginning of your marriage relationship, forgiving your spouse may come easy. That is the time to pray that forgiving each other will *always* be easy—or better yet, unnecessary. However, when you have to be forgiving time and again for the same thing, you wonder if perhaps you are encouraging him (her) by *appearing* to condone his (her) undesirable actions with your forgiveness. You may be hesitant to forgive because you're afraid that in doing so you are setting yourself up for the same thing to happen again. But there is a clear line between enabling and forgiving. In other words, you can still confront your spouse about changing his (her) ways and pray for that to happen. But if he (she) doesn't do it, you can refuse to let it eat at you and make you bitter.

Forgiving does not mean you are giving the offender a free pass to commit the same offense again. It does not mean you are giving that person a license to walk all over you or continue to hurt you. It doesn't make you a doormat.

Forgiveness doesn't make the other person right; it makes you free.

When it is necessary to forgive your spouse for the same thing repeatedly, it becomes harder instead of easier as time goes on. You may know the feeling. You've already said "I forgive you" to your spouse. You've confessed your unforgiveness to the Lord and asked Him to cleanse your heart and set you free of it. But you still have that feeling of not being able to let it go completely. You're trying to be forgiving, but you just cannot seem to do a thorough job of it. The unforgiveness may still be there because you want to see some sign of recognition from your spouse regarding the pain he (she) caused you.

We have to remember that God is the one with the lightning, so we must leave any retribution to Him. It's better to talk to God and tell Him honestly how you feel. Say, "Lord, I confess I am hurt because it seems as though my husband (wife) is never required to change and I *am*." Or, "Lord, why doesn't my husband (wife) have any financial wisdom, and why do I have to suffer for it?" Or, "Lord, why did You let me marry someone with an alcohol problem just like my dad had?" Or, "Lord, why do I have to be the responsible one, and he (she) can just float through life like a child?"

We have to remember that God is so merciful, He doesn't even remember your sins once He forgives them. "I, even I, am He who blots out your transgressions for My own sake; and I will not remember your sins" (Isaiah 43:25). If you are having trouble forgiving your husband (wife), be honest with God about it. Job cried out honestly to God in his pain saying, "I will not restrain my mouth; I will speak in the anguish of my spirit; I will complain in the bitterness of my soul" (Job 7:11). We have a God who understands our pain and wants us to come to Him for comfort.

If you feel you can't forgive someone, ask God to penetrate your unforgiveness with His love. When we are faced with the impossible, God says the way to proceed is "not by might nor by power, but by My Spirit" (Zechariah 4:6). This means certain things will not be accomplished by human strength, but only by the power of God. God's Spirit will enable us to forgive even the unforgivable.

Layers of offenses accumulate, causing layers of forgiveness to be needed. We have to realize that in our lives—and especially in our marriages—forgiveness must be ongoing; possibly daily. We always need the *willingness* to forgive ready in our heart. And only a heart humbled by the forgiveness of God has the ability to completely forgive time and again.

Seven Things THAT ARE TRUE ABOUT Not Forgiving Others

1. ***Not forgiving means you won't be forgiven by God.*** "If you do not forgive men their trespasses, neither will your Father forgive your trespasses" (Matthew 6:15). We need to be right with God in order to receive all He has for us.

2. ***Not forgiving will torture you and rob you of your joy.*** "'Should you not also have had compassion on your fellow servant, just as I had pity on you?' And his master was angry, and delivered him to the torturers until he should pay all that was due to him. So My heavenly Father also will do to you if each of you, from his heart, does not forgive his brother his trespasses" (Matthew 18:33-35). We can't allow ourselves to be tortured by unforgiveness.

3. ***Not forgiving delays the answers to your prayers.*** "If I regard iniquity in my heart, the Lord will not hear" (Psalm 66:18). Keeping unforgiveness in our heart is a sin

that causes God to not listen to our prayers until we get rid of it.

4. *Not forgiving can open the door for the enemy to work in your life.* "Now whom you forgive anything, I also forgive…lest Satan should take advantage of us; for we are not ignorant of his devices" (2 Corinthians 2:10-11). When we harbor unforgiveness, we align ourselves with our true enemy and his plans for our future.

5. *Not forgiving can weaken your own body.* "Confess your trespasses to one another, and pray for one another, that you may be healed" (James 5:16). There is a connection between confession and healing. When you forgive someone, you release matters into God's hands so healing can come in your body as well as your soul.

6. *Not forgiving means violating the two greatest commandments.* "Jesus said to him, '"You shall love the LORD your God with all your heart, with all your soul, and with all your mind." This is the first and great commandment. And the second is like it: "You shall love your neighbor as yourself"'" (Matthew 22:37-39). Not forgiving reveals a lack of love for God and others.

7. *Not forgiving can pollute your soul.* "Does a spring send forth fresh water and bitter from the same opening?" (James 3:11). If you have unforgiveness, the water in your soul will become bitter.

Brace Yourself for This Truth

Now, you need to be sitting down for this. This may be the part where you throw the book across the room and say, "I'm not doing that!" just as some of you did when you read the first chapter of my book *The Power of a Praying Wife*, where I told wives that you have to stop praying the "Change him, Lord" prayer for your husband and start praying "Change me, Lord" instead. Don't blame me for that. It was definitely not my idea. I liked the "Change him, Lord" prayer. Never mind that it wasn't getting answered.

Most of us liked that prayer because we didn't think *we* were the ones who needed changing. But God says we *all* need to be changed, and He will start with whoever is *willing* to be changed. So, if you don't like this next part, take it up with God. This is *His* idea, not mine. But at least hear me out on this because it works. Prayer gets answered this way. And what I have learned is that you will have to accept this truth at some point in your life anyway, so you might as well do it now.

Okay. Here it is. Brace yourself.

The bottom line in saving, improving, and enriching your marriage is that you have to *be willing to have a repentant heart.*

Wait! Don't throw the book. I know what you're thinking. You're thinking, *My husband (wife) is the one who really needs to repent, so why should I have to do it? Besides, I'm a good person. I haven't murdered anyone or robbed a bank. Why do I need to repent?* But God says we *all* need to. That's because we all fall far short of what God wants for us in the way we think, act, and live our lives. And, for the most part, we don't understand the true meaning of having a repentant heart. It doesn't mean you have necessarily done something blatantly bad, although it *can* mean that. Rather, it means you are willing to let God show you where you have not done things perfectly and then respond by humbling yourself before the Lord and asking for His forgiveness.

We have to get to the point in our marriage where we live with a repentant heart all the time. A heart that says, *I am willing to see my errors, and no matter how I have been offended by the things my spouse has done, I will clean house on my own soul. I will pray to have eyes to see the truth about myself before I pray the same for my husband (wife).*

How often does God want to do amazing things in our lives and our marriages, but because we don't pray with a repentant heart, those things don't happen? God said of Israel that *they* would determine whether He could *bless* them or whether they would receive *curses* instead (Deuteronomy 28). He was ready to bless them, but they didn't listen. Instead, they arrogantly went their own way and chased after idols. *We, likewise, determine whether we will have blessings or misery in our marriage by whether we will listen to God as to how we will live, or will we chase after what feels right to us?* Will we self-righteously think we don't ever need to repent of anything because we see worse sins in our spouse, or will we bite the bullet and repent of every bad thought or action as we humbly come before God in prayer?

Learning to Maintain a Repentant Heart

The bottom line is that forgiveness has to do with *repentance* and *love.* You have to *love* your husband (wife) enough to *forgive* him (her) of offenses *and let them go.* And you have to *confess* your attitude of unforgiveness as a sin against God and *repent* of it. You have to be deeply sorry before the Lord that you were unforgiving because you know it displeases Him. You have to choose to forgive because you want to live God's way, because it's the right thing to do, and because it's the best thing for you. Of course, the same thing is true for your spouse, as well.

I know that the last thing you may feel like doing is praying for your husband (wife) if he (she) has hurt you, but that is what God asks you to do. In the process He will heal your pain because He is the God who "heals the brokenhearted and binds up their wounds" (Psalm 147:3). God can help you forgive so completely that you won't really think about those hurtful things anymore. As you pray, God will give you His heart of love.

You always grow to love the person you pray for. Try it; you'll see. God wants you to live "not returning evil for evil or reviling for reviling, but on the contrary blessing, knowing that you were called to this, that you may inherit a blessing" (1 Peter 3:9). God isn't calling you to forgive so He can rub your nose in what offended or hurt you. He is asking you to forgive because when you do, you will enrich your marriage and inherit all that He has for you.

God does not violate a person's will who is determined to have a rebellious heart that refuses to take advice, seek counsel, or be open to the Lord's working in his or her life. But your prayers for your husband (wife) will still be rewarded with healing, release, strength, peace, and blessing for *you* when you pray for him (her), even if he (she) is not responding at the time. The Lord who loves *you* will "comfort *your* [heart] and establish *you* in every good word and work" (2 Thessalonians 2:17).

Forgiveness is not an option in our lives; it is a mandate. It is God's will for us every day. It doesn't depend on whether the person we must forgive is *repentant,* or *deserving* of it. It depends entirely on *us.* It is between *us* and *God.* We do it for the Lord, ultimately. Don't give up on forgiveness because you think you're just going to have to be doing it over and over again. Forgive because it is God's way and great good will come out of it. David said, "I would have lost heart, unless I had believed that I would see the goodness of the LORD in the land of the living" (Psalm 27:13). He wanted God's presence in his life enough to do whatever it took. I believe you want that too. Forgiving your husband (wife) is the best place to start, and the quickest way to enrich your marriage.

PRAYERS *for* MY MARRIAGE

Prayer for Forgiveness to Flow Freely Between Us

Lord, I pray that You would help my husband (wife) and me to always be completely forgiving of one another. Help us to be humble enough to ask for forgiveness of each other when we need to. And give us a heart to forgive freely—whether the other asks for it or not. Help us both to "grow in the grace and knowledge of our Lord and Savior Jesus Christ" (2 Peter 3:18), so that we will become forgiving like You are. Help us to quickly forgive one another so that we will be forgiven by You, Lord (Luke 6:37).

Protect us from ourselves, Lord, so that we will not let our own flesh dictate whether we should hang on to offenses or let them go. Teach us to love one another the way You love us, and to always be merciful to one another. Thank You that we will have Your goodness and mercy following us all the days of our lives as described in Your Word (Psalm 23:6). Thank You that when we love each other the way You want us to, You will bless us and show us Your favor by surrounding us like a protective shield (Psalm 5:12).

Lord, I know Your Word says that "if we say that we have no sin, we deceive ourselves, and the truth is not in us" (1 John 1:8). Help us to be undeceived about our own errors. Help us to live in truth and not be arrogant enough to think we never have any unforgiveness in us. Enable us to be quick to confess our unforgiveness to You and to one another. In Jesus' name I pray.

Prayer for Forgiveness to Come Easily in Me

Thank You, Lord, that I can do *all* things through Christ who strengthens me, and therefore I have the strength to forgive my husband (wife) for anything that has hurt or disappointed me. Thank You that You are the God of forgiveness, mercy, and grace. Thank You that You have released me from any stronghold of unforgiveness. Take away all feelings in me that cause me to think I need to pay back hurt for hurt. Help me to "strive to have a conscience without offense" toward my husband (wife) (Acts 24:16). Where I need to be forgiven, help me to apologize and receive forgiveness from my husband (wife).

Where there are places in me that harbor unforgiveness that I am not even aware of, please reveal those to me so I can confess them to You. I know that "You, Lord, are good, and ready to forgive, and abundant in mercy to all those who call upon You" (Psalm 86:5). I call upon You this day and ask You to forgive me for any unforgiveness I have toward anyone, especially my husband (wife). I know that You, Lord, are the only one who knows the whole story, so I refuse to be the judge of all that happens in my husband (wife). You are the one "who will both bring to light the hidden things of darkness and reveal the counsels of the [heart]" (1 Corinthians 4:5). Break any entrenched unforgiveness in me by the power of Your Spirit. Help me to love him (her) the way You do, so I can release all unforgiveness and be cleansed from all unrighteousness. In Jesus' name I pray.

Prayer for Forgiveness to Come Easily in My Husband (Wife)

Lord, I lift my husband (wife) to You in prayer and ask You to help him (her) let go of any unforgiveness that he (she) harbors. I don't want him (her) to hang on to it and limit what You want to do in his (her) life. Help him (her) to forgive me for anything I have done—or *not* done—that was displeasing to him (her). I pray that You, "the God of patience and comfort," will grant to my husband (wife) the ability to be "like-minded" toward me so that we together may glorify You with a single-minded voice of unity (Romans 15:5-6). Give him (her) a heart of mercy toward me so that he (she) can truly let go of anything I have said or done that has hurt him (her).

You have said, Lord, that if we *don't* forgive people for their sins against us, You *won't* forgive us for *ours* (Matthew 6:14-15). Help my husband (wife) to become aware of anyone he (she) needs to forgive and enable him (her) to forgive that person completely, so that he (she) can move into the wholeness and restoration You have for him (her). Take away all thoughts of revenge or payback and make him (her) to be a forgiving person. In Jesus' name I pray.

TRUTH *to* STAND ON

Whenever you stand praying, if you have anything against anyone, forgive him, that your Father in heaven may also forgive you your trespasses.

MARK 11:25

Confess your trespasses to one another, and pray for one another, that you may be healed. The effective, fervent prayer of a righteous man avails much.

JAMES 5:16

Why do you judge your brother?
Or why do you show contempt for your brother?
For we shall all stand before the judgment seat of Christ.

ROMANS 14:10

If there is any consolation in Christ, if any comfort of love,
if any fellowship of the Spirit, if any affection and mercy,
fulfill my joy by being like-minded, having the same love,
being of one accord, of one mind.

PHILIPPIANS 2:1-2

Be submissive to one another, and be clothed with humility,
for God resists the proud, but gives grace to the humble.

1 PETER 5:5

PRACTICAL STEPS *to* GOING DEEPER

1. Read Ephesians 4:32 in your Bible. In light of this Scripture, how are you supposed to be toward your spouse and why? Write out a prayer asking God to help you always be forgiving toward your spouse.

2. Read Isaiah 43:25 in your Bible. What does this verse say about the way God forgives us? In light of that, how should you forgive your spouse? Have you been able to fully forgive your spouse for every offense? Write out a prayer asking God to help you forgive so completely that offenses don't come to mind anymore.

3. Read Matthew 5:7 in your Bible. The New King James Version says, "Blessed are the merciful, for they shall obtain mercy." If total forgiveness on your part is an act of mercy, what will happen to you if you forgive your spouse? What will God do for you?

4

Pray to Keep Negative Emotions
from Affecting Your Lives

*E*veryone has times of sadness, depression, fear, doubt, and other negative emotions. That's because sad, depressing, and scary things happen, causing us to lose faith. *Temporarily!* But that is not a place where we permanently want to live. We must pray to protect our marriage from that.

I used to be ruled by negative emotions, and I believe that started in the closet. That tiny dark space underneath the stairs in my parents' tiny old ranch house that had no running water, no bathroom, no electricity, and no heat in the bitter freezing Wyoming winters, except what came from an old coal-burning stove in the kitchen and a small stone fireplace in the living room. Upstairs, the two small bedrooms were always freezing, and it took forever till the sheets warmed up. Seeds of anxiety, sadness, fear, loneliness, and rejection were planted there like weeds that would grow deeper and more rampant every year of my early life until they would eventually suffocate all hope within me. I felt as frightened by that as much as I did by my mother.

As far back as I can remember, I had that depressed feeling. I didn't know I was experiencing depression at the time; I thought it was just me. *This is the way I am,* I thought as I grew up. *I am a frightened, hopeless, lonely, hurting, anxious, and depressed person, and there is nothing I can do about it. No one can help me, nor does anyone want to, nor will anyone ever want to, or even be able to.*

I am not talking here about a chemical imbalance, although I probably had one. Terror, dread, sadness, and stress have a way of depleting your mind, body, and soul until you not only have a physical imbalance, but a spiritual and emotional one as well. And that's enough to depress anyone. When I grew up and was out on my own, I went to different doctors and tried various medicines, but nothing ever worked for me. This was a deep wounding of the soul for which there is no true cure outside of the power of God.

It wasn't until I received the Lord and began to learn of the wholeness He has for each of us that I became aware that depressed, anxious, and afraid wasn't the way He made us to be. Depression, fear, and anxiety were not His will for my life. His promise for me was peace—if I would pray fervently and be thankful and worshipful of Him.

The Bible says, "Be anxious for nothing, but in *everything by prayer and supplication, with thanksgiving,* let your requests be made known to God; and the *peace of God,* which surpasses all understanding, will *guard your hearts and minds* through Christ Jesus" (Philippians 4:6-7). I learned that because of Jesus, I had a way out of anxiety, depression, and fear if I would learn to pray about everything. If every negative condition in my heart and mind would respond positively to prayer, then I did not want to settle for less. So I prayed fervently for the power of God to work in me, and I did not stop until I eventually found deliverance and healing from all the negative emotions that crippled me. Sometimes just my own prayers were enough, but often the faith-filled prayers of others, praying *with* and *for* me, paved the way for miracles.

When my husband and I had been married a few months, and I still couldn't shake the grip of depression, fear, and anxiety I was under, my husband suggested I go to our church for help. There were pastors' wives who were deeply knowledgeable of Scripture, were gifted by God to understand the freedom God had for us all, and were well able to pray in power about it.

The first time I saw Mary Anne, the pastor's wife and counselor I mentioned earlier, I noticed she had the most beautiful eyes, which sparkled like the ocean when the sun dances on the water. I had heard she was especially gifted in the understanding of God's Word and of God's power when we pray. She heard my story and asked me to fast and pray for three days—which was no easy feat for someone such as I, who had gone to bed hungry many nights as a child—but I was very willing to do it.

I went back to that same counseling office the following week after not having anything to eat or drink but water for the three days before. Mary Anne had asked me to make a list of all my sins God brought to mind in that week. I was grateful when I took the list back to her office and she didn't want to read it. Instead she asked that I would present the list to God and confess it all at once. I also had to confess my unforgiveness toward my mother and renounce all my occult involvement. Even though I had completely stopped all practice in the occult when I received the Lord, I had never gone before the Lord and actually renounced those practices.

Once I confessed and renounced all that, Mary Anne and another pastor's wife prayed for me, and I literally felt the depression lift off of me. I am not exaggerating this. In fact, I am understating it so it won't be hard for you to believe. But I felt the depression lift off from me as though it were a heavy, wet, dark blanket. And the best part about the story is that it never came back. I am not saying I never felt depressed again. There are many depressing things that happen in life. But I was never gripped or controlled by it again. If I felt depressed, anxious, or afraid, I could always go to God in prayer, and He would take it all away.

This is not to say that if you are taking medication prescribed by a doctor for depression or anxiety that you are to suddenly stop taking it. To the contrary, this can be dangerous. That also doesn't necessarily sentence you to a lifetime of medication, either. I believe you can find mental and emotional wholeness without medicine, but there is no sin in taking prescribed medicine if and when you need it. Taking medicine doesn't make you any less holy than someone else who doesn't take anything. Taking prescribed medicine according to your doctor's instructions does not make you a failure. In a world spinning faster, with pressures increasing and the rigors of life becoming more monumental every day, it is no wonder a body can become out of balance and need help.

Every *body* is different. Every *mind* and *soul* are different. Everyone's past is different, and each person's *reaction* to their past is different. Some of us are born depleted; some of us develop an imbalance later. It doesn't matter. What does matter is that you look to God as your healer and pray for healing. God will heal you in His way and time. If you need prescribed medicine, keep taking it and thank God for it. When it is time to stop, ask your doctor to help you wean off of it if that's what you're supposed to do. If not, keep taking your medicine and praise God that it's working.

Whether you are taking medicine or not is entirely between you and God and your doctor. But I want to tell you that medicine alone will never be totally enough. The only total cure for deep depression I have ever found is the love of God and His power working in you to break all oppression on your life. And the love of God will give you hope. "Now hope does not disappoint, because the love of God has been poured out in our hearts by the Holy Spirit who was given to us" (Romans 5:5).

When the Problem Is Depression

It's normal to feel depressed about the things that happen in life—such as the loss of a job, a loved one, finances, possessions, or the experience of failure, disappointment, severe sickness, or accidents. But when you stay depressed, then it becomes a problem. You were not made to live in depression. Depression every day is not God's will for your life. When every day seems dark and gray and without joy or light, then it becomes a grip of hell in your life and must be broken.

When I received the Lord, I began to finally see a light at the end of the long dark tunnel of my life, but I still had depression. I was born again into the kingdom of God because I received Jesus and I know something happened to me that day, but I still had depression. I felt hope for the first time in my life, but I still lived under a dark cloud of depression. Not everyone is instantly freed of every bondage the minute they receive the Lord. I have no doubt they can be, and I have no doubt that some are, but this is not the experience of most people. There are way too many depressed Christians for this to be true. There are people who adamantly believe that if you are a true Christian you will never have depression. May I politely suggest that the people who are saying this are people who have never been depressed? They have been blinded by their own arrogance, legalism, and lack of mercy, understanding, and compassion toward the plight of others.

I have also heard it suggested that in light of the following verses, if we are really walking in the light then we wouldn't have to go through the darkness of depression. "God is light and in Him is no darkness at all. If we say that we have fellowship with Him, and walk in darkness, we lie and do not practice the truth" (1 John 1:5-6). These people are saying that those verses bring into question our born-again status saying, *Can we really be saved if we have depression?* As one who has been depressed while also being a born-again believer, this attitude makes me mad. Let me get something straight in case anyone has ever suggested that to you. *Yes, you can be born again and depressed at the same time! And that doesn't mean you don't love God and have no faith. Your faith and love for God is what and who is going to get you through this.*

The verses above have to do with the *decision* to walk in fellowship with darkness. Being depressed does not mean you are *choosing* to walk in depression. Depression is something that you can have *on* you once you are a believer, but not *in* you. It can't possess you. It doesn't own you. The Holy Spirit is in you, not depression. Depression is not you. It may be on you like an oppression of the enemy designed to steal your joy and rob you of life, but you are not your depression. You can still have the light of the Lord *within* you and yet have the darkness of oppression settle *on* you and invade your life like an enemy encroaching on the territory of your being. But God has freedom from all that for you, so don't give up on Him setting you free. I have been totally set free from depression, and I know that the Lord did it.

How Depression Feels

In case you have never been depressed yourself, let me describe it for you. It may help you to better understand your spouse if he (she) ever gets depressed. And it may help you to recognize it if it happens to you. Job described what seemed like depression as "a land as dark as darkness itself, as the shadow of death, without any order, where even the light is like darkness" (Job 10:22). When you are depressed, even good things can't be enjoyed because they are tainted through the lens of that dark oppression. Job said, "When I looked for good, evil came to me; and when I waited for light, then came darkness" (Job 30:26). In other words, it seems as though no matter what he did, it never got better.

Perhaps no one ever struggled with depression more openly or wrote about it more clearly than King David. He knew depression well. Listen to what he said about the way he felt and see if this sounds like depression to you. "My life is spent with grief, and my years with sighing; my strength fails because of my iniquity, and my bones waste away" (Psalm 31:10). "Turn Yourself to me, and have mercy on me, for I am desolate and afflicted. The troubles of my heart have enlarged; bring me out of my distresses! Look on my affliction and my pain, and forgive all my sins" (Psalm 25:16-18). "Consider and hear me, O LORD my God; enlighten my eyes, lest I sleep the sleep of death" (Psalm 13:3). "Why are you cast down, O my soul? And why are you disquieted within me? Hope in God, for I shall yet praise Him for the help of His countenance" (Psalm 42:5). I especially appreciate the phrase "cast down" referring to a heavily burdened soul. That's exactly what it feels like—you have fallen in a pit far from hope.

David's solution to all this was to look up and put his hope in God. Sometimes we can feel as though God has abandoned us when we sink in depression and our prayers are not being answered. As a result, we feel separated from Him. But God has *not* abandoned us. He will comfort us when we turn to Him. Paul said, "God, who comforts the downcast, comforted us" (2 Corinthians 7:6).

David expressed it like this, "I said in my haste, 'I am cut off from before Your eyes,'" but he also said, "*Nevertheless You heard the voice of my supplications when I cried out to You*" (Psalm 31:22). David knew deep despair and depression, but he also knew his hope was in God.

David also said, "The pangs of death surrounded me, and the floods of ungodliness made me afraid. The sorrows of Sheol surrounded me; the snares of death confronted me" (Psalm 18:4-5). But then he said,

"You have delivered my soul from death, my eyes from tears, and my feet from falling" (Psalm 116:8).

In the midst of David's sorrow he said, *"Yea, though I walk through the valley of the shadow of death, I will fear no evil; for You are with me; Your rod and Your staff, they comfort me"* (Psalm 23:4). *"Indeed, the darkness shall not hide from You, but the night shines as the day; the darkness and the light are both alike to You"* (Psalm 139:12). God can see plainly into the darkness that hangs over you. He sees the truth about you and your situation, and He wants you to see it too. That means "there is no darkness nor shadow of death where the workers of iniquity may hide themselves" (Job 34:22). That's because we who believe in the Lord have been given authority over all the power of the enemy.

When you feel as David did—"My spirit is overwhelmed within me; my heart within me is distressed" (Psalm 143:4)—then say as David did, *"Hear me when I call, O God of my righteousness! You have relieved me in my distress; have mercy on me, and hear my prayer"* (Psalm 4:1).

This is the way depression feels to me. You feel distant from other people as if you are in another realm when you are around them. You are not on the same plane they are. You can be in the same room with them, but you feel as though there is a wall separating you from them, so you don't really make contact. It seems as if they are fading from you, like the darkness around *you* is swallowing you up and away from them. When you speak, it's almost like an out-of-body experience. It's as if you are outside your body listening to yourself speak, but you are not really connecting to the other person. And there *is* a barrier to their connecting with you. But it is your own depression. It is described in Psalms, saying, "Loved one and friend You have put far from me, and my acquaintances into darkness" (Psalm 88:18).

When you are deeply depressed, it's hard to do anything, even the basic necessities for life. It takes all your energy just being depressed. You're tired all the time because fighting anxiety, fear, and depression is exhausting. You lose interest in activities and doing things that you would normally do. You are pessimistic about most things, and you feel hopeless about everything else because there seems to be no way to rise above your predicament. When you don't believe your miserable situation will ever change, you can't see a reason to live. You wonder, *Why try?* At its worst, depression can make you feel suicidal, which means you see death as the only way out.

When you feel as though you can't do anything that involves the future, even as close as the next day, you live moment to moment. You are unable to plan ahead and prepare in advance. You can't think clearly about things, and you find it hard to get anything done, so it's extremely difficult to keep your home straight or your closet clean. The reason you have a difficult time planning anything is because you never feel good about what you are planning. You see no point to it. Depression can overshadow your ability to make solid and rational decisions. People may tell you to snap out of it, but you are powerless to do so on your own strength. That's why telling a depressed spouse to "get over it" will only make him (her) feel more hopeless.

We can also get depressed from being overextended, exhausted, malnourished, or sick. There is nothing more depressing than being sick or in pain.

When you are depressed, you have a strong need for physical touch and verbal affirmation, but this is the time when you find it hardest to communicate that need. It's difficult to communicate your need for love when you feel unlovable, unworthy, and unable to respond, but love is what you need most.

Don't ever feel that suffering from depression has separated you from God. It hasn't. The enemy wants you to believe that God is far from you and that's why you have to live in the darkness of depression. But God refers to the treasures of darkness saying, "I will give you the treasures of darkness and hidden riches of secret places, that you may know that I, the LORD, who call you by your name, am the God of Israel" (Isaiah 45:3). When you go through the dark times of depression, it forces you to walk closer to God. And that is a good thing. I have been there, and I have found that the treasure we find in darkness is *Him*. It's the promise of God's presence in the midst of our darkness. That means we don't have to be afraid of the dark, because His light will come into our darkness and He will reveal Himself to us.

Ten Things YOU NEED TO KNOW
ABOUT *Depression*

1. ***God is with you in it.*** "Fear not, for I am with you; be not dismayed, for I am your God. I will strengthen you, yes, I will help you, I will uphold you with My righteous right hand" (Isaiah 41:10).

2. ***Even though you are in a struggle, you will not be destroyed.*** "We are hard-pressed on every side, yet not crushed; we are perplexed, but not in despair" (2 Corinthians 4:8).

3. ***God hears when you call to Him about it.*** "In my distress I called upon the LORD, and cried out to my God; He heard my voice from His temple, and my cry came before Him, even to His ears" (Psalm 18:6).

4. ***The Lord will be a light to you at all times.*** "The people who walked in darkness have seen a great light; those who dwelt in the land of the shadow of death, upon them a light has shined" (Isaiah 9:2).

5. ***God will bring you out of darkness.*** "For You are my lamp, O LORD; the LORD shall enlighten my darkness" (2 Samuel 22:29).

6. ***God wants you to trust in Him through it.*** "Who among you fears the LORD? Who obeys the voice of His Servant? Who walks in darkness and has no light? Let him trust in the name of the LORD and rely upon his God" (Isaiah 50:10).

7. ***Jesus understands your sorrow.*** Jesus was "despised and rejected by men, a Man of sorrows and acquainted with grief" (Isaiah 53:3).

8. *God's presence will save you.* "In all their affliction He was afflicted, and the Angel of His Presence saved them; in His love and in His pity He redeemed them; and He bore them and carried them all the days of old" (Isaiah 63:9).

9. *You need to keep praying about it.* "Attend to my cry, for I am brought very low; deliver me from my persecutors, for they are stronger than I" (Psalm 142:6).

10. *Jesus has more for you than living with depression.* Jesus said, "The thief does not come except to steal, and to kill, and to destroy. I have come that they may have life, and that they may have it more abundantly" (John 10:10).

Other Common Negative Emotions

If you or your husband (wife) are suffering from feelings of rejection, anxiety, fear, loneliness, and other negative emotions, the following may help you understand yourself or your spouse better.

Feelings of rejection are often caused by something traumatic that has happened in the past—especially in childhood. Those of us who have been through difficult times as children often have a hard time sharing those things because we fear they might make us appear different. And you don't want to be different in any way when you're young. If you have had trouble feeling accepted or accepting of yourself, you don't want to open the door of possibility for other people to reject you too. You have a constant internal life going on inside you that you don't share with others because you don't want to appear stupid, inferior, or rejectable.

I suffered with deep feelings of rejection because my mother told me from the time I was very young that I was worthless and no good and would never amount to anything. Because I believed her, the constant feeling of never being worth anything—always feeling unloved and uncared for—made me a magnet for every negative emotion there is.

Feelings of anxiety are feelings of intense worry or fear that something bad is about to happen. You have a constant torturous uneasiness about the outcome of many events or situations. In the extreme, you feel anxious even when you are not sure why. At its worst, anxiety leads to panic attacks, which can grip you so strongly that you feel as though you are going to have a heart attack, stop breathing, and die.

When I was working as a singer, dancer, and actress on TV in my early twenties, I would have panic attacks so bad that I would go into the ladies' room and lock myself in a bathroom stall so I could double up against the door and hang on for dear life. If someone was in the room, I would just hold my breath, try to gain control, and make myself breathe in and out. If no one else was there, I would cry. Although I didn't have a relationship with God then, I still said, "God, help me." In my mind I wasn't actually asking this distant being, who I thought might exist, to take the anxiety away, because I believed it was warranted since I was such a failure. (And I was anxious because I feared that people were going to find out what a failure I was.) All I was asking of God was that He would keep me from dying. I truly thought at the time that depressed, anxious, fearful, suicidal, and hopeless was just the way I was, and I didn't think for a moment that God could make me into something I wasn't. That was before I knew who God really is.

Anxiety like this is usually unwarranted in the face of the truth. When you are chronically uneasy because you think something bad is going to happen, you have no peace and it is uncomfortable to be around you. Jesus said not to have an anxious mind (Luke 12:29). Proverbs 12:25 says, "Anxiety in the heart of man causes depression, but a good word makes it glad." *The good word from God is that you don't have to be anxious about anything because you can talk to Him about whatever concerns you.*

Feelings of fear are not something that comes from God. *"God has not given us a spirit of fear,* but of power and of love and of a sound mind" (2 Timothy 1:7). If we lay claim to the *love* God has for us, the *power* He has for us, and the *sound mind* He has for us, there will be no room for a spirit of fear. This doesn't mean we are inviting a spirit of fear every time we are afraid. That only happens when we allow fear to become a controlling factor in our lives. It's good to be afraid of danger. It's what keeps us from walking out into traffic or alone in a deserted place at night. But it's not good to be afraid as a way of life.

The only kind of fear God wants us to have is to fear Him (1 Peter 2:17). That doesn't mean we are afraid of Him, but that we are afraid of what life would be like *without* Him. And the fear He is talking about is a deep reverence for Him and who He is. We don't have to live with fear when God says He has love, power, and a sound mind for us instead. Take all your fears to God and claim what He has for you.

Feelings of loneliness are painful. Loneliness causes an ache in your heart that can be unbearable. But we don't have to live with that either when God is waiting for us to draw close to Him so He can draw close to us. I used to live in the pain of loneliness even after I was married. One day, in an especially painful time of loneliness, God spoke to my heart that whenever I felt lonely I was to come to Him and He would take it away. I did that right then, and the loneliness disappeared. From then on I recognized any feelings of loneliness as a signal that I needed to draw close to God. Let it be that kind of sign to you as well. Jesus said, "Whatever you ask the Father in My name He will give you. Until now you have asked nothing in My name. Ask, and you will receive, that your joy may be full" (John 16:23-24). Ask God to set you and your husband (wife) free from loneliness and all other negative emotions.

Twelve Things TO REMEMBER IN THE FACE OF *Negative Emotions*

1. *God knows what you are going through.* "O Lord, You have searched me and known me. You know my sitting down and my rising up; You understand my thought afar off. You comprehend my path and my lying down, and are

acquainted with all my ways. For there is not a word on my tongue, but behold, O Lord, You know it altogether" (Psalm 139:1-4).

2. *God is there for you in your darkest hour.* "Unto the upright there arises light in the darkness; He is gracious, and full of compassion, and righteous" (Psalm 112:4).

3. *You don't have to live with the darkness of negative emotions.* "I have come as a light into the world, that whoever believes in Me should not abide in darkness" (John 12:46).

4. *God will rescue you when you cry out to Him.* "They cried out to the Lord in their trouble, and He saved them out of their distresses" (Psalm 107:13).

5. *You don't have to be afraid.* "The Lord is my light and my salvation; whom shall I fear? The Lord is the strength of my life; of whom shall I be afraid?" (Psalm 27:1).

6. *God will break through all bondage.* "He brought them out of darkness and the shadow of death, and broke their chains in pieces" (Psalm 107:14).

7. *Even if you fall again, you will rise up yet another time.* "Do not rejoice over me, my enemy; when I fall, I will arise; when I sit in darkness, the Lord will be a light to me" (Micah 7:8).

8. *You have the power to cast off darkness and put on light.* "The night is far spent, the day is at hand. Therefore let us cast off the works of darkness, and let us put on the armor of light" (Romans 13:12).

9. *God keeps His eyes on you when you keep your eyes on Him.* "Behold, the eye of the Lord is on those who fear Him, on those who hope in His mercy, to deliver their soul from death, and to keep them alive in famine. Our soul waits for the Lord; He is our help and our shield. For our

heart shall rejoice in Him, because we have trusted in His holy name. Let Your mercy, O Lord, be upon us, just as we hope in You" (Psalm 33:18-22).

10. ***God will deliver you.*** "He has delivered us from the power of darkness and conveyed us into the kingdom of the Son of His love" (Colossians 1:13).

11. ***He will continue to deliver you until you are completely free.*** "Yes, we had the sentence of death in ourselves, that we should not trust in ourselves but in God who raises the dead, who delivered us from so great a death, and does deliver us; in whom we trust that He will still deliver us" (2 Corinthians 1:9-10).

12. ***God will comfort you.*** "Sing, O heavens! Be joyful, O earth! And break out in singing, O mountains! For the Lord has comforted His people, and will have mercy on His afflicted" (Isaiah 49:13).

If This Has Already Happened to You

If you or your husband (wife) have been already experiencing serious negative emotions, just know that it is possible to get free of them. It doesn't necessarily happen overnight, but it *does happen*. So don't give up.

While it is certainly no fun being depressed, it is definitely no fun being *around someone* who is depressed all the time, either. Life is hard enough on your own without having to deal with someone else's problems. But when you are married, your spouse's problems become yours as well. In my case, my husband and I both suffered from depression and anxiety in the beginning. However, I found healing for it in that first year we were married. Michael struggled with it much longer.

A spouse who is controlled by depression, anxiety, or fear is very self-focused. He (she) is forced to think about himself (herself) most of the time, and therefore has little resource left to give to others—especially his (her) spouse. That's why your husband's (wife's) depression can make *your* life miserable too. And it will definitely affect your children, because they won't understand what it is and will think there is something wrong with them.

Often after a person gets married, all the weaknesses, negative emotions, and emotional disorders they have surface one by one. Those things can't be hidden for long in the closeness of a marriage. If you see that happening in you or your spouse, don't be afraid. God is allowing that so He can set you free from it. Often these things don't come out until you are in a safe place. A marriage is a safe place—or at least it is supposed to be. It means that you are now with someone who loves you enough to commit to you. If there is anything wrong with you, God is not going to let you hang on to it. He won't allow you to continue with depression, anxiety, fear, bitterness, anger, or loneliness. It will be exposed because marriage shines a spotlight on those kinds of things and there is no place to hide. Who you are will be revealed. And God doesn't want you hiding anyway. He wants you free.

When negative emotions surface in you or in your husband (wife), be willing to face what is exposed without fear. *It is not the end of the good times; it is the beginning of the best times.* Be willing to do what it takes to get free and become whole.

If your spouse is often depressed, sometimes the two of you may end up not talking about things that need to be talked about. You might avoid the depressed person because you don't know if what you say is going to make things worse. They can appear weak to you when they don't have the ability to do things they need to do. Because their depression forces you to be the strong one and the full-time decision maker. You can't go to them as a safe place where you can let down and share your thoughts, hopes, dreams, and fears because all the depressed person can focus on is getting through the day.

Anxiety can be just as paralyzing as depression is, because if one of you believes that disaster is one step away, it can keep you from taking a step in any direction at all. Dreams for the future are put aside. The future is only as far as tomorrow.

If your husband (wife) deals with frequent depression or anxiety, don't see him (her) as a *depressed person* who can't get over it. See him (her), instead, as a *person God wants to heal.* If your spouse is on medication for depression, don't tell him (her) to get off of it. This could have serous ramifications and he (she) could end up feeling like a failure if it's necessary to resume taking it. As I said earlier, there is no failure in having to take medicine prescribed by a doctor, as long as it is right for the person who needs it. Some people take it all their lives, and if they are believers I am certain they are still going to heaven and are not walking in darkness.

You may feel as though you don't know what to do to help your depressed husband (wife), but one thing you can always do is pray—*for* and *with* him (her). And it will make a big difference, even if it doesn't seem like it is at the moment. It is a way to show your love and support, which means a lot. Assure your husband (wife) that what he (she) is feeling is only temporary and there will be an end to it. "Weeping may endure for a night, but joy comes in the morning" (Psalm 30:5).

Seven Things DEPRESSION AND *Negative Emotions* ARE NOT

1. Negative emotions are not inevitable.
2. Negative emotions are not a life sentence.
3. Negative emotions are not a sign of failure.
4. Negative emotions are not a sign of God's anger.
5. Negative emotions are not a license to withdraw from others.
6. Negative emotions are not an opportunity to be rude or mean.
7. Negative emotions are not a tool used to control a spouse.

How to Get Out of Depression and Other Negative Emotions

No matter what negative emotion it is, if it grips you or your husband (wife) and is affecting your lives together, do the following things to break the hold it has on you. Read this entire chapter to him (her) if you need to.

Read God's Word every day. Read as much as you can. Speak it out loud. Find an appropriate verse and say it over and over until it is engraved upon your heart and you believe it. Speak aloud the Scriptures on the "Truth to Stand On" page at the end of each chapter in this book. Then say, "Thank You Lord, that Your Word is a lamp to my feet and a light to my path" (Psalm 119:105). "Thank You for the sound mind You have given me." Read it to your spouse if he (she) won't read it to himself (herself).

Determine to take charge of your mind. Refuse to allow your emotions to rule you. Instead, you rule over them. Don't allow negative thoughts to dictate how you act, what you say or don't say, or what you do or don't do. Think about the good and positive things about your life. Write them down if you need to.

Pray without ceasing. Always have a dialogue going with God, but don't do all the talking. Listen, as well. God says you are to give the burdens of your soul entirely to Him. If you pray to God instead of allowing negative emotions to control you, you can have the kind of peace in your heart that is beyond comprehension.

Praise and worship God. This is one of the most powerful things you can do. In fact, every time you begin to feel any negative emotion, worship God right where you are and you will feel that thing lift off of you. The wells of salvation are deep. There is so much that Jesus has saved you from. Draw spiritual water from those wells every day and you will find joy (Isaiah 12:3). Drown out the negative noise in your head with praise and worship music that is louder.

Seek good Christian counseling. If negative emotions are a gripping problem for you or your husband (wife), and they don't respond to prayer as I have suggested here, there are good medical doctors, psychiatrists, and psychologists who can help. If it is serous, don't try to deal with the situation alone. There are also good Christian counselors who will pray *for* you and *with* you, and that is a powerful way to one day saying goodbye to gripping negative emotions forever.

You and your husband (wife) may not have any problems with negative emotions, but you can enrich your marriage by praying that you never will. Let any sign of them be a signal for you both to draw closer to God in order to walk through them, knowing He is glorified when you are set free. If you do have a need for breakthrough in this area, cry out to God in your need for His love, peace, joy, and power, knowing He longs to share Himself with you. Say, "Thank You, God, that You make us 'exceedingly glad with Your presence'" (Psalm 21:6).

Above all, be confident of this, that "He who has begun a good work in you will complete it until the day of Jesus Christ" (Philippians 1:6). And if you don't see the answers to your prayers as quickly as you would like, remember that God won't give up on you, so don't give up on Him.

PRAYERS *for* MY MARRIAGE

Prayer to Keep Negative Emotions from Affecting Our Marriage

Lord, I thank You that You show us the paths of life and "in Your presence is fullness of joy; at Your right hand are pleasures forevermore" (Psalm 16:11). Thank You that when we delight ourselves in You, You will cause us "to ride on the high hills of the earth" (Isaiah 58:14). I pray that You will keep my husband (wife) and me from all paralyzing negative emotions. Help us to clearly see that we never have to live with any of them.

Where we have allowed anything such as depression, anxiety, fear, rejection, or loneliness to influence our lives, deliver us out of all that and keep it far from us. I pray that even though we may go through times where we are hard-pressed on every side, we will not be crushed, nor will we be in despair (2 Corinthians 4:8). We will rejoice in Your Word and the comfort of Your presence. We will not forget that You have the power to set us free.

Your commandments are right and they make our hearts rejoice (Psalm 19:8). We were once in darkness, but now we are in Your light. Help us to always "walk as children of the light" (Ephesians 5:8). I pray we will always look to You and put our hope and expectations in You (Psalm 62:5). In Jesus' name I pray.

Prayer to Keep Negative Emotions from Affecting Me

Lord, I pray that You would "search me, O God, and know my heart; try me, and know my anxieties" (Psalm 139:23). Wherever I have allowed negative emotions to control me, deliver me forever from them. Show me things in my life that have been passed down in my family—attitudes, fears, prejudices, and even depression—and break these strongholds completely. Keep me from falling into bad habits of the mind and heart that are learned responses to life. Lord, I pray for healing and deliverance from any depression, anxiety, fear, rejection, loneliness, or any other negative emotion that would seek to find permanent residence in my heart. You are the lamp of my soul, Lord, and I thank You that You "will enlighten my darkness" (Psalm 18:28). Thank You that You will give me rest from my sorrow and fear (Isaiah 14:3).

Lord, take away all sadness or despair. Heal every hurt in my heart. Give me a garment of praise at all times and take away the spirit of heaviness. Make me to be a tree of strength. Teach me Your Word so that Your glory will be revealed in me. Rebuild the places in me that have been damaged or ruined in the past. Lord, I pray that You would "send out Your light and Your truth! Let them lead me; let them bring me to Your holy hill and to Your tabernacle" (Psalm 43:3). May Your light in me completely evaporate any black clouds around me so that they cannot keep me from sensing Your presence in my life. In Jesus' name I pray.

Prayer to Keep Negative Emotions from Affecting My Husband (Wife)

Lord, I lift my husband (wife) up to You and ask that You would set him (her) free from depression, anxiety, fear, rejection, loneliness, or any other negative emotions that grips him (her). Thank You for Your promise to bring out Your "people with joy" and Your "chosen ones with gladness" (Psalm 105:43). Thank You that because of You, Jesus, "darkness is passing away, and the true light is already shining" in his (her) life (1 John 2:8). Help him (her) to keep his (her) eyes on You and take refuge in You, knowing that You will not leave his (her) soul destitute (Psalm 141:8). Have mercy on him (her) and be his (her) helper! (Psalm 30:10). Anoint him (her) with Your "oil of gladness" (Psalm 45:7). Restore to him (her) the joy of Your salvation, and uphold him (her) "by Your generous Spirit" (Psalm 51:12). Set him (her) free from anything that holds him (her) other than You.

I say to my husband (wife) now, as You, Lord, said to Your people in Your Word, "Be strong and of good courage; do not be afraid, nor be dismayed, for the LORD your God is with you wherever you go" (Joshua 1:9). The Lord *loves* you and has given you *hope* and *grace,* and will *comfort* your heart and *establish* you in all things (2 Thessalonians 2:16-17). In Jesus' name I pray.

TRUTH *to* STAND ON

We do not wrestle against flesh and blood,
but against principalities, against powers,
against the rulers of the darkness of this age,
against spiritual hosts of wickedness in the heavenly places.

EPHESIANS 6:12

He has delivered us from the power of darkness and conveyed
us into the kingdom of the Son of His love.

COLOSSIANS 1:13

He has sent Me to heal the brokenhearted…
to give them beauty for ashes, the oil of joy for mourning,
the garment of praise for the spirit of heaviness;
that they may be called trees of righteousness,
the planting of the Lord, that He may be glorified.

ISAIAH 61:1,3

There is no fear in love; but perfect love casts out fear,
because fear involves torment.
But he who fears has not been made perfect in love.

1 JOHN 4:18

You are my hiding place; You shall
preserve me from trouble; You shall
surround me with songs of deliverance.

PSALM 32:7

PRACTICAL STEPS *to* GOING DEEPER

1. Read Philippians 4:6-7 in your Bible. What are you supposed to do in response to the things that happen, or don't happen, in your life that are upsetting to you? Do you ever feel anxious about anything? Write out a prayer telling God what makes you anxious, and ask Him to take that away and give you His peace. Write a similar prayer for your husband (wife) and any specific anxieties he (she) has. Ask him (her) if you are not sure what makes him (her) anxious.

2. Read 2 Timothy 1:7 in your Bible. The New King James Version of this Scripture says, "God has not given us a *spirit of fear*, but of *power* and of *love* and of a *sound mind*." In light of this Scripture, write out a prayer for yourself completing this sentence: Dear Lord, I thank You that You have not given me _____, but instead You have given me _____. Therefore, I will not allow _____.

Then write out a similar prayer for your husband (wife): Dear Lord, thank You that You have not given my husband (wife) _____ _____ . Help him (her) to understand that, and to remember that You have instead given him (her) _____ .

3. Read 1 John 4:18 in your Bible. What takes away fear in our lives? What does fear do to us? If you have fear, what does that mean for you? It seems that nearly all negative emotions involve some kind of fear. Write out a prayer asking God to help you and your spouse to be so perfected by God's love flowing into your hearts, and through each of you to one another, that all negative emotions are gone.

5

Pray to Keep Your Marriage Strong While Raising Children

*N*othing will change a marriage faster and more dramatically than the birth of a child. When children come along, the demands are so great that you no longer have time to focus entirely on each other the way you used to. It's a lot harder to find quality time to be together because you're so exhausted. You have to sacrifice other things in order to devote yourself to becoming a good parent. All that can be overwhelming. But the good news is that this forces you to grow up, establish firm priorities, make optimal use of your time, and learn to take care of yourself because you can't afford to be sick.

It's important when the size of your family increases that you not lose sight of the fact that children can easily dominate your lives to the exclusion of each other without your even realizing it. Children can come between the two of you because of the amount of time you rightfully need to devote to them. But if the two of you can stay in close communication and share the load, it will bond you more closely together.

The problem is when some parents become so focused on parenting that they think of nothing else, not even their spouse. While God wants us to love and care for our children to the best of our ability, there is a fine line between the care and nurture that gives your children the best chance in life, and the other side of that line, where they become your obsession to the point that it jeopardizes your marriage. Allowing your spouse to feel neglected, overlooked, unimportant, unnecessary, or irrelevant doesn't help your marriage stay strong. And having your marriage fall apart doesn't help your children. We all need wisdom and revelation from God in order to find that balance. It is best to pray about this as early in the marriage as possible—even when you are *thinking* about having children.

Many conflicts can arise between a husband and wife over the raising of their children that are serious enough to lead to divorce. These conflicts may not happen in the busy infancy or toddler stages, but rather later on in the complicated teenage years when so much is at stake. I have found that the best way to raise your children and take the entire burden off the two of you is to pray for them every step of the way. In my first book in the Power of a Praying series, *The Power of a Praying Parent,* I provide 30 ways to pray for your child. Such things as that they be protected, feel loved and accepted, maintain good family relationships, have godly friends and role models, have a desire to learn, maintain a sound mind, not be ruled by fear, not be addicted to anything, grow strong faith in God, and become who God created them to be. Praying this way about your children means you don't have to be Supermom or Superdad, and that takes the pressure off your marriage. Praying *together* about your children is amazingly effective, but praying *alone* has great benefits as well. Doing both is the best. Below are some specific things to pray about with regard to your marriage and raising children.

Pray That You Decide Together on How to Discipline Your Children

How you discipline your children is a very important issue that you and your spouse must decide on together. It should not be one-sided, with one of you strict and the other lenient. If that is the case with you, one of you will become the fun parent and the other one will be the grumpy one, and that will cause resentment in your relationship. If *you* refuse to discipline your children, and you force your *husband (wife)* to be the bad guy, your husband (wife) will become very tired of being labeled "the bad guy" while you look like your child's best friend. It will chip away at the foundation of your marriage until it is weakened or destroyed. Don't think for a moment that this is not a deep issue. I have known too many marriages to break up over this very thing.

In fact, I know a great couple who have been married nearly 25 years and their children are now teenagers. Recently the husband and wife have come into conflict over when and how to discipline their children. The wife feels her husband is too permissive, and the husband believes the wife is too strict. It all came to a head when she found out that their children had experimented with drugs, and he thought it was okay to not discipline them at all for that. Of course she wanted their children to experience some sort of consequence for what they did, before they ended up getting in trouble with the law. She sees her husband's permissiveness as a danger for their children, possibly jeopardizing their future. They have filed for divorce over this. Neither of them knows the Lord, but if they did, they could pray through this and come to a good solution. They could work this out so easily if humility, reliance on God, knowledge about the power of prayer, and truly loving your spouse were to come into play. The wife feels that if she doesn't divorce him, it could be the downfall of her children.

I can understand where she is coming from, but it would be so much better to go to Christian counseling than to break up the family. When she gets divorced, she will have completely lost control over what the children will be allowed to do when they are with the permissive spouse.

There are definitely times when you have a child endangered by the actions or inactions of a parent, but if you both are reasonable people, you should be able to work this out. Especially if you pray together. *Putting one another first before the children doesn't mean neglecting the children in any way.* It's just when raising them becomes a problem between you and your spouse, you have to work it out in a mutually acceptable manner. That takes much prayer and communication.

Seek God for wisdom about how you both are going to discipline your children for each offense. Try to work that out *before* the children arrive if you can. Or at least before something bad happens.

Pray That You Decide Together on What the Rules Are

We had *two* long-haired Chihuahuas. Not by choice. Our daughter got the little dogs just before she went into her second year of college. Caring for her puppies was helpful to me at the time because having joint custody of these two fine examples of God's sense of humor made it easier for me when she left. It was like having a little part of her with us after she was gone, only furry. The one thing I have learned about Chihuahuas is that they are creatures of habit to the extreme. If they get to do something once, they believe they are entitled to do it all the time.

Children are a little like Chihuahuas when they are young. For example, they think that if they can come into your bed to sleep *one* night, they should be able to do it *every* night for the rest of your lives together. Michael and I decided together when our first child was a baby that we did not want our children sleeping in our bed at night. We didn't want to make them feel bad about wanting to be near us, or to think that we were rejecting them, so our policy was that the one of us whose side of the bed the child came to in the middle of the night was the one who would carry or walk the child back to his or her bed and tuck them in and lay down beside them until they could get back to sleep, or at least feel better about being in their own room. It worked very well with each child because it only took a few times of doing that before the trip into our room didn't seem worth it to them. And then when they did come, we knew it was urgent.

It's not that we didn't love our children or didn't want to be with them. It's just that neither of us could sleep very well with them in bed with us. As a result we would wake up tired, grumpy, and barely functioning. We discovered a long time ago that not getting enough sleep wasn't good for our marriage. We also knew that "Chihuahua syndrome" in kids means that if you do it once, it immediately becomes a habit that is extremely hard to break.

Some people truly like their kids sleeping with them every night. I know one couple who has their three children and their big dogs sleeping in their bed with them, and it doesn't bother them. Personally, that sounds like a nightmare to us. But if that works for them, then great. The point is to agree on what the rules are for your children. You have to come to some common conclusions so that there is balance in your boundaries.

Pray that you and your husband (wife) can always talk things out concerning your children. When you strongly disagree about something, pray that you both can get the mind of God on the issue. Often it's not a matter of wrong or right, but of personal preference. So if the two of you don't agree, there needs to be the working out of a compromise. And if you can't see how a compromise will ever work for you, know that God can change both of you so you will do the right thing.

Communicate clearly with your children about what the rules are and why. Teach them God's ways every day and pray with them about everything. Help them to see that prayer is a lifestyle, not something you only do in an emergency. If you are allowing your children to do things that your spouse objects to, and you continue doing it, that is putting your children before your husband (wife). What matters most is that your marriage stays strong and your intimacy isn't sacrificed on the altar of child obsession. You have to put each other first and come to some kind of mutual understanding or compromise. Divorce is not good for a child, either.

Pray That You Can Find Quality Time to Be Alone Together

Everything you do affects your children. If you live God's way, they will benefit from that. "Oh, that they had such a heart in them that they would fear Me and always keep all My commandments, that it might be well with them and with their children forever!" (Deuteronomy 5:29). When we live God's way, our children will be kept free from the enemy's hand. "The posterity of the righteous will be delivered" (Proverbs 11:21). Likewise, if we live unrighteous lives, our children will suffer the consequences.

One of the right things to do is to work on your marriage and find ways to make it better. Even though raising children can take up all of your time, you still must find time to be alone together away from your children once a week, even if it's only for a couple hours to go to dinner or take a walk together. Pray that you can find someone you trust who will watch your children for those hours once a week so that the two of you can go someplace where you are able to enjoy each other. Or take the children to someone else's house while you have quality time alone together at your own home. Even such a small amount of time can make an enormous difference in your marriage.

Michael and I have two close friends, Bob and Sally, whom we met in church shortly after their first baby and ours were born. Sally and I traded babysitting favors, which was convenient for us because our children were the same age and so we were set up for it. I took her daughter for three hours once a week, and she took my son on another day for the same amount of time. Sometimes it was in the morning, sometimes in the afternoon, and sometimes it was an evening, which allowed for a date night. It was a lifesaver for all of us because none of us had any family members close by to help out the way many families do. And we all know how difficult it is to find trustworthy people who are willing and available to take care of our children.

Ask God to lead you to one or two trustworthy people who could take good care of your child for two or more hours once a week. Pay them an agreed amount, or trade with them if they have children too, so they will be more likely to say yes. Only God knows the truth about potential babysitters, so always ask Him for His peace—or lack thereof—with regard to whoever takes care of your child. Trust what the Holy Spirit whispers to your soul. It's better to have a date night in your own home after your little darlings are in bed than it is to take a chance on a flaky babysitter.

Pray That You Can Agree on How Many Children— if Any—to Have

It's important that you and your husband (wife) come to some kind of agreement on how many children your hearts have room for— while always staying open to the plans of God and His surprises. Keep in mind that not having children can bring pressures too.

When one of you does not want to have any children, or you both want children but for one reason or another are not able to have them, this can also be a great source of stress in a marriage. I know a couple who decided not to have children because the husband had already raised a family with his first wife and didn't want to do it again. The wife in that marriage had to pray, "Lord, take away my desire for children if this is Your will. If it is not Your will, take away whatever fear my husband has that makes him not want children." In this case, the wife was able to come to terms with the fact that children were not in her future. Not every woman can accept that decision. But at least they came to an agreement about that and they were able to travel the world, which they loved doing together.

Another woman I know in the same situation devoted herself to mentoring spiritual children instead of having her own. In another case, the husband eventually changed his mind and they now have a child. Many couples agree to adopt or foster a child. Whatever your situation, and for whatever reason, pray that you and your husband (wife) will be in unity and at peace with each other regarding this important matter.

Pray That the Two of You Can Stay Connected

In the beginning, when you first have a child, you both have to accept the fact that you are going to be too tired most days to sit down and discuss your feelings and dreams. You may be too exhausted at the end of the day to talk about much more than what the children need right now and how you can juggle the responsibilities of meeting those needs. Ask God to help you *both,* in the midst of all that, to stay connected to each other and still be good parents. Start praying about that before the baby arrives if possible.

We all change through the seasons of life, and if you and your husband (wife) have not made any meaningful contact for years, then when the last child leaves home it will be especially difficult. You will feel like strangers and the house will be extremely empty. If you already have spent years totally focused on your careers, raising children, paying for and maintaining a house, and just keeping up with life, and you have lost contact with each other, just know that it is never too late to regain that feeling of connection—or establish it if you feel it was never there in a satisfactory way in the first place. In order to do that, you have to spend time alone talking and listening to each other and making a great effort to reconnect.

If you're married to someone who is stubborn, stuck in his (her) ways, refusing to change, and incapable of stepping out of his (her) rut, then pray for him (her) to be set free. For his (her) own sake, as well as for yours, pray that he (she) will be delivered from stubbornness. Your future happiness together depends on it.

If This Has Already Happened to You

One of the best things you can do if you and your husband (wife) are not on the same page about how to raise your children is to be praying parents together. We can all become prideful if we think we can be *perfect* parents and devote ourselves to becoming that. We can get even *more* prideful if we buy into the belief that we have raised perfect children. In fact, this is actually dangerous ground to walk on because God blesses those who are humble and He resists those who are prideful (James 4:6).

If you already feel that you don't know how to be a perfect parent on your own, then be glad because you will have to depend on God to help you raise your children. He is the perfect parent. And He will always act in response to your prayers because you have more authority over your child in prayer than you may know.

It is actually better for your marriage if you both accept that you are not perfect parents, but *God* is. He is the only one who knows what is best for your children. So consult Him every day and ask Him to help you to be the best parent you can be. This is far better than trying to figure it all out on your own. The best thing you can do for your children is pray *for* them and *with* them. Also teach *them* to pray. Make prayer a natural part of their lives—and yours—and it will serve them well all the days of their lives. Being a *praying parent* is the best kind of parent of all, and it will take the pressure off either of you trying to be the *perfect parent.*

Turn to God whenever you become discouraged while raising your children—or if the two of you are not in agreement about raising your children. Seeking God is a great common denominator. God understands our weaknesses and temptation to give up. The Bible says, "You're blessed when you're at the end of your rope. With less of you there is more of God and his rule" (Matthew 5:3 MSG). He wants you to come to Him and find His grace to help you with whatever you need. The more you experience God's love and grace, the more you are able to extend His love and grace to each other. The more you seek God—as the perfect parent— for His guidance, the less you will think of yourselves as the know-it-all parents.

Ten Great Things TO REMEMBER WHEN Raising Your Children

1. ***Start training them as soon as they are old enough and when they are older they will know better.*** "*Train up a child in the way he should go*, and when he is old he will not depart from it" (Proverbs 22:6).

2. ***Discipline them fairly whenever they need it.*** "*Foolishness is bound up in the heart of a child*; the rod of correction will drive it far from him" (Proverbs 22:15).

3. ***Teach your children something from God's Word every day.*** "These words which I command you today shall be in your heart. *You shall teach them diligently to your children*, and shall talk of them when you sit in your house, when you walk by the way, when you lie down, and when you rise up" (Deuteronomy 6:6-7).

4. ***Trust that your children are not destined for trouble.*** "*They shall not labor in vain, nor bring forth children for trouble*; for they shall be the descendants of the blessed of the LORD, and their offspring with them" (Isaiah 65:23).

5. ***Pray fervently day and night for your children.*** "Arise,

cry out in the night, at the beginning of the watches; pour out your heart like water before the face of the Lord. *Lift your hands toward Him for the life of your young children*" (Lamentations 2:19).

6. ***Give them godly training, not angry commands.*** "*You, fathers, do not provoke your children to wrath*, but bring them up in the training and admonition of the Lord" (Ephesians 6:4).

7. ***When you do what's right, your children will be blessed.*** "The righteous man walks in his integrity; *his children are blessed after him*" (Proverbs 20:7).

8. ***Keep praying when things get difficult and refuse to give up.*** "I would have lost heart, unless I had believed that I would see the goodness of the LORD in the land of the living. *Wait on the LORD*; *be of good courage*, and He shall strengthen your heart; wait, I say, on the LORD!" (Psalm 27:13-14).

9. ***Know that your children are God's reward to you, no matter what it feels like sometimes.*** "Behold, *children are a heritage from the LORD*, the fruit of the womb is a reward" (Psalm 127:3).

10. ***Trust that the Lord hears every prayer for your children.*** "*For this child I prayed, and the LORD has granted me my petition* which I asked of Him" (1 Samuel 1:27).

Pray That You Both Can Release Your Child into God's Hands

It's important when you are praying for your children to release them to God so that you will have the peace of knowing they are in good hands. The following excerpt is adapted from *The Power of a Praying Parent*, where I describe what it means to release our children to God:

We don't want to limit what God can do in our children by clutching them to ourselves and trying to parent alone. *If we are not positive that God is in control of our children's lives, we'll be ruled by fear.* And the only way to be sure that God *is* in control of our children's lives is to invite Him to be and surrender our grasp on them. The way to do that is to live according to His Word and His ways and pray to Him about everything. We can trust God to take care of our children even better than we can. When we release our children into the Father's hands and acknowledge that He is in control of their lives and ours, both we and our children will have greater peace (page 33).

That doesn't mean you abdicate all responsibilities as a parent and say to God, "They're Your problem now." It means you trust God and ask for His help in raising them. That will take the burden of raising them off your shoulders. It will give you greater peace about your children, and bring greater peace in your marriage. And that is worth praying about.

PRAYERS *for* MY MARRIAGE

Prayer to Keep My Marriage Growing Strong

Lord, I pray for your protection over our marriage and our children. Help my husband (wife) and me to learn how to pray for our children so that we never leave any aspect of their lives to chance. Your Word says that "unless the LORD builds the house, they labor in vain who build it" (Psalm 127:1). So I invite You right now to build and establish our house, our marriage, and our family. Give me and my husband (wife) great wisdom and revelation about how to raise our children. Help us to talk things through and be in complete unity about how to teach and discipline them. Your Word says that You will reveal things we need to see when we reverence You (Psalm 25:14). Show us specifically what we need to see about ourselves and each child.

Help us to always put You first in our lives and to make each other and our marriage a priority as we are busy raising our children. Show us any time that we sacrifice each other to a point that is detrimental to our relationship. I know You are with us to save us, and Your love in us will bring peace and joy to our family (Zephaniah 3:17). Teach us to remember Your promise that whatever we ask in Your name, You will give to us (John 16:23). In Jesus' name I pray.

Prayer to Keep Me from Neglecting My Marriage or Our Children

Lord, help me to be balanced in my parenting. Help me to not be obsessive about my children, but rather to relinquish control over their lives to You as I partner with You in raising them. Enable me to find the perfect balance between focusing too much on my children to the neglect of my husband (wife), and the other extreme of neglecting my children in any way. Wherever there are disagreements between me and my husband (wife) as to how to raise and discipline our children, help us to be able to communicate well with each other and resolve whatever conflict we have.

Give me Your wisdom, revelation, and discernment. Give me Your strength, patience, and love. Teach me how to truly intercede for my children without trying to impose my own will when I pray. Show me how to pray so I can lay the burden of raising them at Your feet and have joy in the process. Increase my faith to believe for all the things You put on my heart to pray about for them. Lord, I know that I don't have the ability to be the perfect parent, but *You* do. I release my children into Your hands and pray that You would protect and guide them. Help me not to live in fear about my children because of all the possible dangers, but to live in peace because I pray for each child and trust that You are in control of their lives. In Jesus' name I pray.

Prayer to Keep My Husband (Wife) from Neglecting Our Marriage or Our Children

Lord, I pray for my husband (wife) to find the perfect balance between being focused solely on the children, and not spending enough time with them. Help him (her) to be willing to discuss with me about the raising and disciplining of each child so we can be in complete unity about everything. Let no issues of child rearing change his (her) heart toward me or undermine our relationship. Help him (her) to see the need for us to spend time together alone so that we can stay strong and connected as a married couple.

Lord, You have said in Your Word that whatever we ask we receive from You, because we keep Your commandments and do things that are pleasing in Your sight (1 John 3:22). Help my husband (wife) to obey You and do what is right in Your sight so that his (her) prayers will be answered. Give him (her) wisdom and revelation about all aspects of being a good father (mother) as well as a good husband (wife). In Jesus' name I pray.

TRUTH *to* STAND ON

The mercy of the LORD is from everlasting to everlasting
on those who fear Him, and His righteousness to children's
children, to such as keep His covenant, and to those who
remember His commandments to do them.

PSALM 103:17-18

If you then, being evil,
know how to give good gifts to your children,
how much more will your Father who is in heaven
give good things to those who ask Him!

MATTHEW 7:11

He has strengthened the bars of your gates;
He has blessed your children within you.

PSALM 147:13

My grace is sufficient for you,
for My strength is made perfect in weakness...
For when I am weak, then I am strong.

2 CORINTHIANS 12:9-10

All your children shall be taught by the Lord,
and great shall be the peace of your children.

ISAIAH 54:13

PRACTICAL STEPS *to* GOING DEEPER

1. Read Psalm 127:3 in your Bible. Do you always think of your children as a reward from God? Does your husband (wife)? If not, write out a prayer asking God to help you always think of them that way. If you already think of them as a gift from God, write out a prayer of thanks and praise to God for your children.

2. Read Proverbs 22:6 in your Bible. Do you and your husband (wife) agree on how to raise and discipline your children? What are the ways you agree or disagree? Write out a prayer asking God to help you and your spouse agree on everything that has to do with raising your children.

3. Read Deuteronomy 5:29 in your Bible. What do you two as parents need to have and do in order for your children to be blessed? Write out a prayer asking God for that for you both.

Read 1 Samuel 1:27 in your Bible. Write out a prayer asking God to help you both become powerful praying parents. Ask God to help you pray for your children and raise them so you can have more peace, energy, and quality time for each other.

6

Pray to Keep Finances from Becoming Out of Control

ne of the greatest burdens on any marriage is having financial problems. The deeper the problem and the longer it goes on with no end in sight, the greater the stress. And what worse financial crisis can there be than sinking heavily into debt with no way to pay all the bills? Not having enough money for necessities—rent, mortgage, electric bill, water, or food—is unbearably frightening. The sense of being caught in a vise that is always closing in on you is a horrible feeling that is unsustainable. Those who have been there know how important it is to do whatever it takes to stay debt-free and live within your means. In order to make sure that happens in a marriage, however, you need to pray that both you and your husband (wife) will be of one mind with regard to handling money.

Some experts say that the number one cause of divorce today has to do with financial difficulties. Money is a source of life. Without it we can't have a home, food, clothing, security, or a good future. So being married to someone who is irresponsible, foolish, selfish, stupid, or careless when it comes to money can cause you to feel as though your life is being sucked away. You fear that no matter how hard you work, you will never have anything to show for it. It can cause any person to feel desperate enough to do whatever is necessary to stop the bleeding—even if it means getting a divorce. That's why it is important to pray about this issue as a preventative measure as soon as you are married—or better yet, way *before* you're married.

In any marriage where one person is working hard to make a living and conserve their finances wisely, and the other is foolishly spending money faster than it is coming in, there will be major problems. If one person would rather save money for the future instead of spending on luxury items, and the other wants to buy everything they want, the moment they want it, without any thought for the future, there will be problems. If one person tells lies and manipulates in order to hide his (her) expenditures so the other one won't find out, there will be problems. If one person doesn't care what the other wants or thinks, there will be problems. If one person is responsible and the other isn't, there will be problems. These problems are enough to ruin any marriage.

The stress caused by spending foolishly, making unwise investments, and accumulating debt with never enough money to pay it off, is beyond what any marriage can tolerate. If two people are going to live together successfully, they have to come to an agreement about how money is earned, spent, saved, given, and invested.

The Message Bible says, "The one who stays on the job has food on the table; the witless chases whims and fancies" (Proverbs 12:11). That same verse in the New Century Version says, "Those who work their land will have plenty of food, but the one who chases empty dreams is not wise." Chasing whims, fancies, and empty dreams can ruin a person's life. When it comes to finances, some people are in dreamland. They can't put two and two together. That's why communication between a husband and wife about their finances is vital. You must have the same financial goals, the same mind about how money is handled, and be living in the same reality. And that should be established as soon as possible in a marriage. You can always adjust that as you go along. The important thing is to agree together.

Ten Things TO ASK GOD FOR REGARDING *Your Finances*

1. To give you wisdom concerning financial matters.

2. To teach you to make good decisions with regard to spending.

3. To enable you to get out of debt and stay debt free.

4. To eliminate any craving for unnecessary material possessions.

5. To help you plan ahead for future expenses.

6. To open doors for you to find good work that is secure.

7. To bless your employer so that you can be blessed as well.

8. To remove any fear of giving to God as He has instructed.

9. To show you how to give to others according to His will.

10. To embolden you to trust Him to meet all your needs.

Be Content and Work Hard While Waiting for Your Finances to Be Blessed

Being content doesn't mean resigning yourself to financial struggles and thinking, *This is as good as it gets and nothing will ever change.* Or, on the other hand, thinking, *Our finances are great and they always will be.* It means being content with what God has given you while you pray about your finances and wait patiently for His leading and future blessings. "Godliness with contentment is great gain...And having food and clothing, with these we shall be content" (1 Timothy 6:6,8). Being content doesn't mean doing nothing. Working hard is one of the ways God blesses us. When you work hard to provide for your family, that is not a sign of loving money. Putting the making of money as a higher priority *before* your family *is*. I know that is hard when one or both of you are walking a fine line between providing for your family and causing them to feel neglected in order to get ahead. It is the position of your heart with regard to finances that matters most.

Seven Things TO REMEMBER ABOUT THE *Work You Do*

1. *Begin all the work you do by seeking the Lord.* "In every work that [Hezekiah] began in the service of the house of God, in the law and in the commandment, to seek his God, he did it with all his heart. So he prospered" (2 Chronicles 31:21).

2. *Commit your work to God.* "Whatever you do, do it heartily, as to the Lord and not to men" (Colossians 3:23).

3. *Work hard and your work will be rewarded.* "You, be strong and do not let your hands be weak, for your work shall be rewarded" (2 Chronicles 15:7).

4. *Pray for God to establish your work.* "Let the beauty of the LORD our God be upon us, and establish the work of our hands for us; yes, establish the work of our hands" (Psalm 90:17).

5. *Work diligently and your wealth will increase.* "He who has a slack hand becomes poor, but the hand of the diligent makes rich" (Proverbs 10:4-5).

6. *Take a day to rest from your work each week.* "Six days you shall labor and do all your work, but the seventh day

is the Sabbath of the LORD your God. In it you shall do no work" (Exodus 20:9-10).

7. ***Ask God for success in your work and He will lift you up.*** "Do you see a man who excels in his work? He will stand before kings; he will not stand before unknown men" (Proverbs 22:29).

Seek God First to Get Out from Under Financial Stress

Always remember that God is the one who supplies all your needs and keeps your life from being sucked dry with one financial scare after another. That's why you must recognize where your provision comes from. "My God shall supply all your need according to His riches in glory by Christ Jesus" (Philippians 4:19).

The devourer, by contrast, comes to steal and destroy all you have. The list of ways for him to gobble up your life is endless. You can have one problem after another, such as the car breaks down, the house needs repair, you get sick and have to miss work, you have unexpected medical expenses, or the washing machine breaks down and you need to replace it. But when you submit to living God's way with regard to your finances, He provides for you and protects you from many of these things. It's not that these things will never happen, but He blesses you in different ways that make a big difference, and in ways you may not even realize until you start praying for His guidance. He hides you in His shadow and keeps you from disaster far more than you may realize (Psalm 91:1).

Jesus said, "Do not lay up for yourselves treasures on earth, where moth and rust destroy and where thieves break in and steal; but lay up for yourselves treasures in heaven, where neither moth nor rust destroys and where thieves do not break in and steal. *For where your treasure is, there your heart will be also*" (Matthew 6:19-21). He is not saying you can never have anything, just that your heart must be with Him first and not these things.

Seven Things TO DO CONCERNING Your Money

1. ***Keep in mind that all you have comes from God.*** "What do you have that you did not receive? Now if you did indeed receive it, why do you boast as if you had not received it?" (1 Corinthians 4:7).

2. ***Pray about every aspect of your finances.*** "Ask and it will be given to you; seek, and you will find; knock, and it will be opened to you. For everyone who asks receives, and he who seeks finds, and to him who knocks it will be opened" (Matthew 7:7-8).

3. ***Stay out of debt.*** "Owe no one anything except to love one another, for he who loves another has fulfilled the law" (Romans 13:8).

4. ***Be faithful with what God has given you.*** "He who is faithful in what is least is faithful also in much; and he who is unjust in what is least is unjust also in much" (Luke 16:10).

5. ***Spend wisely.*** "Why do you spend money for what is not bread, and your wages for what does not satisfy? Listen carefully to Me, and eat what is good, and let your soul delight itself in abundance" (Isaiah 55:2).

6. ***Give and you will be blessed.*** "Remember the words of the Lord Jesus, that He said, 'It is more blessed to give than to receive'" (Acts 20:35).

7. ***Love God, not money.*** "The love of money is a root of all kinds of evil, for which some have strayed from the faith in their greediness, and pierced themselves through with many sorrows" (1 Timothy 6:10).

Reaping the Rewards of Giving to God

One of the greatest keys to financial freedom is giving. The first and most important place to start is giving to God. I know that this can seem like a monumental sacrifice, especially if you and your spouse are working hard, and it always seems like you are barely scraping by. But God blesses you greatly when you give to Him. Talk to Him and ask Him to help you. This has to be settled in your minds between you and your spouse and God. This is a big part of getting your finances under control. Here are five things to remember about *giving to God*:

1. If you give God 10 percent of what you bring in, He will pour great blessings on you. " '*Bring all the tithes into the storehouse*, that there may be food in My house, and try Me now in this,' says the LORD of hosts, '*If I will not open for you the windows of heaven and pour out for you such blessing that there will not be room enough to receive it.* And I will rebuke the devourer for your sakes, so that he will not destroy the fruit of your ground, nor shall the vine fail to bear fruit for you in the field,' says the LORD of hosts" (Malachi 3:10-11). God will not only bless your finances, but also He will not allow the enemy to steal from you. He will prosper the work you do.

But be sure you and your spouse are in unity on this. If your spouse is not a believer and he (she) objects to tithing, he (she) may not understand the principle of it, and it won't make sense to him (her). In that case, ask what amount he (she) would feel comfortable giving and try to come to some agreement about it. Don't let this become a point of strife. Seeing him (her) come to know Jesus is more important than tithing his (her) money against his (her) will. I have seen great strife in marriages over this very thing. Don't let it happen to you.

2. Don't work to build your own house and not contribute to building God's house, or it will seem as though you will never get ahead. " 'You have sown much, and bring in little; you eat, but do not have enough; you drink, but you are not filled with drink; you clothe yourselves, but no one is warm; and he who earns wages, earns wages to put into a bag with holes... You looked for much, but indeed it came to little; and when you brought it home, I blew it away. Why?' says the LORD of hosts. 'Because of My house that is in ruins, while every one of you runs to his own house'" (Haggai 1:6,9). If it ever seems as though you work hard and never get ahead, or that money is always slipping through your fingers, ask God if you are giving toward the building of His church and kingdom in the way He would have you do.

3. *You have to be faithful with what you have before God will bless you with more.* In responding to a servant who wisely invested his money, the Lord said of the servant, "Well done, good and faithful servant; you were faithful over a few things, I will make you ruler over many things. Enter into the joy of your lord" (Matthew 25:21). If you are faithful to give a portion of your money to God, He will be faithful to trust you with more.

4. *If you truly believe that everything you have belongs to God or came from God, you will want to be a good steward of the things He has given you.* "Yours, O LORD, is the greatness, the power and the glory, the victory and the majesty; for all that is in heaven and in earth is Yours...Both riches and honor come from You, and You reign over all...For all things come from You, and of Your own we have given You" (1 Chronicles 29:11-12,14). When you believe that everything you have comes from God, you will want to give back to Him.

5. *You will always receive from God far more than you give.* "Give and it will be given to you: good measure, pressed down, shaken together, and running over will be put into your bosom. For with the same measure that you use, it will be measured back to you" (Luke 6:38). God's law is that you will reap a great blessing because of what you give to Him, and you can test Him on that.

Understanding the Value of Giving to Others

After giving to God, giving to others who have nothing, who can't help themselves, and who don't have enough food or clothes or a home is extremely important to God and crucial to your own financial peace and freedom. Don't give only to rich people's causes; give to those who can do nothing for you or for themselves. God sees you giving to others and considers that as something you are giving to Him. Jesus said that when He returned He would invite certain people to partake of what had been prepared for them from the foundation of the world. He will say, "I was hungry and you gave Me food; I was thirsty and you gave Me drink; I was a stranger and you took Me in; I was naked and you clothed Me." And we, the believers, will say, "When did we do that?"

And Jesus will answer, "Assuredly, I say to you, inasmuch as you did it to one of the least of these My brethren, you did it to Me" (Matthew 25:35,39-40). Anything we do for others, we have done it for the Lord, and that brings great rewards.

Here are five things to remember about *giving to others*:

1. *Ask God to show you a person in need you can help in some way.* You will be surprised at what will be revealed to you. There are always people around you who you may not even realize have great needs, and God is waiting to show you who they are. Be on the lookout for where God wants you to put your time, effort, and money.

2. *Ask your husband (wife) to be a part of any giving you do, so he (she) can share in the blessing.* Tell your husband (wife) what you're feeling about who you want to give to and why. If he (she) is reticent when it comes to giving, don't let that stop you from helping others. Just because your spouse doesn't understand how to open up the flow of God's blessings into his (her) life by giving doesn't mean you have to limit what God wants to do through you. There are things you can do or give that won't affect your mate.

For example, you can give food, clothes, furniture, and household items to people who can use them. Perhaps all you have to give someone at this moment is a ride, some kind of help or assistance, a meal to eat, or an encouraging word. You can't imagine how much of a blessing doing something like these things can be to others. You never know what can bless someone else until you offer it to them.

3. *Give from what you have.* Even if you don't have much money to give, you may have other things that can help meet the needs of others. Do you have a talent you can use to bless someone? Ask God to show you. If you have a skill you have been using for 40 hours a week, it may be that this is the last thing you want to do when you get off work, but ask God to show you where there is a need for your skill or talent that would bless someone greatly. "Do not forget to do good and to share, for with such sacrifices God is well pleased" (Hebrews 13:16).

God doesn't require that you give money you don't have. If you owe a debt to someone and when money comes in you give it to someone else instead of paying the person you owe, that is not right. Paying your debts is part of being a good steward. One of the great things about being out of debt is being able to give to others as God directs you. Give to God and get out of debt first. Take care of what you owe and don't rob God or others. Instead, ask God to show you how you can bless others. For some people, a ride to the doctor's office may be the biggest blessing of all.

4. *Give to God, not to impress others.* I know someone who was so into giving that he gave away practically everything at the expense of his wife and children. But his giving was not for God so much as it was to impress other people. It was giving to be admired. "Take heed that you do not do your charitable deeds before men, to be seen by them. Otherwise you have no reward from your Father in heaven" (Matthew 6:1). It's good to have a giving spirit, but when you are married you have to be considerate of your mate and come to an agreement together about giving.

5. *You have to give in order to receive.* If you are in need of financial blessing, give something of yourself to others today. Often, just the act of giving will break whatever has a hold on your finances. You will always have enough for what you need if you give to God and others. "He who sows sparingly will also reap sparingly, and he who sows bountifully will also reap bountifully. So let each one give as he purposes in his heart, not grudgingly or of necessity; for God loves a cheerful giver" (2 Corinthians 9:6-7). Give generously and you will receive generously from God.

If This Has Already Happened to You

If you are already married to someone who has no business sense or wisdom about finances—who can't add, subtract, or count, and has no financial discipline or responsibility in handling money—then I suggest you invest in knee pads for your frequent prayer vigils.

There has to be financial honesty in marriage. You and your spouse need to be up-front with one other about income and spending. You must always consider the other when buying anything. If your spouse is secretly spending money faster than either of you can earn it, then it feels as though he (she) has no consideration of your future and what you need (who doesn't need financial security?). It puts up a wall of separation and kills love between you.

If you or your spouse has a bad habit of accumulating debt, ask God to open your eyes so you can clearly see the truth. Pray for discernment about what you don't really need and ask God to give you the strength to resist buying it. We have all bought things in our lives that we recognized later were a waste of money, and now wish we had the money back instead of those things. Pray that God will give both of you the wisdom to make sound financial decisions in advance. Ask Him to help you be wise about the things you buy. Pray He will help you avoid getting into debt in the first place. If you are already in debt, ask God to show you how to pay it all off and get back on track.

Financial stress always takes a great toll on a marriage, but you can either let it tear you apart or make you stronger. One good thing financial stress *can* do for you is force you to draw closer to God, to depend on Him to get you through and turn things around. It also encourages you to work more closely with your spouse so you will be on the same team financially. This is extremely important.

Another thing a financial crunch will do is help you learn how to simplify. Learning to live more simply takes stress off your marriage and financial pressure off both of you. God will show you how to live without certain things and be wise about every purchase. I was raised extremely poor. And even after I was out on my own, completely supporting myself, I was still poor to the point that every penny, nickel, dime, and quarter counted. Sometimes it meant having food for dinner, being able to do a load of wash at the Laundromat, or paying the light bill. This is not a good way to live, so ask God to enable you to stay out of that kind of gut-wrenching poverty. The Bible says God does not want His children begging bread, but He also doesn't want us to kill ourselves working for material possessions either (Proverbs 23:4).

We have to find that perfect balance. And the way to find it, God says, is to understand that we don't have because we don't ask. He wants us to pray about the things we need.

Ask God to give you and your spouse the wisdom to not purchase anything you don't need. Ask Him to help you establish an emergency savings account. Ask Him to guide you *before* you spend money on anything so you won't make a mistake you will regret. Remember that whatever you want to buy that your spouse *strongly* opposes will not be worth the toll it will take on your marriage. "Take heed and beware of covetousness, for one's life does not consist in the abundance of the things he possesses" (Luke 12:15).

You have to be able to enjoy your life, and unless you have lost all contact with reality, it is impossible to enjoy life if you are heavily burdened with debt or are struggling to just survive. You need to have money to live and also to do some things that are enjoyable, such as take a day off to do something fun, or go out to dinner together, or do what you must do to take care of your health. Say no to things you don't absolutely need to have so that you can get out of debt and never be a slave to it again. That is the best feeling.

My husband and I try constantly to simplify our lives. We are not successful at it all the time because our lives can become too busy and complicated very easily. But when we can eliminate something we don't need, we are eager to do it and are richer for it. "*Aspire to lead a quiet life*, to mind your own business, and to work with your own hands" (1 Thessalonians 4:11). Ask God to show you ways you can work at what you love and simplify your lives together.

Seek Advice from Financial Experts

If you and your spouse desperately need financial help and wisdom about how to get on top of your financial situation, seek the advice of an expert or professional. There are many good Christian financial advisers, plus excellent Christian books, radio programs, recorded teachings by financial professionals, and seminars on the subject. If you and your husband (wife) can attend one of these seminars, or listen to radio programs or read books about this together, it will be greatly beneficial for you. Half the battle will be won if you can face all financial matters full force together. Look up the words "financial peace" on the Internet and see what comes up.

One of the things financial experts advise is to not sustain credit card debt if you can avoid it. Instead, pay off your credit cards each month. I know there are times when you need to purchase something big that is a necessity and pay it off monthly, such as a new refrigerator, tires for your car, or repairs on your home. And you do need to put vacation expenses on a credit card because it is unwise to travel with large amounts of cash. But even then, be sure you can pay it all off right away. Paying huge finance charges for credit card debt is like throwing your money down the drain. If buying things on credit puts you under a mountain of debt that you can't get out from under, it doesn't make you feel good about your life—or your spouse, if he (she) is the one causing the problem. A professional can help you see where you have gone wrong and how to change it.

If One of You Gambles

There are many types of bad habits that have to do with finances, but none is as destructive as gambling. If one person is conserving and saving and denying themselves and doing all they can to stay out of debt, and their husband (wife) is gambling money away, the result is a heartbreaking sense of futility. And it is at epidemic proportions in families right now because of the easy access to gambling on the Internet and the numerous gambling places within driving distance from most cities.

If you gamble, remember you are gambling with the Lord's money. It's hard to think that God would want to bless you with riches so that they can be given to gambling casino owners. Actually, gambling casinos are betting on people losing, and the reason they are so successful is because they are winning that bet.

Gambling can be addicting, and it is one of the enemy's plans for your life and a pit he has prepared for you to fall into. Some people try gambling a few times and when they win it is like an elixir, always drawing them back to experience the thrill of the win again. But the truth is they have a strong discontent with what they have, and an unwillingness to look to God to provide what they need. When God promises us that He will never leave or forsake us, He means that in the way He provides for us too. "Be content with such things as you have. For He Himself has said, 'I will never leave you nor forsake you'" (Hebrews 13:5).

Gambling may *seem* like the solution to a debt problem, but it never is. "There is a way that seems right to a man, but its end is the way of death" (Proverbs 14:12). Even if you win, you will eventually lose in every way. The money won't be blessed and will slip through your fingers, and you will have nothing lasting to show for it. Nothing good will come out of it.

Marriage is building a life together—a home, a family, and a future—and that cannot happen without financial security. When a husband or wife is foolishly gambling their money, a breakdown of trust happens that is extremely hard to repair. If you are trying to build a life and your spouse's out of control gambling problem is tearing down all you have built, you feel as though you have no future. No marriage can survive that.

Gambling doesn't have to occur in a casino or in online gambling. It can happen when one person is always investing in risky schemes that fail because they are easily talked into it by a family member or a not-so-good-friend who fancies themselves as a clever investor. This is the way to lose large chunks of money.

If either you or your mate have a problem with gambling, stay in God's Word and fast and pray periodically until you are set free. Jesus said, "If you abide in My word, you are My disciples indeed. And you shall know the truth, and the truth shall make you free" (John 8:31-32). You need a miracle from God, and when you lay all else aside and seek Him for that miracle, you can see Him work one in your life. Seek help if you need it. Seek the freedom in Christ that you have been given and get back on the path toward life and blessing.

It was said of Uzziah, one of the kings of Judah, that "as he sought the Lord, God made him prosper" (2 Chronicles 26:5). It is the same for you and your spouse in your marriage today. *Seek God's guidance in acquiring, giving, spending, saving, and investing.* "If riches increase, do not set your heart on them" (Psalm 62:10). *Set your heart on God*, be in His Word, and live His way, and He will prosper you. *"This Book of the Law shall not depart from your mouth*, but you shall meditate in it day and night, that you may observe to do according to all that is written in it. *For then you will make your way prosperous, and then you will have good success"* (Joshua 1:8).

Pray that you and your husband (wife) will always be able to think *God's* way about money. If you have any bad habits with finances, ask Him for a transformed heart so you can overcome them. Ask God to renew your mind about finances so that your finances can be renewed. Don't live like the world, always trying to get out of *yesterday's* debt. Live wisely *today* and plan for your *future*. Thank God that He promises to supply everything you need. And in time when you look back over your life, you will see how He has done that.

PRAYERS *for* MY MARRIAGE

Prayer for God's Blessing on Our Finances

Lord, help my husband (wife) and me to remember that it is You who gives us the ability to produce wealth (Deuteronomy 8:18). And that the earth is Yours and everything in it belongs to You (Psalm 24:1). And that You, Lord, own every animal and creature and "the cattle on a thousand hills" (Psalm 50:10-11). All silver and gold and all things valuable belong to You (Haggai 2:8). Everything we have comes from You, so help us to be good stewards of the finances you give us. Help us to always be calm and wise in handling money so that we may prosper and not make hasty, rash, or impulsive decisions (Proverbs 21:5).

Help us to work diligently, to be content with what we have, and to learn to give (Proverbs 21:25-26). Help us to always discern between the dream of something more or better that is in line with Your will for our lives, and the lusting greed for material possessions that is not Your will at all. Enable us to stay out of debt and pay off any debt we have quickly. Help us to not be drawn in by the ways of the world, but instead seek after what truly satisfies our soul (Romans 12:2).

I know that having good health, a loving and supportive family, a solid marriage, great friends, good and satisfying work, and a sense of purpose in helping others is the richest life of all. Help us to always put our sights on those clear priorities. Lord, I pray that You would bless us with provision and help us to always be wise in the decisions we make regarding our spending. Give us the wisdom and the courage to resist spending foolishly. Help us to faithfully tithe and give offerings to You, and show us how you would have us give to others. Teach me and my husband (wife) to completely agree on our spending as well as our giving. In Jesus' name I pray.

Prayer for Financial Wisdom in Me

Lord, I pray that You will give me wisdom with money. Help me to be able to generate it and also spend it wisely. Teach me to give according to Your will and ways. Thank You that any charitable deed I do in secret, You will reward openly (Matthew 6:1-4). Show me when I am tempted to buy something I don't need and will regret later. Show me what is a waste of money and what is not. Help me to avoid certain places that are traps for me, where I will be tempted to spend foolishly. Help me not to be drawn toward things that will not add to our lives.

I submit our finances to You and ask that You would reveal to me all that I should know or do. I don't want to look back in regret, but rather to be able to look forward to a secure future. Reveal to me anything I need to see in myself that are bad habits with regard to spending. Help me to glorify You with the money I spend. I acknowledge You as the Lord who gives us the power to gain wealth, and I thank You that You give no burden with it (Deuteronomy 8:18). I know that I must not trust in uncertain riches but in You, for it is You "who gives us richly all things to enjoy" (1 Timothy 6:17). "Oh, how great is Your goodness, which You have laid up for those who fear You, which You have prepared for those who trust in You" (Psalm 31:19). In Jesus' name I pray.

Prayer for Financial Wisdom in My Husband (Wife)

I thank You, Jesus, that You are the power and wisdom of God (1 Corinthians 1:24). I pray that You would give my husband (wife) wisdom about our finances. Help him (her) to trust You with all his (her) heart and not depend on his (her) own understanding (Proverbs 3:5). Help him (her) to not be wise in his (her) own eyes, but to fear You and stay far from evil (Proverbs 3:7). Give him (her) a good business sense and the ability to be responsible with money. Show him (her) insight into Your truth and give him (her) the power to resist temptation when it comes to needless spending. Where he (she) has made mistakes with money, I pray that You would reveal Your truth to him (her) so it doesn't happen again.

When he (she) is feeling financial strain, I pray You would take the stress of that burden away. Enable him (her) to get free of all debt and understand how to avoid it in the future. Help him (her) to know that "there is nothing too hard for You" (Jeremiah 32:17). Enable him (her) to know that even though there are times when he (she) is not seeing the desired fruit of his (her) labor, he (she) can still rejoice and say, "The LORD God is my strength; He will make my feet like deer's feet, and He will make me walk on my high hills" (Habakkuk 3:19). Help him (her) to be anxious for nothing, but to pray about everything and be thankful (Philippians 4:6). Teach him (her) to trust in You and Your promise to provide for those who love You and look to You for everything.

Enable my husband (wife) to excel in his (her) work and be recognized by many for the work he (she) does (Proverbs 22:29). Teach him (her) to not be lacking in diligence, but to be fervent in spirit, serving You in everything he (she) does (Romans 12:11). Establish the work of his (her) hands (Psalm 90:17). In Jesus' name I pray.

TRUTH *to* STAND ON

Set your mind on things above,
not on things on the earth.

COLOSSIANS 3:2

The Lord your God will make you abound
in all the work of your hand.

DEUTERONOMY 30:9

Prepare your outside work,
make it fit for yourself in the field;
and afterward build your house.

PROVERBS 24:27

Oh, taste and see that the Lord is good;
blessed is the man who trusts in Him!

PSALM 34:8

The Lord will open to you His good treasure, the heavens,
to give the rain to your land in its season,
and to bless all the work of your hand.

DEUTERONOMY 28:12

PRACTICAL STEPS *to* GOING DEEPER

1. Read 2 Corinthians 9:6-7 in your Bible. In light of this Scripture, what kind of person does God love? What is the principle of giving in these verses? Write out a prayer asking God to help you and your spouse to be in total agreement about giving to God and to others.

2. Do you and your spouse ever have disagreements about how your money is to be spent? Write out a prayer asking God to help you and

your spouse be able to quickly resolve any conflicts between you with regard to spending money. Pray that when there needs to be compromise between you, you will both peacefully communicate and work these things out.

3. Read Luke 6:38 in your Bible. What is the one principle God gives to guide us if we want to see financial blessings in our life? Do you feel you and your spouse live by that principle of generosity to God and to others in need? If not, write out a prayer asking God to help you both remember that everything you have comes from God, and so giving back to Him the way He requires is a must. If you already give to God and to others, write out a prayer of thanksgiving to God for providing for you and ask Him to help you continue to do that.

7

Pray to Keep Destructive Behavior from Establishing a Stronghold

marriage is for two people only and exclusively. Outside of including God in your relationship, any other third party breaks the marriage bond. Drugs, alcohol, or any other promoter of destructive behavior will always be a third party in any marriage. It will be an intruder in your relationship together.

There is a price to pay for everything we do that is not God's will for our lives. God says, "*I, the Lord, search the heart*, I test the mind, even to give every man according to his ways, according to the fruit of his doings" (Jeremiah 17:10). There is also a reward for every attempt we make to do the right thing. "He will reward each according to his works" (Matthew 16:27).

Destructive behavior—or simply behavior that constantly annoys your spouse to the point of desperation—is not good, and there will always be a serious consequence for it in your marriage and personal life. But every attempt you make to discover and clearly see that behavior in yourself, and to do what's right to rid yourself of it, will bring reward.

You may not have a single bad habit, and neither does your spouse, but you still must pray about this issue. There are countless couples who are now divorced because in a weak moment in their lives, one of them resorted to some kind of destructive behavior that they eventually couldn't (or wouldn't) get free of. And it became their downfall. Pray that God will protect your marriage from destructive behavior in either of you.

We can all have an annoying habit that drives our spouse crazy, but we have to be strong enough to recognize it in ourselves—especially if it is pointed out to us specifically enough times. If we see something like that in our spouse, we can pray about that before we speak and ask God to give him (her) ears to hear and the ability to get free of whatever annoying habit it is that you feel could destroy your marriage. Pray, don't nag. Nagging doesn't work. Ask God to give you words to say that are kind and productive.

We are not created by God to destroy ourselves. We are built to preserve our lives. We have a survival instinct in us. We don't willingly let ourselves drown, step in front of a train, jump off a high building, or put a gun to our head and pull the trigger unless we are not in our right mind or we are under the influence of something other than God.

Pray to Be Free from Destructive Behavior

If you are the one struggling with destructive behavior of some kind, then you know that trying to get free of any kind of destructive habits can feel like an impossible task when the pull is so strong and your willpower seems weak. But that is exacerbated by the enemy speaking to your mind, saying, "Do this. You deserve it after all you have been through." "You can't help it. It's just the way you are." "It's in your genes. It's in your family." "There is no power greater than this, and so you have to surrender to it." Identifying these lies and the source of them will help you see what you're facing from the proper perspective.

There can be an aspect of rebellion that should not be ignored in this. Any time *your* will is exerted over God's will, you are in rebellion against Him. You may not seem to be blatantly rebellious, but there is something that rises up within you that says, "*I* am in charge. I *will not* be told what to do. I *will* do *what* I *want* to do and *when* I *want* to do it." I'm not saying you are necessarily being rebellious if you can't control your destructive habits, but I believe a rebellious spirit comes to everyone at some point as a child, and if a parent allows rebelliousness to have a place in that child's behavior instead of teaching and disciplining them away from it, this rebellious attitude or mind-set stays with them and influences their decisions and choices from then on. It causes them to say to themselves, without even consciously realizing they are doing it, "I will do what I want."

Whenever you *won't*—or *will not*—stop doing what you are doing, even though your loved ones have asked you to repeatedly to do so, you are in rebellion. You are not only in rebellion toward your spouse, but, most of all, in rebellion toward *God*. The first way to break down a stronghold of rebellion is to resist it in prayer.

If you and your husband (wife) have any uncontrollable habits, God has healing for you both. But in order to get free and move into all God has for you, you must believe that when you received Jesus as Savior, He became your Savior in *every way*. He even *saves* you from *yourself* when you ask Him to. You must believe that the Word of God has life and liberty for you. You need to believe that God hears your prayers and will answer them. You must have *faith* that the only limits to what God can do in your life are the limits *you* put on Him when you don't have *faith*. You have to understand that God has the power to set you free from whatever binds you, but He has given you a free will, and so you still have to choose to *ask* for His power to manifest on your behalf.

God has also given you authority over all the power of the enemy (Luke 10:19). Jesus gave His 12 disciples "power over unclean spirits, to cast them out, and to heal all kinds of sickness and all kinds of disease" (Matthew 10:1). The key words here are "all kinds." There wasn't a disease, sickness, or unclean spirit that was greater than the healing power of God. Jesus came as *your* healer and deliverer. He is the same yesterday, today, and tomorrow. Why would He bother coming as your healer or deliverer if you could always be completely healed and delivered on your own?

If your father or grandfather was an alcoholic, it doesn't mean *you* have to be. But it may mean that any weakness you have was inherited. The good news is that Jesus has broken every curse in our lives, including any that came down through our family. But we still have to make an effort to stop doing anything that misses the mark God has for us.

When you truly realize the purpose God has for you, you won't allow any self-destructive behavior to control you. You will take whatever steps are necessary to get free of it. You will remember that Jesus is your *healer* and *deliverer* and you won't accept less than the freedom He has for you (Mark 16:17-18).

Why Do We Do Things We Don't Want to Do?

Read these encouraging words the apostle Paul said that have been powerfully and beautifully translated by Eugene H. Peterson in *The Message*. See if this doesn't speak to anyone who has ever struggled with a behavior that they wished they didn't have:

> What I don't understand about myself is that I decide one way, but then I act another, doing things I absolutely despise. So if I can't be trusted to figure out what is best for myself and then do it, it becomes obvious that God's command is necessary.
>
> But I need something *more*! For if I know the law but still can't keep it, and if the power of sin within me keeps sabotaging my best intentions, I obviously need help! I realize that I don't have what it takes. I can will it, but I can't *do* it. I decide to do good, but I don't *really* do it; I decide not to do bad, but then I do it anyway. My decisions, such as they are, don't result in actions. Something has gone wrong deep within me and gets the better of me every time.
>
> It happens so regularly that it's predictable. The moment I decide to do good, sin is there to trip me up. I truly delight in God's commands, but it's pretty obvious that not all of me joins in that delight. Parts of me covertly rebel, and just when I least expect it, they take charge. I've tried everything and nothing helps. I'm at the end of my rope. Is there no one who can do anything for me? Isn't that the real question?
>
> The answer, thank God, is that Jesus Christ can and does. He acted to set things right in this life of contradictions where I want to serve God with all my heart and mind, but am pulled by the influence of sin to do something totally different (Romans 7:15-25).

It cannot be said any clearer or better than that. The point is, when you try to get free and do the right thing on your own, sometimes you just can't. But with Jesus, you can do all the things you need to do because He will strengthen you and enable you to do them (Philippians 4:13). And if God is for you, who on earth can be against you? (Romans 8:31). Ask God to show you what steps to take to find all the healing, deliverance, and wholeness you and your spouse need.

That's why you must pray in advance that you and your husband (wife) will be addicted only to God's presence and His Word. Pray neither of you will ever be a slave to this kind of behavior, but rather a slave to God (Romans 6:16). That's where freedom comes from.

If you or your husband (wife) cannot stop this behavior, seek professional help immediately. Don't live with this problem one more day. It won't get better on its own. And don't even try to handle it alone. You need all the love, support, and help from others you can get.

When Someone Is Drawn Toward Destructive Behavior

Some people start taking drugs or drinking as a social activity, just to follow the crowd. Some do it because they feel hopeless, insecure, or overwhelmed, and an intoxicant makes them feel better. Others want to "*be in control*" of their situation, and they mistakenly feel as though they have control when they drink or take drugs. They let themselves get *out* of control doing something bad for them so that they can feel *in* control. "To a hungry soul every bitter thing is sweet" (Proverbs 27:7).

People who do self-destructive things are often doing them to feel better about themselves, but the truth is, partaking in something that alters their mood and makes them think it's fulfilling them is actually luring them into a trap of delusions that keeps them from experiencing the fulfillment *God* has for them. We all have a spiritual hunger. Whether we understand it as that or not, the truth is we can only truly be satisfied by God and nothing else.

When I was in my twenties, before I became a believer, I used to drink and take drugs because doing so made me less anxious. Drugs and alcohol seemed to release my spontaneity and sense of humor. Feeling inadequate and uncomfortable in a group of people made me afraid, and drinking took that fear away. I also wanted some relief from the pain and terrible insecurity I felt about myself and my future. Drugs and alcohol seemed to do that temporarily. And they were so readily available through the Hollywood circles I traveled in that they became like a spring well of water that never ran dry.

It's not that I felt all-powerful when I drank or took drugs; I just felt *less powerless*. I did stupid and dangerous things while under the influence of those substances, and it's a miracle I lived through that period of my life. At least I had enough sense to not drink and drive. Nor did I drink when I was alone, and definitely not when I was working. I did not have an addictive personality, so I never *craved* any kind of drug or alcohol—ever. I just took them to try to feel normal in a social situation.

When I received the Lord and discovered God had a purpose for my life and a hope for my future, I did not drink like that again. That was it. I found in Jesus what I had been looking for in alcohol and drugs, and so those things instantly lost their appeal. I had seen God do miracles for me and so I didn't want any part of something that was not God's will for my life. I refused to find false relief in the self-destructive behaviors that had nearly killed me so many times in the past. I wanted to stay alive and find out what God had for me.

Having a mother who is mentally ill is similar to having a parent who is an alcoholic. My best friend in high school had an alcoholic mother, and we realized that we shared the same struggles. For example, we both learned to never bring a friend home because we never knew what we would find. Her mother might be passed out on the floor, and mine might be having an episode of insane rage. Our mothers were entirely unavailable to us, and we could never connect with them emotionally. We both had pacifistic fathers who worked hard to support the family, but they never rescued us from our mothers. Because of that, we felt doubtful about ourselves and fearful about the future. We felt insecure, unloved, and empty inside and didn't know how to fill that emptiness.

Our situations were swept under a rug at home. We didn't talk with our dads, families, or friends about what was happening. We only talked with each other. We felt unimportant, confused, and sad. We had little sense of purpose in life, and there was no hopeful expectation. I turned to drugs and alcohol, which I was able to get free of with God's help. But my friend developed an eating disorder that eventually killed her. It was very sad. Since that time I've known many people who had alcoholic parents, and every single one of them struggled greatly in their lives because of it.

If you or your husband (wife) have a problem stopping any kind of destructive behavior, you need to get help immediately because this will not only take its toll on you, but also your marriage and your entire family. Destructive behavior will always be an intruder in your relationships with your sons or daughters. It will make them feel abandoned because it doesn't seem as if you love them enough to quit. Next to abuse, this is the ultimate destroyer of children.

Drugs and alcohol become an idol when it's something a person loves more than *God*, who has said not to do it, and more than a spouse, who has asked him (her) not to do it, and more than *children*, who are frightened by a parent doing it. The Bible says, those who practice drunkenness are "not wise" (Proverbs 20:1), do not "walk properly" (Romans 13:13), "will not inherit the kingdom of God" (Galatians 5:21), and will ultimately be the loser (Proverbs 23:31-32). Pray that this will not happen to you.

Five Ways TO RISE ABOVE YOUR *Weaknesses*

1. ***Invite the Holy Spirit to fill you afresh each day.*** "[I pray] that He would grant you, according to the riches of His glory, to be strengthened with might through His Spirit in the inner man, that Christ may dwell in your hearts through faith" (Ephesians 3:16-17).

2. ***Ask Jesus to help you crucify your fleshly desires.*** "Those

who are Christ's have crucified the flesh with its passions and desires. If we live in the Spirit, let us also walk in the Spirit" (Galatians 5:24-25).

3. *Resist worldly temptation.* "Denying ungodliness and worldly lusts, we should live soberly, righteously, and godly in the present age" (Titus 2:12).

4. *Don't be intoxicated with anything other than the Holy Spirit.* "Do not be drunk with wine, in which is dissipation; but be filled with the Spirit" (Ephesians 5:18).

5. *Decide every day to sow to the Spirit and not the flesh.* "He who sows to his flesh will of the flesh reap corruption, but he who sows to the Spirit will of the Spirit reap everlasting life" (Galatians 6:8).

If This Has Already Happened to You

Any kind of destructive behavior your spouse cannot seem to gain control over is addictive. Even if he (she) doesn't do it every day, if it is on any kind of regular basis, then it is a problem that has to be addressed. When it affects the quality and success of his (her) work or physical health; when it causes him (her) to be unpleasant to others and have poor judgment or lack of control; when it does terrible things to you, your children, and other family members and friends, he (she) has a problem and needs help. If your spouse lives in denial that there *is* a problem, or thinks that what he (she) is doing is not really all that bad, ask God to do what it takes to reveal the truth to him (her) in the clearest way possible.

When he (she) has a *true revelation from God* that any self-destructive compulsion or behavior is a ploy of the enemy designed to keep him (her) from realizing his (her) purpose and becoming all God created him (her) to be, those behaviors will begin to be resisted. And when he (she) gets free, there will be a time when it is only in the weakest moments under enemy fire that he (she) even considers giving place to them again. Ask God to show him (her) what his (her) purpose is. He (she) may not be able to understand it in full detail, but he (she) will sense that God has something great ahead, and he (she) needs to be completely available to the Lord in order to be in the right place at the right time.

If your spouse cannot stop using drugs, alcohol, or being involved with any other addictive or destructive behavior, seek *professional help* for him (her). This kind of serious addiction does not get better on its own. It is a sickness and must be treated as such. There are some people who are users but are not addicted and can stop on their own, and I have seen many success stories where reality hit and they were able to just lay it down completely and never look back. But for those who have the addiction, they must have outside help.

If your husband (wife) struggles with any kind of personality disorder—for example, an eating disorder—pray that the *spirit* of wisdom and revelation will open his (her) eyes to the truth. This is not just having wisdom about a few things, or having some things revealed, this is having *the Spirit* of *wisdom and revelation* so that he (she) is able to understand *all things* needed in order to get free.

Any kind of destructive behavior involves choice. To deliberately choose something that will do damage to yourself or destroy your body is a disorder of the mind. People who have these kinds of disorders and practice any kind of self-destructive behavior that they cannot control must have professional help. I am not talking about addictions, alcoholism, or eating disorders here. Those kinds of situations need immediate medical attention. Don't even attempt to handle these problems on your own.

It's possible to be a normal person and still fall into the trap of substance abuse and other destructive behaviors. You can even be a mature adult who has never had a problem before, and you try something once in a weak moment and find it comforting, empowering, or stress-relieving. Then every time you need comfort, relief from stress, or the feeling of empowerment, you try it again. Soon you may need to take more than before, because there is a tendency toward diminishing returns when it comes to this kind of behavior. Just as a gambler will place bigger and bigger bets in an attempt to regain what he has lost, an addict will take in more and more in order to gain that sense of euphoria, control, freedom, or whatever it was they experienced in the first place.

In some cases, there is an altering of chemistry in the brain, and eventually that person has a biochemical dependency. It may be that the connection between feeling good and the drugs or alcohol they consumed establishes some kind of a pattern in the brain. A person can also be predisposed to do something like that, or by inheriting a tendency or a weakness from a family member.

Alcohol and drug addiction are considered diseases of the mind. Being addicted in any way is a form of mental illness. A person who drinks or does drugs and doesn't have control over the addiction appears to care more about himself (herself) and what *he (she)* wants than about what his (her) family's needs are. An alcoholic or drug addict may feel he (she) loves his (her) spouse and children, but he (she) doesn't have what it takes to get rid of all self-destructive behavior for his (her) family's sake, as well as his (her) own. That kind of addiction will always take priority over other people.

If you are around a husband (wife) who is addicted to alcohol, drugs, or any other destructive behavior, their *insanity* affects your *sanity*, and you can start to feel as though you are losing your mind. That's why you must get professional help for yourself too. Don't try to go through this alone. Your love for your troubled and sick spouse has to be strong enough to not accept what is unacceptable. You need the support and prayers of others so you can stand strong through this to complete freedom and victory for you both.

People don't change unless they want to. Pray for your spouse to desperately *want* to change. The only changes that are lasting come when we surrender our lives completely to the Lord and give Him free rein. When we invite God to make big changes in us, He will do that. It may not happen overnight, so don't give up.

If none of this has never happened to either you or your husband (wife), then thank God and keep praying to prevent this from ever happening in the future.

PRAYERS *for* MY MARRIAGE

Prayer to Keep Me and My Husband (Wife) Free from Destructive Behavior

Lord, I pray that You would protect my husband (wife) and me from any kind of self-destructive behavior. Open our eyes to see if we have allowed habits into our lives that have the potential to harm us or others. Bring to light anything we need to see so that we will have nothing hidden from one another. If we ever open ourselves up to bad or destructive habits, help us to get free quickly. Give us the ability to cope with any frustration or anxiety we may be dealing with by taking all concerns to You and each other and not looking for relief from outside resources.

Lord, You have promised that "if we confess our sins" You are "faithful and just to forgive us our sins and to cleanse us from all unrighteousness" (1 John 1:9). Help us to confess any sin the moment we see it in ourselves so that we will be cleansed from it before it can establish a hold on us. Thank You that we are "predestined to be conformed to the image" of Your Son (Romans 8:29). That's what we want. Help us to understand that the power that raised Jesus from the dead is the same power that will raise us above all that tempts us away from Your best for our lives (Ephesians 1:19-20). Lift us above anything that would bring us down. In Jesus' name I pray.

Prayer for Me to Be Free from Any Destructive Behavior

Lord, I pray You would reveal to me any habit I have embraced that is not Your will for my life. Break any spirit of rebellion in me that causes me to feel that I can do what I want, when I want, without regard for the consequences. Enable me to understand clearly how what I do affects my husband (wife) and family. Where You or other people have tried to warn me, give me ears to hear and receive the truth. Bring me to complete repentance before You for ever ignoring those warnings.

Help me not to hold resentment toward anyone who tries to confront me on any problem, especially my husband (wife). Enable me to remember that "faithful are the wounds of a friend" (Proverbs 27:6). I know that "You desire truth in the inward parts, and in the hidden part You will make me to know wisdom" (Psalm 51:6). Help me to become a person of truth and wisdom who does not have a secret life.

Thank You, God, that You are my healer, my refuge and strength, and "a very present help in times of trouble" (Psalm 46:1). Thank You, Holy Spirit, that You are my Comforter and Helper. I cast my burden on You, Lord, knowing You will enable me to get free of anything that influences me in a bad way and to "stand fast therefore in the liberty by which" You have made me free. Keep me from being "entangled again with a yoke of bondage" (Galatians 5:1). I willingly present myself to You as a slave of righteousness (Romans 6:19). I know that I depend on the excellence of Your power to set me free (2 Corinthians 4:7).

Thank You that "I have been crucified with Christ; it is no longer I who live, but Christ lives in me; and the life which I now live in the flesh I live by faith in the Son of God, who loved me and gave Himself for me" (Galatians 2:20). So even though I may be weak in and of myself, Jesus in me is strong enough to set me free and help me to resist all temptation. Thank You that I can do what I need to do because You enable me to do it (Philippians 4:13). My soul waits quietly for You to save me from myself (Psalm 62:1). In Jesus' name I pray.

Prayer for My Husband (Wife) to Be Free from Any Destructive Behavior

Lord, I pray that my husband (wife) will have eyes to see the truth and ears to hear Your voice speaking to him (her). May Your will always be done in his (her) life. Keep him (her) free from any destructive habits. I pray that You, "the God of our Lord Jesus Christ, the Father of glory," will give to my husband (wife) "the spirit of wisdom and revelation" in the knowledge of You, that the eyes of his (her) understanding would be enlightened, that he (she) would "know what is the hope of His calling, what are the riches of the glory of His inheritance," and "what is the exceeding greatness" of Your power toward him (her) who believes, according to the work of Your mighty power in his (her) life (Ephesians 1:17-19).

If my husband (wife) is ever drawn toward any kind of destructive behavior, give him (her) the ability to take responsibility for his (her) actions and not live in denial about them. I pray he (she) will always be completely honest with me about everything he (she) is doing. Let there be no secrets. Tear down any walls that may have been erected between us.

Help him (her) to understand his (her) worth in Your sight, and to see that his (her) life is too important to waste. Help him (her) to seek You as his (her) healer and deliverer, so he (she) can find total restoration in You. To my husband (wife) I say, "Sin shall not have dominion over you, for you are not under law but under grace" (Romans 6:14). I say that God has deliverance and healing for your life. I say, "The God of peace will crush Satan under your feet shortly" (Romans 16:20). I say, "Stand fast therefore in the liberty by which Christ has made us free, and do not be entangled again with a yoke of bondage" (Galatians 5:1). In Jesus' name I pray.

TRUTH *to* STAND ON

I can do all things through Christ
who strengthens me.

PHILIPPIANS 4:13

Do not be conformed to this world,
but be transformed by the renewing of your mind,

that you may prove what is that good and
acceptable and perfect will of God.

ROMANS 12:2

All things are lawful for me, but all things are not helpful.
All things are lawful for me, but I will not be brought
under the power of any.

1 CORINTHIANS 6:12

Being confident of this very thing,
that He who has begun a good work in you
will complete it until the day of Jesus Christ.

PHILIPPIANS 1:6

My brethren, be strong in the Lord and in the power of His
might.
Put on the whole armor of God,
that you may be able to stand against the wiles of the devil.

EPHESIANS 6:10-11

PRACTICAL STEPS *to* GOING DEEPER

1. Read Galatians 6:8 in your Bible. Do either you or your spouse have any habits that give place to fleshly desires that annoy one another? If you are not sure, ask God to show you anything that could become a potential problem. Write out a prayer asking God to show both of you any annoying habits or behavior you need to be free of, and ask Him to free you of it.

2. Read Psalm 32:7 in your Bible. Where can we go to find safety from potentially troubling habits? When we seek the Lord about such things, what does He provide around us?

Read Lamentations 3:22-23 in your Bible. What attitude does God have toward you? How often does He have that attitude toward you? Write out a prayer thanking Him for His mercy that is new every morning. (For example; "Thank You, Lord, for Your mercy and _____, especially with regard to _____.")

3. Read Philippians 4:13 in your Bible. In light of this Scripture, why can you and your spouse be certain that you are able to gain victory over any annoying, unwise, or less-than-beneficial behavior? Write out a prayer thanking God that, because you have received Christ in your heart, you can do all things because He will give you the strength and ability to do it.

8

Pray to Keep Ungodly Attractions from Entering Your Mind

*L*ust of the eyes and heart is epidemic in our culture, and it's so pervasive that we cannot think we can ignore this problem because "we are not the type of people" who would ever be swayed by anything like that. The truth is it can happen to anyone in a weak, unguarded moment—in thought if not in action. And the thought life is where trouble starts. That's why we must pray not only for ourselves to be protected from this onslaught from the enemy of our soul, but also for our spouse as well. Again, we should pray about this as soon as we know we are getting married.

There were two important things I prayed for in a marriage partner. One was that he must have a strong personal relationship with God through Jesus Christ. It was out of the question for me to think of sharing my life with someone who didn't share my love for the Lord. I couldn't imagine how to make a marriage work without it. The other important thing I prayed for in a husband was that he would always be faithful to me. I knew I could never tolerate sexual sin in marriage. It was an unimaginable violation of trust, and I wouldn't be able to live with it. God answered my prayers and gave me a husband who loves the Lord and has always been faithful. Michael's faithfulness to me and to the Lord is his most admirable quality in my mind, and he has never given me any reason to doubt it. Even so, I have prayed throughout all of our more than 48 years of marriage that the enemy would never be able to destroy us with any kind of temptation—even in our mind. I believe those prayers have not only kept us strong, but also away from danger. This is something we all need to pray in advance of anything bad happening so our marriage is protected.

The Truth Is, It Can Happen to Anyone, but It Doesn't Have To

Don't think for a moment that you could never fall into an adulterous trap. It is a strong, heady thing that can wrap around you like an invisible python, and when the time is right it will constrict your good sense until you can't breathe. And it can happen with someone you never dreamed it could. Or it might happen suddenly with someone you just met. It's insidious, treacherous, and devious, a deceitful entrapment that can sweep you away and entice you to do things you will regret. That's why no married man or woman can ever entertain any infatuation, possible soul connection, or even a flirtation with another person.

An ungodly attraction can happen to anyone, but won't happen to everyone. That's because it won't be allowed to happen to those who learn to keep their heart with all diligence, and who understand the plan of the enemy and how to stand against it. These people recognize the signs to watch out for. For example, they realize that any persistent desire to be around a certain person other than their spouse, or thinking about that person too often, is not good.

When we entertain someone in our home, we *invite* them *in,* give them a *place* to stay, and provide something of sustenance for them. It's the same with images or thoughts that come across our mind. We can *invite them in to stay awhile,* give them a *place to reside* in our heart, and *sustain them with unholy longings.* We must stay aware of what is happening and not allow ourselves to even go there. We must learn to pray about this in advance for ourselves as well as our husband (wife).

If you ever see this happening to you, command these thoughts to leave, by the authority given to you in Jesus' name. That might seem rude to a guest in your home, yet if your guest was doing something that would destroy your marriage, or close the door to God's best for your life, you would demand that this person leave immediately. And so you must do with ungodly attractions that want to stay in your mind. Throw them out, close the door to your heart against them, and lock it.

Pray that you and your husband (wife) will each have a godly person in your life who you are able to be honest with and who will pray with you about any ungodly attraction you may have, even if it is just in thought. Thoughts turn into actions. Pray to have trusted friends who do not have a spirit of gossip. It is one of the sorriest sins. The heartbreak of sharing a confidence and asking for prayer, only to discover the person who was told the confidence then goes and tells others, is terribly damaging. Their sin of gossiping is as great as the sin they are gossiping about. Gossip in the church keeps people from sharing what needs to be shared in order to find prevention, or healing and renewal. It keeps them from seeking the prayer support they need.

What You See Can Innocently Affect Your Relationship Negatively

Have you ever been to a film that is supposed to have a decent rating and yet something indecent flashes suddenly in front of your eyes? And even if you close your eyes the moment you realize what it is, that scene will play over and over in your mind and infect your soul. You end up feeling shock, repulsion, guilt, disgust, or attraction—all of which take up way too much space in your brain. You now have to spend time and energy dealing with these thoughts and feelings that you wouldn't have had to do if you had never seen those images in the first place. You have to seek God for cleansing so that this mental infection doesn't spread to your good sense. This kind of assault on our senses has become so widespread that we can, unfortunately, grow increasingly used to it.

The Bible says, "I will set nothing wicked before my eyes" (Psalm 101:3).

Someone cannot be possessed by anything if they have received Jesus as their Lord and Savior, but they can certainly invite evil into their lives by the things they allow, and that will keep them from realizing the fullness of the good life God has for them. It offends God when His children choose to open up to that which separates them from Him. Pray that will never happen to you or your husband (wife).

Jesus said, "If anyone desires to come after Me, let him deny himself, and take up his cross, and follow Me" (Matthew 16:24). Refusing to allow anything evil to come before your eyes is part of denying yourself and taking up *His* cross and following Him. If anything tempts you, get rid of it. Throw out any videos or magazines that have any ungodly images or language on them. If necessary, stop going to movies, get rid of the Internet, have your cable disconnected, disconnect your television if you are in a hotel room alone and are tempted by the "adult" channels. Block them the minute you walk in the room. Get rid of anything that is not of God. Do what it takes to cut off the source of whatever is causing you to be tempted to limit all God has for you.

The good news is that Jesus' death on the cross broke the power of death and hell. Understand your God-given authority over anything that tries to poison your life and soul.

God warns us in His Word over and over that we are to flee such things. We are to turn away from it and not look at it. Change the channel the minute you see it. Get up and walk out of the theater. Close the magazine. Look away from the billboard. "A prudent man foresees evil and hides himself; the simple pass on and are punished" (Proverbs 27:12). God wants purity to reign in your sexual relationship. That means not allowing outside influences to pollute and infect it, or shake its foundation.

Any deviation from the path God has established for us will set a snare for your soul, even if it's only happening in your own mind "by accident." Looking at any form of suggestive images in photos and films is a snare that will have to be dealt with on a spiritual level in order to reestablish yourself on solid ground. Even if you don't realize at the time that you are in disobedience to God's laws, your soul will reap the consequences of that unintended violation.

Five Things YOU SHOULD Never Look At

1. ***Don't look at anything that draws you away from obeying God.*** "If your eye causes you to sin, pluck it out and cast it from you. It is better for you to enter into life with one eye, rather than having two eyes, to be cast into hell fire" (Matthew 18:9).

2. ***Don't look at worthless things.*** "Turn away my eyes from looking at worthless things, and revive me in Your way" (Psalm 119:37).

3. ***Don't look at the world's attractions.*** "For all that is in the world—the lust of the flesh, the lust of the eyes, and the pride of life—is not of the Father but is of the world" (1 John 2:16).

4. ***Don't look at the dark side of life.*** "The lamp of the body is the eye. Therefore, when your eye is good, your whole body also is full of light. But when your eye is bad, your body also is full of darkness" (Luke 11:34).

5. ***Don't look away from the path God has for you.*** "Let your eyes look straight ahead, and your eyelids look right before you" (Proverbs 4:25).

It Is Unfair to Compare

One of the greatest threats to any marriage is having your mind filled with visions of perfect people on television, in films, or in photographs. These images are an illusion, and they set up a dangerous trap of comparison you can fall into. When you compare your spouse or yourself to the images you see, it can make you think that *you* either fall short of what you are supposed to be, or that you are missing something great in your husband (wife).

Let me tell you something about looking at others and feeling inadequate. When I was a teenager I used to look at pictures of beautiful people and feel ugly. But when I was in my twenties, I started working on television with some of the biggest stars at that time, and I saw how they really looked when they came into the studio for makeup early in the morning. It was shocking. I quickly realized that anyone who has a good makeup artist, a great hair stylist and colorist, an expert to give facials, a personal trainer, a nutritionist, enough money to eat well, a great photographer who understands the necessity of good lighting, an excellent wardrobe person, a good plastic surgeon (who can make you look rested and happy and not stretched and contorted), and a nanny for your children—who can watch your kids while you have all these things done—can look good. I guarantee that if you were to have all these things for a month, you would look fantastic too. How these "beautiful people" get into a position to have all these things is that they have talent and charisma.

I'm not saying there weren't any naturally beautiful people. There were. But they were far rarer than you might think. And even those people saw flaws in themselves. They, like the rest of us, always have something they don't like about their body, face, abilities, and talents. The point is, seeing how most people *really* look helped me to not be so hard on myself. It helped me to stop focusing on everything I saw that was wrong with me. It was freeing.

Don't set yourself up for negative comparisons by letting photos, films, magazines, and billboards influence your own self-image. Anything you dislike about your body, face, hair, personality, or talent can inhibit you with your spouse as well. By all means do what you can to feel good about yourself, but don't hold yourself to a standard set forth in magazines, movies, and television. Don't put this kind of added pressure on yourself, because these images aren't completely real and will only undermine your relationship with your husband (wife).

Keep Your Eyes from Evil

Of the countless people I have heard from regarding the trouble in their marriages, one of the most common issues is pornography. I have frankly been shocked at how epidemic these problems are, even among believers. Pornography is one of the most insidious tactics of the enemy to destroy lives and marriages today. And because it is just a few clicks away on the Internet, it is too easily accessible. A common complaint I have heard from women whose husbands are heavily into pornography is that they have watched it together as a couple hoping to enhance their sex life, but instead it destroyed their marriage.

This horrible habit starts a little at a time. Just seeing a suggestive magazine cover in an airport, gas station, or grocery store can plant a seed in the mind that grows into something insidious. The more one is exposed to it, the more seeds are planted and the deeper they grow. When a person becomes drawn to it, they start to seek it out. They become secretive, not forthcoming, and not full faced before the Lord. They don't have clear-eyed laughter anymore. Blindness covers their eyes so they cannot see the truth.

When I was young I received a wood-burning set. I plugged in the handheld wood burner, and whenever I pressed it to the wood it burned an image that was there permanently. Pornography is like that. It burns an image into the brain that stays there. It can cause a person to be obsessed with it to the point of destroying their soul.

It doesn't matter how old or young you are, you can be susceptible to it at any age. When exposure to pornography happens to a young child, it plants a seed in his or her heart that will keep growing long after the event has taken place. Somewhere down the road in adulthood it will surface. That's because behind every lustful thought is a seducing spirit that wants to draw its victim away from the things of God and toward the vile and evil that brings destruction. And it will continue silently waiting to surface in a moment of weakness to ensnare a person and destroy their life.

Even if you and your spouse are not tempted in the least by pornography, there are still countless sexual images everywhere that may be thrust before your eyes, and that alone can open the door to this problem. I have seen legitimate news magazines that have images in an advertisement for some products that border on pornographic. There are TV shows, movies, and videos you can easily see that have suggestive material in them. I'm not talking about going to an adult bookstore and asking for the brown paper-wrapped magazines in the back room. I am not even talking about clicking on a pornographic sight on the Internet. I am talking about racy and explicit images in easily seen commercials, print ads, videos, and films. When we let our eyes focus on these images or hear suggestive or off-color dialogue, it pollutes our mind.

Jesus said that sin happens just by looking (Matthew 5:28). But Jesus also gave the solution. "If your right eye causes you to sin, pluck it out and cast it from you; for it is more profitable for you that one of your members perish, than for your whole body to be cast into hell" (Matthew 5:29). That means if something comes on the TV that is suggestive, turn it off. If it presents itself in a scene of a film, walk out. Don't even stare for a moment. Make it an instantaneous reaction. Don't let the enemy burn a path to your mind.

Four Warnings TO REMEMBER ABOUT *Lust*

1. ***Lust is always against God's will.*** "He no longer should live the rest of his time in the flesh for the lusts of men, but for the will of God" (1 Peter 4:2)

2. ***Lust always destroys peace in your soul.*** "Beloved, I beg you as sojourners and pilgrims, abstain from fleshly lusts which war against the soul" (1 Peter 2:11).

3. ***Lust wars against your spirit.*** "The flesh lusts against the Spirit, and the Spirit against the flesh; and these are

contrary to one another, so that you do not do the things that you wish" (Galatians 5:17).

4. *Lust in your heart sets a trap for your soul.* "The righteousness of the upright will deliver them, but the unfaithful will be caught by their lust" (Proverbs 11:6).

If you ever find you can't stop thinking about a certain thing or person in an unhealthy way, go before God immediately and confess it. Pray to be set free from those thoughts. Stay before the Lord until this obsession is gone. There is no good that will come out of it, and the consequences for pursuing it, or allowing it to overtake you, can ruin your life. If you can't get rid of the image, ask someone you trust to pray with you about it. It's possible that you could tell your husband (wife), but then after your ungodly attraction is gone—which it will be if you stay before the Lord long enough—then your poor husband (wife) is left having to sort through all the rejection and hurt feelings. It's not worth it. I say, go to the Lord and prostrate yourself on the ground. Fast and pray. Stay there before Him until this thing is broken. It will be.

Every time these kinds of feelings come back, humble yourself before God again in that same way. If that doesn't work and this attraction becomes an obsession, call in a close friend—a godly friend who doesn't gossip—to stand with you in prayer and break this stronghold of the enemy. If even that fails, *then* tell your husband (wife) and go to counseling together. You're going to need it.

If you find you are attracted to someone, by all means don't tell that person. It only opens up feelings in him (her) of being appreciated in the wrong way. It inspires an intimacy between the two of you because of a secret you now share. At the first sign of an attraction, don't fool yourself with fancy words like "attraction" and "affair" that make it sound like flowers in spring. Call it what it is—adultery of the heart and fornication of the mind. Don't create a sexual tension or inspire an attraction in the other person, or force that person to have to fight one off. Leave them out of it. This is between you and God. And possibly a godly and trustworthy friend or counselor.

An ungodly attraction is a strong and heady feeling, and it may make you think you have finally found the one you have been waiting for and the fulfillment of a perfect life ahead. But it is all an illusion. The one you have been waiting for is actually at home waiting for *you*. And you need to go back and give your marriage all your efforts to make it work. You need to give God a chance to do a miracle.

I know a young pastor's wife who was having a strong attraction toward someone other than her husband in her church. She had come to the point where she felt her marriage was not anything like what she thought it would be. She came to me for help, and I suggested she call two other women she trusted to pray with her as well. Between the three of us, we agreed to stand with her, talking with her and praying for and with her, until we saw that thing completely broken.

We are all vulnerable to being attracted in our mind to people around us, but the three of us were convinced beyond any doubt that for this young woman, it was a ploy of the enemy to destroy the great ministry she and her husband had. We prayed that this work of hell in her life would be broken completely. The attraction persisted for months until we were finally able to break through it. And she and her husband went on to have a great marriage and many years together in a highly successful ministry. They raised a wonderful family with children and grandchildren. No one else ever knew about it, not even her husband, and definitely not the person she was attracted to. This was entirely a battle in the spirit, and the enemy lost.

If you find yourself attracted to another person other than your husband (wife), ask God to break that attraction like severing the head off of a snake so that there is no way it can ever regenerate. You have authority over evil in your life. "Sin lies at the door. And its desire is for you, *but you should rule over it*" (Genesis 4:7). The enemy wants to entice you away from the life God has for you, but God has given you the power to put a stop to it.

You will be able to tell if there is still a residue in your heart with regard to any ungodly attraction if you are sad when you don't see that person. Or if you are excited when you do. You will know you are free when you see that person one day and you thank God with all your heart that you didn't act on your attraction. You will be grateful that you didn't sacrifice your marriage, your children, or your life for it. You will wonder, *What in the world was I thinking?* And you will thank God that He rescued you away from it.

If This Has Already Happened to You

It can be difficult to spot an ungodly attraction in your spouse if your lives are busy and you give each other latitude and you believe for the best in each other. But if you ever sense that something is wrong and you don't know what it is, trust the instincts God has given you and ask God to show you what it is you are sensing. I know of situations where a wife felt something was wrong, even though she had no hard evidence. She only sensed the divided attentions of her husband and said it seemed like she saw something different in his eyes.

It can be that we don't see what's wrong because we don't *want* to see it. We want to see what's *right*. We want to see the *good*. We want to think the best. We don't want to see what we fear it might be because we can't bear for it to be that. We understand that everything in our life will be affected, and we can't face it. But the good news is that you are never alone when you have Jesus, who is Immanuel—the God who is with you. He has sent His Holy Spirit to come alongside of you to be your Helper and Comforter and to guide you in all things—even to face anything you need to see in your marriage.

When a wife discovers that her husband is into pornography, it makes her feel betrayed, inadequate, unattractive, full of self-doubt, grieved, hurt, and like a failure. But the truth is, it has nothing to do with her. It is not her fault in any way. No one forces someone else to become perverted. The enemy has planted a seed of lust in her husband's flesh—whether it happened to him as a child or he has allowed it as an adult—and it has trapped him.

So if you ever find that your husband (wife) has dabbled into pornography, please know it is not your fault. It really has nothing to do with you. It affects you terribly, but you are not responsible. But don't desert your spouse if he (she) is willing to try to get free. The fact is, he (she) needs your support more than ever. That doesn't mean you have to suppress your feelings of anger and disappointment, but don't allow those feelings to persist and get in the way of having your prayers answered.

You may become angry that you have to think about this problem at all, that your mind has to even be occupied with such depraved thoughts, and you will rightfully be upset about having to ever wonder about whether or not the problem is really gone. There is nothing wrong with expecting human decency, and when you find a lack of it in your spouse, you grieve for the person you thought you married. Give yourself the right to grieve and be angry, but remember that it is your spouse who has the problem and you can be part of the solution. Your prayers can help him (her) get free, and you can guide him (her) to get professional help. There are experts who know what to do, and your spouse has to be held accountable by someone besides you.

You can also seek godly prayer partners and commit to working and praying through this to build a new life together. No force of hell can stand against the power of God manifesting on behalf of a husband and wife who pray together, and who have highly trusted people to pray with them. There are certain churches that have great programs to help people get free of this intrusion into their life. Check that out in your area.

If your husband (wife) is caught in a stronghold of the enemy, the power of your prayers for him (her) is greatly enhanced when you *fast* and pray. Even after a simple 24-hour fast where you drink only water and you pray every time you get a hunger pang, you can see God do miracles. God says that the purpose of fasting is *"to loose the bonds of wickedness,* to *undo the heavy burdens,* to *let the oppressed go free,* and that you *break every yoke"* (Isaiah 58:6). That is exactly what you need to combat a problem of this magnitude. Keep praying for your husband (wife) to get free and don't give up.

The Power of God's Word Is Greater

I learned years ago that quoting Scripture, especially in your prayers, is powerful, and it is the only thing strong enough to silence the voices of temptation, despair, and desperation. The words of Scripture have power on their own, but when you speak them out loud, they increase your faith and give you strength to face whatever *seems* greater.

Your mind can be renewed and transformed as you read God's Word because it aligns your heart and mind with God's. If you are *not* doing that, you can find yourself drifting away from God without even realizing it. And the drift will be subtle and almost imperceptible until one day you realize you fell and God wasn't there to catch you—because you fell into temptations far outside the parameters God has established for your life.

While outside counseling is extremely important and can make a tremendous difference with ungodly attractions, only God can fully heal the inside of us. Counseling can help us change our behavior—which definitely needs to be changed—but it can't transform us into the people God created us to be. Only the Holy Spirit can do that. Along with counseling, you still have to establish and deepen your relationship with God. You have to stay in His Word and in communication with Him through prayer, praise, and worship. "Before I was afflicted I went astray, but now I keep Your word" (Psalm 119:67). Don't stop praying until you have the freedom you need.

If you ever face any ungodly attraction, look totally to the Lord for everything, especially freedom from things you don't want in your life. Being tempted is not a sin. Giving in to it *is.* Once you are set free, you don't need to keep punishing yourself. "They looked to Him and were radiant, and their faces were not ashamed" (Psalm 34:5). The Bible says people "should repent, turn to God, and do works befitting repentance" (Acts 26:20). Works befitting repentance means that you stop doing what you have repented of and live the way God wants you to.

If you are in any kind of Christian leadership or place of influence, prominence, or work for the glory of God and His kingdom, you will be tempted in some way because of it. Don't try to face the temptation alone. Everyone needs two or more strong believers to stand with them ongoingly to resist the plans of the enemy for their destruction. "Though one may be overpowered by another, two can withstand him.

And a threefold cord is not quickly broken" (Ecclesiastes 4:12). Find strong believers who are in the Word, who live godly lives and who are not gossips, who will be prayer partners with you and your spouse. "Confess your trespasses to one another, and pray for one another, that you may be healed. The effective, fervent prayer of a righteous man avails much" (James 5:16).

You also need to be connected to the body of Christ through your local church (see 1 Corinthians 12:12). You are not fully under God's covering if you are not submitted to a godly body of believers. When you are not connected, you lose the power that comes in multiple people worshiping and praying together. I am not talking about being mind-controlled; I am talking about letting your heart find a home in a church where you become part of the church family there. Don't just go to church to watch what's going on. Go to be connected to what God is doing there. Make contact with the people and serve the church in some capacity. Your faithfulness will become part of your protection.

If you and your husband (wife) have not experienced any of the pollution described in this chapter, thank God and pray that you never will.

PRAYERS *for* MY MARRIAGE

Prayer to Protect Your Marriage from Ungodly Attractions

Lord, I pray You would protect my marriage from any kind of ungodly attractions in either of us. Keep those temptations so far from both of us that they never find a place in either of our minds or hearts. Pour Your wisdom and knowledge into us so that we are too wise and too smart to allow the enemy to sneak up on our blind side and throw temptation in our path. I pray You would not allow temptation to even come near us.

Lord, I know that in You "are hidden all the treasures of wisdom and knowledge" (Colossians 2:3). Give us the ability to see danger in advance and the wisdom to not do anything stupid. Help us to "walk properly" (Romans 13:13). Bless our marriage in every way. Help us to always put each other first and never sacrifice one another out of selfish disregard for the other's needs. Keep our eyes from looking at anything that would compromise our relationship. Keep our hearts from being enticed and drawn away from each other. Help us to walk properly and not in lust or strife (Romans 13:13). Enable us to always live in the Spirit so we don't fulfill the lust of the flesh (Galatians 5:16). Open our eyes to recognize ungodliness and worldliness so that we can reject those enticements and learn to live Your way.

Lord, help us to become so committed to You that nothing else matters to us more than living in obedience to Your ways. Enable us to see things from Your perspective. Teach us to recognize in advance what will lead to temptation in us so that we always take steps to avoid it. Keep us away from anything that could tempt us to view evil. Reveal everything in either of us that needs to be seen. Where we are blind to the true nature of the things we allow ourselves to look at, open our eyes to see the truth. Where we are in darkness about this, shine Your light on our attraction to disobedience (Isaiah 42:5-7).

I know that "to be carnally minded is death, but to be spiritually minded is life and peace" (Romans 8:6). I know that if we live in the flesh we cannot please You (Romans 8:8). Help us learn to live in a way that pleases You. Establish us in our faith. Keep us from being deceived by the world and the enemy (Colossians 2:6-8). Thank You, Lord, that we are complete in You and need not seek anything outside of what You have given us in each other and in You (Colossians 2:10). In Jesus' name I pray.

Prayer for Me to Keep Clear of Ungodly Attractions

Lord, help me to love You with all my heart, soul, mind, and strength, and help me to love my husband (wife) the same way (Mark 12:30). Keep me far from the broad way that leads to destruction, and help me to always choose the narrow gate that leads to life (Matthew 7:13-14). Thank You for my husband (wife) and for the marriage You have given us.

Lord, I pray that You would search my heart and reveal any evil thoughts, attractions, or fantasies I harbor so I can be free of them completely (Psalm 139:23-24). Show me the root of any kind of problem in me so that I can totally eliminate it. I love Your laws, Lord, and I don't want to have conflict in my mind that brings me into captivity to sin. Thank You, Jesus, that I can find freedom from my flesh, which serves the law of sin, so that I can serve Your laws instead (Romans 7:22-25).

Lord, I lift my eyes up to You in heaven and deliberately take them off the things of earth (Psalm 123:1). I take comfort in the fact that You are my refuge that I can go to any time I am tempted to look at anything ungodly, or when I see in my mind that which does not please You (Psalm 141:8). Take away all that is in me that holds the door open for sinful and lustful thoughts. I rebuke the devourer, who would come to destroy me with temptation, and I say that I will serve only You, Lord. Thank You, Jesus, that You understand temptation and are well able to help me when I am tempted (Hebrews 2:18). Help me to be a wife (husband) who is faithful and true in thought and deed. "O LORD, You have searched me and known me...You understand my thought afar off" (Psalm 139:1-2). "Show me Your ways, O LORD...on You I wait all the day" (Psalm 25:4-5). In Jesus' name I pray.

Prayer for My Husband (Wife) to Keep Clear of Ungodly Attractions

Lord, I pray for my husband's (wife's) mind to be protected from all lies of the enemy and open to Your truth. Take all blinders completely off of him (her) so that he (she) can clearly see everything tempting him (her) to live outside of Your will as a set-up for his (her) demise. Help him (her) to fully understand what damage any degree of giving in to temptation to allow ungodly attractions does to our marriage. Open his (her) eyes to that danger and give him (her) strength to avoid situations and people that could draw him (her) into it.

Turn his (her) eyes away from worthless things (Psalm 119:37-39).

If he (she) ever fails in this area, help him (her) understand the greatness of Your power on his (her) behalf (Ephesians 1:17-19). Cause him (her) to desire freedom, healing, and restoration. Help me to not feel betrayed. Show me all I can do to help him (her) get free.

Lord, do whatever it takes to help my husband (wife) see the truth about everything he (she) does. Enable him (her) to put off all conduct that is not in alignment with Your will and reject all corruption that comes from "deceitful lusts" (Ephesians 4:22). Don't let him (her) be taken down a path that leads to death (Proverbs 5:3-5). Deliver him (her) completely, and we will say, "This was the Lord's doing, and it is marvelous in our eyes" (Mark 12:11). Give him (her) wisdom and revelation so that the eyes of his (her) understanding will be enlightened to always know the truth. In Jesus' name I pray.

TRUTH *to* STAND ON

Each one is tempted when he is drawn away
by his own desires and enticed.
Then, when desire has conceived, it gives birth to sin;
and sin, when it is full-grown, brings forth death.

JAMES 1:14-15

No temptation has overtaken you except such as is common to man;
but God is faithful, who will not allow you to be tempted
beyond what you are able, but with the temptation
will also make the way of escape, that you may be able to bear it.

1 CORINTHIANS 10:13

How can a young man cleanse his way? By taking heed
according to Your word.
With my whole heart I have sought You; oh, let me not wander
from Your commandments!
Your word I have hidden in my heart, that I might not sin
against You.

PSALM 119:9-11

When wisdom enters your heart, and knowledge is pleasant to
your soul,
discretion will preserve you; understanding will keep you,
to deliver you from the way of evil.

PROVERBS 2:10-12

Do not be conformed to this world, but be transformed by the
renewing of your mind,
that you may prove what is that good and acceptable and
perfect will of God.

ROMANS 12:2

PRACTICAL STEPS *to* GOING DEEPER

1. Read Psalm 101:2 in your Bible. What should you be careful to do? How should you live in your home? Write out a prayer asking God to help you and your husband (wife) to walk in a perfect way with a perfect heart. Tell Him you recognize that only He can help you do that. Ask Him to help you avoid anything that is not right in His sight.

2. Read 2 Timothy 2:22 in your Bible. What are you supposed to run from? What are you to pursue instead? Write out a prayer asking God to help you and your husband (wife) always recognize any temptation that either of you experience as something to strictly avoid.

3. Read 1 Thessalonians 5:22, Romans 12:21, and James 4:7 in your Bible. What is the common thread in these three Scriptures that you and your husband (wife) should do? Write out a prayer asking God to help you and your husband (wife) always be able to do these things.

Read Philippians 4:8 in your Bible. What kind of things are you supposed to think about instead? Write out a prayer asking God to help you both think about these things. Be specific.

9

Pray to Keep Love Alive and Hardness of Heart from Developing

When you get married, your heart has found a home. But your heart can always become a home for whatever is allowed into it. The home of your heart can be warm, loving, kind, comforting, joyful, grateful, and full of life and light. It can also be cold, hard, uncomfortable, unkind, unloving, ungrateful, joyless, and miserable. Taken to the extreme, that home can become locked up because one person has shut out the Lord, or their spouse, or both. But you can unlock the door again if you have the right key. Jesus said, "I will give you the keys of the kingdom of heaven, and whatever you bind on earth will be bound in heaven, and whatever you loose on earth will be loosed in heaven" (Matthew 16:19). God has given us keys of authority when we pray, and also the power to change things according to His will—even our hearts. This is something we must pray about as soon as we can in our marriage.

It is up to each of us to do everything we can to see that hardness does not find a way to move into our heart, because if it does, bad things are sure to follow. "Happy is the man who is always reverent, but he who hardens his heart will fall into calamity" (Proverbs 28:14). When a husband and wife harden their hearts toward one another, they have hardened them toward God as well. That causes them to stand on shaky ground.

This is an all too common and subtle trap people can fall into, so it is important to start praying about it before anything like this happens.

And don't think it can't happen to you. First of all, don't trust your heart because it can grow hard over something you believe is completely justified. The Bible says, "He who trusts in his own heart is a fool, but whoever walks wisely will be delivered" (Proverbs 28:26). God never sees hardness of heart as being justified. That's because when you receive the Lord, He sends the Holy Spirit to live in your heart and soften it. God said in the Bible to His people that He would "put a new spirit within them and take" away their stony heart (Ezekiel 11:19). Anyone allowing their heart to become like stone has not given the Holy Spirit free reign in it. When you invite the Holy Spirit to flow freely through you, your heart will be watered and good things will grow.

It is imperative that you continually remind yourself that when anything goes wrong in your marriage—no matter what it is—Jesus has given you the power and authority to take charge of it in the spirit realm through prayer. That doesn't mean you attempt to dominate your spouse or get heavy-handed and make ultimatums. It means you recognize the enemy's footprint, and take charge of what is happening, by praying for God to break through the atmosphere of your marriage and the condition of your heart with His love and power. Every time you pray, you are opening the door to welcome in God's healing, deliverance, transformation, and restoration.

God Can Soften the Fabric of Your Heart

Do you remember the amazingly forgiving Amish people who instantly forgave the murderer who killed their children in a schoolhouse? How loving they were to even be able to say the words "I forgive you" after such a senseless and horrific tragedy. But surely there will need to be layers of forgiveness in the years to come as the extent of those violations unfold over time. Perhaps forgiveness has to be extended on every birthday that this child never celebrated, at the family gatherings this child never attended, for this child's wedding that the family never got to witness, for the grandchildren that were never born, and the dreams for this child that would never be realized. Surely all that must have to be forgiven over time. And I am certain with the deep faith of the Amish people they will do that if they haven't already.

As I wrote in chapter 3, forgiveness isn't always a one-time thing. There are layers of forgiveness that need to be recognized in any situation—especially in a marriage. Sometimes we think we have forgiven, but we don't realize how many layers there are. And if we don't deal with each layer, hardness of heart can set in and build up to monumental proportions. Only a heart that is soft toward God, and the things of God, can forgive that much pain so readily.

King David spoke of his heart often, saying such things as, "My heart pants" (Psalm 38:10), "my heart fails me" (Psalm 40:12), "my heart is severely pained" (Psalm 55:4), "my heart is overwhelmed" (Psalm 61:2), "my heart is wounded within me" (Psalm 109:22), "my heart within me is distressed" (Psalm 143:4), and "reproach has broken my heart" (Psalm 69:20). When we have suffering in our heart like that in a prolonged and unresolved way, our heart can grow hard. But David's heart didn't grow hard, and the reason for that is his heart was filled with *repentance* and *worship* of God. Those two heartfelt attitudes will always soften a heart or keep it from getting hard in the first place.

A hard heart doesn't happen overnight. It happens little by little, as layer upon layer of crustiness builds up. Then it can become covered with a seemingly impenetrable and invisible coat of armor that is designed by necessity to protect it from being pierced through or broken again. Sometimes hardness of heart doesn't fully manifest until later in life. It is possible your heart can get broken too many times, causing forgiveness to stop flowing so there is thick scar tissue forming that eventually hardens like a callus around the heart.

The good news is that no matter how long those scars have been there, they can be completely removed by being in the presence of God. "The LORD is near to those who have a broken heart, and saves such as have a contrite spirit" (Psalm 34:18). We need a heart of repentance and worship that says, "I confess where I have not had a perfect heart toward You, Lord, or my husband (wife) either. I worship You and praise You for Your forgiveness of me. Because You have forgiven me, I can do nothing less than forgive him (her) too."

A Heart Is Never Too Hard for God to Soften

God asked Abraham, "Is there anything too hard for the LORD?" (Genesis 18:14). He wanted to know if Abraham doubted what God could do. Our heart can get hard because we doubt that God can and will actually do what seems impossible to us when it comes to our marriage. When we start believing that God cannot change the situation, or our spouse, or us, we lose heart and hardness sets in.

The Bible talks about Rachel laboring in childbirth, saying that she had "hard labor" (Genesis 35:16). Sometimes we have hard labor trying to bring forth new life in our marriage, and year after year it can feel as though nothing ever changes. When we have hard labor and we don't see the birth of anything, our heart can become hard. But Rachel did give birth to something great. His name was Benjamin, and he would eventually be the head of one of the 12 tribes of Israel. The bad news is that she died in the process. Often we have to die in the process of giving birth to something great. We don't have to die physically because Jesus already did that, but our selfishness and pride do have to die.

The Israelites became bitter because of the hard bondage they were under. All their work was difficult and fruitless and caused them to feel defeated. They saw no hope for the future. You may someday feel as though you have worked so hard in so many ways to try to make your marriage what you know it *can* be and what God *wants* it to be, and yet you feel defeated because you don't see results in a certain area. Even though you may be justified in having those thoughts, God says you are not to entertain them. Your heart was not designed to carry loads of discouragement or bitterness. That will not only cause your heart to grow hard, but it will also make you sick.

If God can make heaven and earth by the power of His outstretched arm, then He can stretch His arm toward you and soften your heart in an instant. When you become discouraged, say to the Lord, "There is nothing too hard for You" and ask Him to soften your heart (Jeremiah 32:17).

Six Good Ways to Keep Your Heart Soft

1. *Every day ask God to speak to you through His Word.* You can become hard of hearing when it comes to God's Word, and if that

happens, your heart will grow hard as well. If you shut off yourself to God's truth, you will lose understanding. It happens like that. When you don't open your heart to hear God speak to you through His Word, you lose the opportunities He has for your blessing and healing. God's Word also reveals what is in your heart. "The word of God is living and powerful, and sharper than any two-edged sword, piercing even to the division of soul and spirit, and of joints and marrow, and is a discerner of the thoughts and intents of the heart" (Hebrews 4:12). You can be blind to what is really happening in your heart if you don't allow the Word of God to penetrate it and reveal it to you.

2. *Prepare your heart by seeking after God each morning.* The Bible says of King Rehoboam, one of the kings of Judah, that "he did evil, because he did not prepare his heart to seek the LORD" (2 Chronicles 12:14). God looks for the person who will seek Him faithfully so He can show Himself strong on their behalf. "The eyes of the LORD run to and fro throughout the whole earth, to show Himself strong on behalf of those whose heart is loyal to Him" (2 Chronicles 16:9). Prepare your heart by inviting Him to reign powerfully in you and touch your heart every day. When you seek after God with all that is in you, you will find Him and He will soften your heart (Deuteronomy 4:29).

3. *Ask God for a wise and understanding heart (1 Kings 3:12).* God put wisdom in Solomon's heart because he asked for it (2 Chronicles 9:23). If you want a heart of love, compassion, wisdom, and understanding, ask God for it. He can take away any hardness of heart and replace it with all that, and also give you a soft heart toward your spouse. That means no matter what condition your heart is in, God can fix it (1 Chronicles 29:18).

4. *Ask God to give you a repentant heart so that you are quick to see your own sin.* David did some terrible things—adultery and murder being the worst. But he said, "I acknowledge my transgressions, and my sin is always before me. Against You, You only, have I sinned and done this evil in Your sight—that You may be found just when You speak, and blameless when You judge" (Psalm 51:3-4). As a result, God looked upon his heart of repentance and forgave him and blessed him. God always looks at our heart, even when we do wrong things accidentally or stupid things on purpose. "The LORD does not see as man sees; for man looks at the outward appearance, but the LORD looks at the heart" (1 Samuel 16:7). If you don't want God to see a stone when He looks at your heart, have a repentant heart that is always willing to say, "I see where I have missed the mark for the way You want me to live, and I ask You to forgive me."

5. *Ask God to instruct you even as you sleep.* If you ask Him to, God will teach you in the night and you can wake up in the morning with a different heart (Psalm 16:7-9). I have seen it happen many times in my own life where I have gone to bed feeling a hardness creeping into my heart toward my husband, and I have confessed it to God and asked Him to take it away. Each time I have awakened in the morning feeling totally the opposite. Only God can change a heart that way. The Bible says that God gave Saul another heart (1 Samuel 10:9). If you ask God, He can give you a new heart too.

6. *Praise God throughout the day no matter what is happening.* When you worship God, you invite His presence in greater measure into your life. *In His presence your heart is changed.* Always! The hardness melts away. "The sacrifices of God are a broken spirit, a broken and a contrite heart—these, O God, You will not despise" (Psalm 51:17). When we have a pure heart toward God, we can stand in His presence and receive a new heart from Him (Psalm 24:3-5).

If This Has Already Happened to You

I want to warn you about something. There can come a point in any marriage when you may lose patience with waiting to see some kind of change in your spouse that you have been desiring. You've forgiven again and again over this, and you've become weary of the struggle. You've grown tired of being disappointed and waiting for a breakthrough that never comes. Your heart can begin to close a door that was once open between you. The years have taken their toll, and you subconsciously (or consciously) decide you are not going to try anymore. You no longer feel love for your husband (wife) the way you did, and you don't even care about getting it back.

This can happen in any marriage where one spouse is working to make things better and it seems the other doesn't seem to be trying nearly seriously enough. Your heart can grow cold and hard like a stone, and it will seem as if the love you once had has died. But the good news is that God has the power to completely turn things around. He is the God of miracles and restoration who makes all things new. Jesus—the ultimate source of resurrection power—can resurrect love that has died and soften your heart toward your spouse. He can bring your marriage to life again, and it can happen quickly.

If there is any strife, anger, sadness, despair, hopelessness, resentment, or bitterness in your marriage relationship, you can take authority over the spirits behind those negative emotions and declare that your *heart* and your *home* are established for *God's glory*. And God's enemy doesn't have the right to be there. That's because Jesus paid the price to give you full authority over "all the power of the enemy" (Luke 10:19). If he torments you with suggestions that your authority has been compromised because you haven't been to church lately, haven't read your Bible, or haven't obeyed all of God's laws, then again declare, "Those are issues between me and my heavenly Father, and my authority comes from what *Jesus* did, not what *I* do." Then invite God's Spirit of love, joy, peace, forgiveness, and hope to be the guest of honor who is poured out in your heart and your marriage relationship.

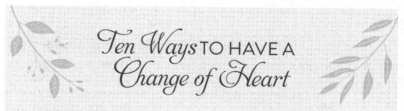

Ten Ways TO HAVE A *Change of Heart*

1. ***Believe in God.*** "He who believes in Me, as the Scripture has said, out of his heart will flow rivers of living water" (John 7:38).

2. ***Draw near to God with your whole heart.*** "These people draw near to Me with their mouth, and honor Me with their lips, but their heart is far from Me" (Matthew 15:8).

3. ***Confess all sin before the Lord.*** "If our heart condemns us, God is greater than our heart, and knows all things. Beloved, if our heart does not condemn us, we have confidence toward God" (1 John 3:20-21).

4. ***Seek God with all your heart.*** "Blessed are those who keep His testimonies, who seek Him with the whole heart!" (Psalm 119:2).

5. ***Pray about everything.*** "He spoke a parable to them, that men always ought to pray and not lose heart" (Luke 18:1).

6. ***Trust in God more than your feelings.*** "Trust in the LORD with all your heart, and lean not on your own understanding" (Proverbs 3:5).

7. ***Value the Lord above all else.*** "Where your treasure is, there your heart will be also" (Matthew 6:21).

8. ***Pour out your heart before the Lord.*** "Trust in Him at all times, you people; pour out your heart before Him; God is a refuge for us" (Psalm 62:8).

9. ***Praise God with your whole heart.*** "I will praise You, O LORD, with my whole heart; I will tell of all Your marvelous works" (Psalm 9:1).

10. ***Tell God that you love Him with all that is in you.*** "Jesus said to him, 'You shall love the LORD your God with all your heart, with all your soul, and with all your mind'" (Matthew 22:37).

A Simple Prayer Can Result in a Softened Heart

You know how bad you feel when your heart is not right toward your husband (wife). That's because "a sound heart is life to the body" (Proverbs 14:30). If your heart is not sound, it will harden and drain life away from you. When your heart is hard and unrepentant, you can sense that something bad will happen if you don't straighten it out (Romans 2:5).

We mistakenly believe our thoughts are harmless, but they're not. We think we can have our thoughts to ourselves and no one will know the bitterness sheltered there. But our thoughts are viable and a deep well from which we either draw life or from which we are poisoned. "Both the inward thought and the heart of man are deep" (Psalm 64:6). *God knows the deep secrets of your heart* (Psalm 44:21). The truth is that you will become what you think. "As he thinks in his heart, so is he" (Proverbs 23:7). If you think bitter thoughts, you will become bitter. Your thoughts affect who you are.

When we pray for someone, our heart softens toward them. But whenever you want to break through any kind of hardness in your heart, *fasting* and praying can do miracles. That's because fasting unleashes the power of God to break the strongholds that keep your heart captive. God says, "Turn to Me with all your heart, with fasting, with weeping, and with mourning. So rend your heart, and not your garments; return to the LORD your God, for He is gracious and merciful, slow to anger, and of great kindness; and He relents from doing harm" (Joel 2:12-13). Your heart always changes when you fast. It's amazing how something so simple can be so powerful.

If you ever try to make yourself stop caring so much about your spouse so that your heart won't hurt every time you feel disappointed, you can end up toughening up and steeling yourself for the next offense. Your hard heart then becomes a place of safety, an impenetrable security blanket, your coat of armor to protect you from inevitable arrows. This makes your heart harder over time until there is nothing that will soften it except a touch of the Holy Spirit.

When we become hard-hearted, we extend no grace or mercy. We become righteous in our own eyes. We think we know the truth. We not only put up an impenetrable wall between ourselves and our spouse, but also between us and God. In fact, we blame God, which is a foolish and twisted way to live. "The foolishness of a man twists his way, and his heart frets against the LORD" (Proverbs 19:3). We no longer move from a place of love. You can't truly be in good standing with God and still resent your husband (wife). That's sin. It's missing the mark God has for you.

Remember the psalm I mentioned earlier in this book that said, "If I regard iniquity in my heart, the Lord will not hear" (Psalm 66:18). That means if you have unconfessed sin in your life, God will not hear your prayers. That doesn't mean He *can't* hear your prayers. It means He *won't*. He will wait until you get right before God by confessing what is in your heart that shouldn't be there and repenting of it. That means you intend to stop entertaining attitudes toward your husband (wife) that are not right. This is a very important situation to consider. You absolutely must have your prayers heard.

When you've been hurt enough times and you have hardened your heart for self-protection, it takes great courage to want to feel again. To possibly set yourself up to be hurt again. But when you allow yourself to let go of all hardness in your heart and confess it to God as sin, God can change it. We are the clay; God is the potter, and He will mold us however He wants if we fully submit to Him (Isaiah 64:8). Jesus rebuked His disciples for "their unbelief and hardness of heart" (Mark 16:14). You don't want Him to rebuke you for yours. Pray that you will never be able to hang on to a hard heart.

Ask God every day to show you if there is anything in your heart that shouldn't be there. And also what isn't in your heart that should be. Then ask Him to make the home of your heart a showplace for His love. Ask Him to keep His love alive in you both for one another.

PRAYERS *for* MY MARRIAGE

Prayer for Freedom from Any
Hardness of Heart in Our Marriage

Lord, I thank You that You are "a sun and a shield" to us and because of Your grace and glory there is no good thing that You will withhold from us when we live Your way (Psalm 84:11). I pray that You would protect my marriage from any hard-heartedness that could develop between me and my husband (wife). Show us how to keep filled with Your love so our love never dies.

Help us to not be stubborn or rebellious, refusing to set our hearts right before You (Psalm 78:8). Teach us both to "number our days"—to value the time you have given us together—so that we each may gain a heart of wisdom as you have promised in Your Word (Psalm 90:12). Take away any perversity in our heart, so there is never a wrong attitude taking root in either of us (Psalm 101:4).

If ever our hearts start to become hard, soften them toward one another. Cause Your rivers of living water to flow in and through us at all times to soften, mend, and restore (John 7:37-38). Heal any brokenness so that the damage is not irreparable, and take away any scars that form. I ask that we will always feel genuine love for one another. In Jesus' name I pray.

Prayer to Change Any Hardness of Heart in Me

Lord, show me any hardness of heart in me toward my husband (wife). I want to confess it to You as sin and repent of it. Melt it like ice in the presence of the hot sun. Burn any solid, cold, heavy, frosty lump within me until it pours out like water before You. Take my heart of stone and give me a heart of love and compassion. Break up the fallow ground where nothing good can grow and life gets choked out. I confess to any sin of anger, resentment, unforgiveness, or criticism toward my husband (wife). Forgive me and cleanse my heart completely.

Lord, I pray that You would give me a pure heart toward You so that I may stand in Your holy place. Give me clean hands so that I may rise above my situation. Help me to not lift my soul toward an idol or speak words that are not true in light of Your Word so that I can receive all You have for me (Psalm 24:3-5). You know what is in my heart (Psalm 44:21). So take away all negative thoughts and feelings, and overflow my heart with good things (Psalm 45:1). May the good thoughts in my heart cause my mouth to speak wisdom and not harshness (Psalm 49:3). Create in me a clean heart, and make my spirit right before You

(Psalm 51:10). I want to bring to You the sacrifice of a broken spirit and a humble heart (Psalm 51:17).

Don't let me succumb to being stubborn or prideful in my heart. I want to walk in Your counsel and not my own. Cut away from my heart all that is not of You, so that I can serve You with all my heart and soul (Joshua 22:5).

Give me the wisdom to do what's right so that I will walk in my house with a perfect heart (Psalm 101:2). Help me to seek You with my whole heart and hide Your Word in my soul, and keep all of Your commandments (Psalm 119:11). Teach me to understand and keep Your law (Psalm 119:34). I want to stand strong in all I understand of You, knowing that You will strengthen my heart (Psalm 27:14). Give me a full heart of love for my husband (wife) every day. Thank You that You are a God of new beginnings. Help me to take steps that signify a new beginning in me today. In Jesus' name I pray.

Prayer to Change Any Hardness of Heart in My Husband (Wife)

Lord, I pray that You would give my husband (wife) a heart that longs to know You better so that his (her) heart will be soft toward both You and me. Where his (her) heart has already become hard, I pray that he (she) will turn to You and find Your presence waiting for him (her) (Jeremiah 29:13). Open his (her) heart to hear what You are speaking to him (her) (Acts 16:14).

Help my husband (wife) to have a heart filled with truth and not open to the lies of the enemy. Keep him (her) from having any kind of a rebellious or stubborn spirit so that his (her) heart is always right before You (Psalm 81:12). Take away any pride or bitterness in him (her) so that he (she) will not displease You. Give him (her) a heart that is strong in faith and not afraid of the future (Psalm 112:7). Give him (her) a big heart of love for me so love is always alive in our hearts for one another.

Lord, I know that pride is an abomination to You, so I pray that You would do whatever it takes to remove all pride from my husband's (wife's) heart so there is no need to suffer the punishment that comes with it (Proverbs 16:5). I know that "he who is of a proud heart stirs up strife, but he who trusts in the LORD will be prospered" (Proverbs 28:25). Don't let pride in either of us stir up strife in our marriage. Help our relationship to prosper because we look to You. Keep love from dying in his (her) heart for You and for me.

Lord, help me to be sensitive to any heaviness in my husband's (wife's) heart. Show me what his (her) burdens are and how I can help ease them. I pray that the heart of my husband (wife) will trust me so that our marriage will always be blessed (Proverbs 31:11). In Jesus' name I pray.

TRUTH *to* STAND ON

The heart is deceitful
above all things, and desperately wicked; who can know it?

JEREMIAH 17:9

Keep your heart with all diligence,
for out of it spring the issues of life.

PROVERBS 4:23

Wait on the LORD; be of good courage,
and He shall strengthen your heart;
wait, I say, on the LORD!

PSALM 27:14

I will give you a new heart and put a new spirit within you;
I will take the heart of stone out of your flesh
and give you a heart of flesh.

EZEKIEL 36:26

Let us not grow weary while doing good,
for in due season we shall reap if we do not lose heart.

GALATIANS 6:9

PRACTICAL STEPS *to* GOING DEEPER

1. Read Proverbs 28:14 in your Bible. What can happen to you when you let your heart get hard? In light of this Scripture, how can you keep your heart from becoming hard?

Read Jeremiah 32:17 in your Bible. Write out a prayer praising God that there is nothing too hard for Him—even the softening of any hardness in either your heart or your husband's heart toward one another.

2. Read Hebrews 4:12 and Psalm 119:11 in your Bible. In light of these verses, what can reading the Bible do for your heart? Write out a prayer thanking God for His Word. Ask Him to help you keep His Word in your heart so it never grows hard. Ask the same for your husband (wife) as well.

3. Read Psalm 73:26 and Psalm 4:7 in your Bible. What can God do for your heart? Write out a prayer thanking God for what He can do for your heart—be specific according to what those two Scriptures say. Ask Him to work that in your heart and in your husband's (wife's) heart also.

10

Pray to Keep Your Priorities Clear and in Order

Another common way a marriage can fall apart is if even one of the two people in it does not have right priorities. It is deeply hurtful when a wife (husband) realizes that her (his) spouse clearly prefers his (her) career, his (her) friends, his (her) activities, or just about anything else to spending time with her (him). It almost doesn't have to do as much with the amount of time spent as where their heart is in this relationship.

Even Delilah in the Bible knew it wasn't really love if her boyfriend's heart was not in it. And how did she know? Because Sampson would not do what she asked him to do. When Samson wouldn't tell her what she wanted to know, she said, "How can you say, 'I love you,' when your heart is not with me? You have mocked me these three times, and have not told me where your great strength lies" (Judges 16:15). Of course, the fact that he wasn't married to her and they were living outside the will of God should have indicated something to him. He knew the Lord and she didn't. He knew better, and he should not have put himself in the position of being pressured to tell her this information in the first place. And when he did tell her where his ultimate strength came from, that was his downfall. The point is, she knew that his whole heart had to be with *her* or it wasn't love. Never mind that her heart wasn't with him and she was trying to destroy him.

When it comes to priorities, Jesus made it crystal clear what ours should be. He said we should love God first and love others second

(Matthew 22:37-40). Putting God first doesn't mean you neglect your spouse and children. It doesn't mean you abandon your family and spend all your time in church. It doesn't mean you yell at your family and tell them to fend for themselves because you're going to the mission field. Jesus said, "If you love Me, keep My commandments" (John 14:15). Putting God first means you love Him enough to always do what He asks. Next to loving God, the most important thing He wants you to do is to love others (1 John 3:10-18). But we find we are far better able to love others if we love God first.

There are priorities within the "love others" command too. You must love your husband (wife) first and your children second. The reason for that is if you don't put your spouse before your children, you may end up not having a spouse, and that is not good for your children. It doesn't mean you love your children less. It means you understand the order of things. It doesn't mean you neglect your children and spend all your time with your husband (wife). It means you spend as much time as you need to in order to take good care of your children, but you make sure you do not neglect your husband (wife) in the process. It has to do with letting your husband (wife) know he (she) is still a top priority in your life, no matter how much time you need to spend with your children.

The great thing you will find is that when you love God and truly put Him first in your heart, the other priorities fall into place. Loving God doesn't mean just having occasional warm feelings for God. It means loving Him with all that is within you. It means your heart is always with Him. The same is true for you and your spouse. You cannot be half-hearted about him (her) either. But when you love God with all your heart, loving your spouse the way you are supposed to will be so much smoother. It's about having right priorities.

Keeping those two priorities straight is not that hard until children come along, and then it becomes much more complex—especially if both of you work to support the family. So much time is needed to raise children and keep a home in order, plus all the other things we need to do in order to stay healthy, be in church, and have meaningful contact with family and friends. How can we do all of this without violating what our top priorities should be? It seems we are always going to be neglecting something or someone. And most likely we will be neglecting our spouse in favor of our children. He (she) is the adult after all and will understand. Hopefully. But it doesn't have to be a big problem if our hearts are right with God. It is actually a matter of communication.

Communicating your great love for God is done in many ways. Your worship and praise tell God how much you love and adore Him. Praying to Him, listening to Him, and obeying Him also demonstrate your love for Him. Communicate your love for your husband (wife) by letting him (her) know that even though the children require so much time, you still love him (her) as much as ever. And of course always communicate your love to your children.

Loving God Is the Perfect Foundation for a Great Marriage

The first of the Ten Commandments says we are to have no other God but our God. He wants us to love Him with *all* our heart, soul, and mind, and acknowledge Him as everything to us. That means we love Him with our whole being and not just with the words we say. That means praising Him *with all that we are* because we love Him *with all that is in us.*

Every law of God is fulfilled by love. Love is what leads us to obey God in the first place. The Bible says, "Love does no harm to a neighbor; therefore love is the fulfillment of the law" (Romans 13:10). We were created by *love* to *love* and be *loved.* But our love and affection must be directed toward God first of all. We are to love nothing *more* than Him. God wants us to love Him first so that He can pour His love into us and infuse us with more of His character. By doing that, we are able to love others better.

Loving God will cause us to resist any kind of temptation that comes into our lives to draw us away from what is most important. When God is our first priority, we are not going to allow anything to weaken our relationship with Him. We will refuse to let anything dilute our attention away from Him.

This demand for attention that comes from other places is similar to when commercials come on TV that are so much louder than the regular program that you are forced to reach for the remote to adjust the sound. I don't know about you, but if I have to reach for the remote to adjust the sound because of a commercial that is too loud, then I will either mute the sound, change the channel, or turn the TV off completely. I'm amazed that some TV programmers don't yet realize we have remotes and seem to think we are going to just sit and take their volume abuse.

The same is true for you. When you love God and you notice the enemy trying to pollute your thoughts in any way, you can, by the power of Jesus' name, turn him off completely. You don't have to listen to his abuse because you have the power to change the channel of your focus. You can turn down the volume on the voice of your flesh that screams "I want what I want." You can put God first because you love God most. If your heart is divided—in other words, you are pulled in different directions by other things—you can choose to focus on setting your priorities in a way that pleases God.

Ask yourself, "Is there anything I am doing that has a higher place in my heart than God, my spouse, or my family?" If everything you do flows from your love for God, that helps you to always keep your priorities straight. He will guide you.

Showing love for your husband (wife) is one of the ways you demonstrate your love for God. The Bible says, "If someone says, 'I love God,' and hates his brother, he is a liar; for he who does not love his brother whom he has seen, how can he love God whom he has not seen?" (1 John 4:20). Jesus said we should love others as we *love ourselves*. But we all know there is a self-love that is selfish, prideful, greedy, and not born out of love for God at all. That kind of self-love is corrupt. The kind of loving ourselves that Jesus is talking about appreciates your own God-given gifts, talents, and uniqueness, and the wonderful way He has made you. It motivates you to be a good steward of your body, mind, soul, and life. You will be better able to love others as yourself if you learn to love yourself the way God wants you to. He wants you to take care of yourself—get enough rest, eat health-filled food, drink pure water, exercise regularly, and take care of your health needs. He does not want you working yourself to death for obvious reasons. He wants you to dedicate your work to Him, no matter what it is, so He can help you, lead you, and bless you.

Nothing is more important than loving God and your neighbor. And your spouse is the closest neighbor you will ever have. If you love your spouse the way you love yourself, you will never do to him (her) what you would not want done to you.

Have You Looked to See Where Your Treasure Is Lately?

The way you live out those two most important commandments, which fulfill all the laws of God, is to first seek God every day so you can be led by His Spirit. If you cannot hear God guiding you, through His Word or in prayer, you will end up having misplaced priorities. Only God can tell you what your priorities should be in the way you live out each day. He says to seek Him and His kingdom first, and all the things you need shall be added to you (Luke 12:31). When you seek Him first, everything falls into place. Everything you need will come to you.

Our priorities can get off track when we pursue other things before God. Jesus said, "Do not worry about your life...for it is your Father's good pleasure to give you the kingdom" (Luke 12:22,32). Jesus told a religious scholar—who understood this principle of loving God and loving others—that he was not far from the kingdom of God (see Mark 12:32-34). We, too, will be as close as possible to God's kingdom on earth when we better understand this principle. And once we do, God will help us keep our priorities straight. *He says to store up treasures in heaven because they don't fail* (see Matthew 6:20). He also says that *your heart will be with whatever you treasure most* (Luke 12:34). If you can see your marriage as being your greatest treasure next to your relationship to God—a treasure in which you will invest your whole heart—it will transform your marriage. When you put your spouse first under God, you can better keep your marriage strong, free of strife, and more pleasant in every way. And that in turn will be the greatest blessing for your children.

In order for us to stop being prideful, selfish, and sinfully oversensitive, we have to ask God to help us be humble, selfless, and kind. That means we must be able to exhibit the fruit of the Spirit. And we can't do that unless we are walking *in* the Spirit every day. Each morning you have to wake up and say, "Fill me afresh with Your love, Lord, and help me to be led by Your Holy Spirit today. Help me to exhibit the fruit of Your Spirit in everything I say and do."

Nine Ways TO DISPLAY THE FRUIT OF THE SPIRIT IN *Your Marriage*

The Fruit of the Spirit Is:	With Regard to My Marriage:
1. Love	I will show love to my husband (wife) every day.
2. Joy	I will invite the joy of the Lord to rise in me continually.
3. Peace	I will walk in peace and not in stress and anxiety.
4. Patience	I will be patient with my husband (wife) and not lose my temper.
5. Kindness	I will show kindness to my husband (wife) no matter what.
6. Goodness	I will do good for my husband (wife) in every way.
7. Faithfulness	I will be faithful to my husband (wife) in all I do.
8. Gentleness	I will be gentle and not harsh with my husband (wife).
9. Self-Control	I will not allow myself to get out of control.

GALATIANS 5:22-23 NCV

Three Ways to Assure Your Husband (Wife) That He (She) Is Your Priority

1. *Ask God to help you show love and commitment to your spouse in some tangible way every day.* Showing affection to your spouse should be high on your priority list. Your spouse needs to know that he (she) is loved for who he (she) is. Do things for him (her) that will make him (her) miss you whenever you are gone. Jesus said, "Greater love has no one than this, than to lay down one's life for his friends" (John 15:13). Ask God to show you how to lay down your life—selfish desires—for your husband (wife) in some way every day.

2. *Say no to certain things whenever possible in order to spend time alone with your spouse.* Try getting away together, even for a few hours, if not overnight. Drive somewhere that will take at least half an hour in the car so that you can have time alone without interruption. If you are married to a workaholic, try to convince him (her) that time away alone would be the best thing for *him (her)*. Time alone together can make a major difference in your relationship.

Michael and I have been to a number of marriage retreats, and during a particular one we found that even after 34 years of marriage we were still learning new things. Not that we had never heard these things before, but this time there was actual breakthrough. My husband likes to stay home, so we used to have two semiannual dates a year outside of birthdays. What my husband took away from this retreat was that he needed to take me out on a date night once a week. I had stopped hoping for that years ago, but something clicked with him when the leaders of the retreat suggested that, and now we go to dinner and sometimes to a film almost every week—although it is a lot harder to find a decent film than it is to find a good restaurant. Doing this has made all the difference in our relationship. We try to make time for that, and it's something we look forward to. It seems like such a simple thing, but it is an impactful way to put each other first. So no matter how busy we are during the rest of the week, we know we will have that time alone for a few hours.

3. *Have a devotional time together with your spouse as often as you can.* If you can't do it every day, then try for at least a couple times a week. If your husband (wife) is resistant to that, ask if you can just read a verse or two of Scripture to him (her) periodically and see if he (she) will let you pray for him (her). Praying together is one of the most life-changing things you can do for each other—even if only one of you does the praying. That is more common than you might think. I know that a lot of men feel they will be judged if they don't pray perfectly. They feel they will be compared to the pastor at church or those on television. (I have heard of this often.)

We all have to put aside some things to make time for what is most important at the moment. If something comes up that takes up all of your time—a sick child, an injured elderly parent, the finishing up of a big project—communicate with your spouse that this is just temporary and you will both be back spending quality time together as soon as the situation is under control.

If This Has Already Happened to You

If you feel you or your husband (wife) have priorities that are not in right order, pray first that you can talk this out together. Try to establish where each of you think your priorities *are right now* and what you think they *should be.* Determine what needs to change. Come to a complete understanding about the situation you're in. Decide how you can come to an agreement. For example, there are seasons in business that are more demanding than others, and perhaps you both can agree that during this busy season a lot more time has to be put into work. Decide how you can best compensate for that loss of time together. If you are in total agreement about this, then there will be more understanding and no permanent damage done.

Another example is when you have young children at home who haven't started school yet. The smaller they are, the more moment by moment attention they need. Talk to your spouse and agree that this is a season where there is not as much free time for the two of you, and so you really have to make a concentrated effort to find time together to be alone and make it count.

Still other examples are when you have an important project or assignment due and you need to complete it as successfully as possible.

Or when there are seasons of special interests happening, and it's either do it now or not do it at all. Talk it out and say something like, "I have to work hard on this project, but it will be completed in eight weeks and then I'll be home more." Or if you are worried about your spouse's time away from home, say something like, "Until the children start school, let's be home together as much as possible for their sake." If you can communicate and come to an understanding about these things, it will become clear that your greatest priority is still God, spouse, and children. It will set the record straight in your hearts and minds. The most important thing to remember is that communication is key.

If you feel your commitment to the marriage has remained strong but your husband's (wife's) has not, it is a terribly hurtful and disappointing situation. But don't let yourself become resentful. That only makes matters worse, and it will hurt you more than it does your spouse. It may cause you to blurt out words you will later regret, and it will further distance you from one another.

Instead, ask God to show you what the real problem is. Is your husband (wife) just too busy with work, establishing a career, raising children, or being active in the church or community? Is he (she) too preoccupied with outside interests, sports, friends, or hobbies? Is it a sign of someone who is *careless—or clueless?* Is it that he (she) truly doesn't care? Or is it actually that he (she) just can't see the truth about his priorities or can't figure it out on his (her) own?

There is an important thing that will always cause us to lose track of our right priorities, and that is pride. Pride in either you or your husband (wife) will always cause strife between you (Proverbs 13:10). "Pride goes before destruction, and a haughty spirit before a fall" (Proverbs 16:18). God doesn't want us to think or act as though we are better or more important than anyone, *especially our spouse.* Pride always causes a person to think that he (she) is right, and so it's not necessary to listen to their spouse's input. This is dangerous ground to be walking on. "Be of the same mind toward one another...Do not be wise in your own opinion" (Romans 12:16).

When we get "puffed up with pride," we become like the enemy

(1 Timothy 3:6). If you see pride in yourself or your spouse, pray that it will be broken. If priorities are out of order in your marriage—whether it is you, your spouse, or both of you—"come boldly to the throne of grace" that you "may obtain mercy and find grace to help in time of need" (Hebrews 4:16). Then say, "Lord, take away any pride in us so that we can see what is most important." If you can pray this together about yourselves, it will be powerful. If one of you is not ready to see it, then the one who does recognize that pride is causing a problem should pray for the other to have his or her eyes opened to see the truth.

When the Pressure at Work Affects Your Relationship

Everyone wants to feel significant—as if what they do matters and that they can make a difference in the world in some good way. That's why the work we do is important to us. A man's work is especially important to him, in some ways more than it is for a woman. That's because a man's identity and feelings about himself are often wrapped up in his work to the extreme. He throws himself into it because he continually senses the pressure to be successful. And he senses it even more when he is *not* working. A man out of work feels as though his entire life is on the brink of disaster. He may feel discouraged, angry, sad, depressed, hopeless, irritable, oversensitive, and like a failure. This tremendous stress he carries too often spills over into the atmosphere of his home and marriage.

A woman, on the other hand, often seems to have a greater sense of herself as a person of value aside from her work. Her work is very important to her, and she absolutely wants to excel and succeed, but her sense of identity and personal value does not rise and fall with the success of her work. She feels a sense of accomplishment in raising great children or creating a lovely, safe, comfortable home, or doing good for others. How many times do you hear of a woman committing suicide because she lost her job or her finances crashed? How many times have you heard that about a man?

The pressure a man feels about his work adds to the pressure in his home. If he works too long, too hard, too focused, or too obsessed, his wife feels that she is being replaced by a faceless mistress. Because the pressure a man senses about work is something he feels all the time and is such a big part of him, yet he may not be able to see it in himself. That's why it is crucial for a wife to pray that her husband will find fulfillment in his work. And also that he will be able to use his talents and gifts according to God's will, and that his work will be appreciated and blessed. A husband should pray for his wife's work to be successful as well, but if your husband (wife) doesn't want to do that, find a good prayer partner and pray about this for each other.

Don't Drink the Enemy's Kool-Aid

"Drinking the Kool-Aid" is a phrase that comes from the 1978 Jonestown massacre in Guyana, in which some members of the Peoples Temple cult committed suicide by drinking cyanide-laced Kool-Aid. For those of you too young to remember this incident, in the 1970s a guru rose up named Jim Jones. I was aware of him early on because my housekeeper, Rosa, who worked for me every Saturday for about five years, went to his church. She was a Christian, but somehow she and her church got into following Jim Jones instead of Jesus, the Messiah. She started talking about Jim Jones every week and how great he was, and I sensed right away that she had an unhealthy esteem for this suspicious "spiritual leader." When she started wearing a long necklace attached to a 2" x 4" plastic photo holder with a photo of Jim Jones encased in it, I told her in detail about my reservations regarding her allegiance to him. In our conversation she told me that Jim Jones had acquired land in Guyana and was asking his followers to go there and work the land, and he would take care of their needs. She was seriously considering going.

I had a terrible feeling about that for her sake, and told her so. I prayed fervently for her to come to her senses, but she was drawn to this false prophet. The more I prayed, the more strongly I felt that this was a plan of the enemy for evil. Thanks be to God, the next time I talked to her about it I succeeded in convincing her not to go. I persuaded her on the grounds that it was a big mistake for her to leave her son. I knew she'd had a hard life, and she wanted someone to take care of her and allow her to serve the Lord at the same time. And she thought that her son at age 19 was old enough to be on his own.

"But he still needs you," I said. "You can't just leave him. Besides, I don't believe this is what God wants you to do."

She finally decided not to go because of travel expenses, and it wasn't many months after that when Jim Jones gave his followers in Guyana the poisoned Kool-Aid. Except for a very few who escaped, Jim Jones and his followers died. It was sad beyond belief. Rosa knew it was God who kept her from that disaster.

The point is, the devil always has some kind of poison waiting for us to drink. Don't ever partake of the enemy's drink of death and destruction—especially with regard to your priorities and your marriage. Remember that the devil "is a liar and the father of it" (John 8:44). *The enemy will tell you that everything in your life is more important than your marriage*—your work is more important, and so are your dreams, your children, your friends, your relatives, your recreation, your interests, your career, or even what you do with your own time. Don't drink in those lies. They are poison to you and will prove to be your downfall. Instead, drink the "same spiritual drink" from "that spiritual Rock" which is Christ (1 Corinthians 10:4). Overcome the enemy's lies with God's truth, because *God "who is in you is greater than [the enemy] who is in the world"* (1 John 4:4).

After that terrible incident happened, Rosa grieved terribly for all of her friends who died in Guyana. It was an unbearable disaster that shook her life tremendously, but she might have been one of them. Had I not taken a strong stand against her going, I would have regretted that for the rest of my life. I am taking a strong stand against the devil's plans for you too. I don't want you to buy into the trap he has set for you and your marriage by enticing you to let your priorities get out of order. Love God, love your husband (wife), and love your children, and all else will fall into place.

PRAYERS *for* MY MARRIAGE

Prayer for Us to Establish Clear Priorities in Our Marriage

Lord, I pray You would help my husband (wife) and me to always make You our top priority, and to make each other our priority under You. Enable us to live in Your love so that we can learn to love each other the way You want us to. Make us to be vessels through which Your love flows. Show us how to establish right priorities in our marriage so we can be better for one another and better parents for our children.

I pray that we will not do anything "through selfish ambition or conceit, but in lowliness of mind" may we esteem each other better than ourselves (Philippians 2:3). Help us to always find time for one another to be a help, support, encourager, uplifter, lover, companion, and sharer of good things. Enable us to always bear the burden of the other concerning the difficult things that happen in life. Help us to choose each other and our children over the many seemingly important things that vie for our attention. I know that putting one another first does not mean neglecting our children in any way, but it is a position of our heart that says a good marriage is a gift we work to preserve *for* our children.

Teach us to set aside time to be together alone and to reaffirm each other as our top priority under You. In our seasons of necessary busyness, help us to be understanding of one another and in agreement as to how to handle those times successfully. Thank You that You have chosen us to be people for Yourself, "a special treasure" for Your glory (Deuteronomy 7:6). Help us to always find our treasure in You above all else so we can give our children a solid home and family and our undying love. In Jesus' name I pray.

Prayer for Me to Keep My Priorities in Right Order

Lord, help me to always put You first in my life and to put my husband (wife) next above everything else. Show me how to do that and how to let him (her) clearly know that this is what I am doing. I look to You to teach me the way I should walk and what I should do (Psalm 143:8). Reveal to me any place where my priorities are off. Show me where I have put other things, people, or activities before You or my husband (wife). If I have made my husband (wife) feel as though he (she) is less than a top priority in my life, help me to apologize to him (her) and make amends for it. Where damage has been done to our relationship because of it, I pray You would heal those wounds. Restore us to the place where we should be.

Help me to put our children in highest priority, just under You, Lord, and my husband (wife), for I know that the greatest blessing for them is that we stay together and our relationship be good, and that we are pleasant, loving, and nurturing for them to be around.

Thank You that Your love for me is everlasting, and that in Your lovingkindness You are always drawing me closer to You (Jeremiah 31:3). Help me to seek You first in all things, to keep Your commandments, and to abide in Your love (John 15:9-10). Thank You that before I chose You, You chose me that I "should be holy and without blame" before You in love (Ephesians 1:3-6). I know my holiness and blamelessness comes from all that Jesus *is,* being attributed to me. I am forever grateful, and I long to please You in every way—especially in the way I prioritize my life. In Jesus' name I pray.

Prayer for My Husband (Wife) to Keep His (Her) Priorities in Right Order

Lord, I pray that You would penetrate my husband's (wife's) heart with Your love. Help him (her) to understand the greatness of it. Deliver him (her) from any lies of the enemy that have caused him (her) to doubt Your love for him (her). Jesus, You have said, "God is love, and he who abides in love abides in God, and God in him" (1 John 4:16). Help my husband (wife) learn to abide in your love and to love You above all else so that he (she) walks with You every day. Let everything he (she) does be done in love (1 Corinthians 16:14).

Where his (her) priorities are out of order, I pray You would help him (her) to realize he (she) needs to put You first, me second, and our children next before everything else. Help him (her) to see where he (she) must make necessary changes in the way he (she) spends time. Help him (her) to not feel so pressured by his (her) work that it overtakes his (her) life and our family suffers. Bless his (her) ability to work so that he (she) can accomplish more in less time. Enable him (her) to say no to the things that do not please You and are not to be high on his (her) priority list. Don't let him (her) be led astray by delusion, and don't let his (her) fears come upon him (her) (Isaiah 66:4). Help him (her) to clearly see what is most important in life and what is not. Help him (her) to choose the path of humility and righteousness. Thank You that whatever we ask in Your name, and according to Your will, You will give us (John 15:16). In Jesus' name I pray.

TRUTH *to* STAND ON

Seek first the kingdom of God and His righteousness,
and all these things shall be added to you.

MATTHEW 6:33

Humble yourselves under the mighty hand of God,
that He may exalt you in due time,
casting all your care upon Him, for He cares for you.

1 PETER 5:6-7

I call heaven and earth as witnesses today against you,
that I have set before you life and death, blessing and cursing;
therefore choose life, that both you and your descendants may live.

DEUTERONOMY 30:19

If it seems evil to you to serve the LORD,
choose for yourselves this day whom you will serve...
But as for me and my house, we will serve the LORD.

JOSHUA 24:15

Cause me to hear Your lovingkindness in the morning,
for in You do I trust; cause me to know the way in which I
should walk,
for I lift up my soul to You.

PSALM 143:8

PRACTICAL STEPS *to* GOING DEEPER

1. Read Matthew 22:37-40 in your Bible. What are the two most important commandments of all? Write out a prayer asking God to help you and your husband (wife) keep your top two priorities straight. Tell God where either of you struggles with that, and where each of you need His help most.

2. Read Matthew 6:31-34 in your Bible. What should you not worry about and why? What are you supposed to do instead of worry? What are you supposed to seek first? Write out a prayer asking God to help you both to seek Him first above all else. Ask Him to help you always trust that He will provide for you. Ask Him for the things you want Him to provide and be specific.

3. Read Galatians 5:22-23 in your Bible. Write out a prayer thanking God for the fruit of the Spirit He gives you, and ask that He would help you and your husband (wife) to manifest it in a powerful way to each other. Be specific as to which fruit you especially need to see.

11

Pray to Keep Loss and Grief
from Defining Your Future

We can experience many losses in life. Some are worse than others, but all can be devastating. The loss of a loved one is always terrible. And in that category, the loss of a child is the worst of all. I have personally seen that loss break up a marriage. If one person blames the other for the loss of a child, that makes it unbearable for the one who is being blamed. The grief over the loss is already too much without adding guilt and blame for it as well. It is no wonder many marriages don't survive that.

We can also suffer traumatic loss in many other ways, such as the loss of an ability to do something, the loss of an important job, or the loss of a very close friend. The loss could be caused by a disease, accident, surgery, or injury that results in the loss of an important body part—an event that is life-changing. It can also be the loss of a home or finances, which can seriously affect our ability to take care of ourselves and our family.

Every one of us is going to experience some kind of loss and grief at some time. It's a part of life. Things happen, people die, unexpected changes occur. We can't predict them. We can pray about these things, but we cannot control them. When bad things happen that result in a sudden and tremendous loss to us, that loss can cause such grief in our heart that it greatly affects our marriage if we don't handle it correctly.

Whatever the loss is, we grieve because we have lost that which we cared about so much, and it's now no longer part of our life. And life will never be the same, never what it was. Loss forever alters how we view our future—without the child, the person, the ability, the work, the freedom, the home, the financial stability or security. Such life-changing loss can be unbearable, or at least more painful than we ever imagined. Coping with it at some point can seem impossible, and you wonder if you will ever know life without that crippling pain. Will you ever feel normal again?

Everyone deals with grief differently. A husband and wife may handle their grief in opposite ways. One person may not be able to understand how the other one is handling it when they are doing so in a way that doesn't make sense. For example, one person may draw inward and clam up and drown themselves in their work, finding it hard to be around others. They don't want to talk about it and be reminded of it.

The other one may desperately need to be with people—hopefully their spouse—in order to talk it out again and again to get that horrible pain to subside. That's how they try to get their arms around it all and deal with the devastation. So if their spouse is emotionally unavailable to them, it seems like a punishing rejection right when a listening ear is needed most.

Every marriage *can* go through difficult or upsetting times of loss, so it is helpful to pray in advance that these times do not happen, or if they do, that they do not destroy you as a couple. Prayer may not keep something bad from happening, but it can help you to better weather this storm. Pray that if something bad does happen, you will grow together through it instead of apart—that you will be strong for one another and not become bitter or angry. Personally, I believe that constantly praying for the safety of our family members and friends, and all the possible things that can happen to us, has got to make a difference. It is worth the effort to do so.

When Michael and I were first married, I was still a fairly new believer of about a year. Our church started having home group meetings in individual leaders' homes, where we would meet once a month. The size of that group was about ten—five couples along with their children. The husband and wife who led our group were strong and faithful leaders in the church. They were merciful, loving, kind, and faithful to each other, their children, and God. We were in their group for more than a year and grew to love and respect them greatly. We were grateful for all the godly wisdom they poured into us.

One week just before we were to meet again, we got a call from one of the other members of the group saying that our home group meeting was canceled because the leader couple's eight-year-old son was sick and in the hospital. Of course we prayed for him, but within a day or two we were called again and told that this son had died. It was a great shock to us all—especially to the poor parents and the younger brother and sister. He had suffered from a respiratory disease, and the mom had given him an over-the-counter medicine to bring his fever down, but that medicine caused him to have Reye's syndrome and he died from that. This was before it was known that this medicine could cause death in children at that age. Now it is marked on every package of it.

We all prayed continually for them in their shock, grief, and mourning, and we did what we could to help them have what they needed. About a week later we were called again and told by the same person close to them that the home group was canceled entirely. The father had left his family because he apparently blamed his wife for their son's death. It was unthinkable to all of us that this could happen and turn out so badly.

I had never before been so horrified as I was by this tragic turn of events. It was devastating enough that this sweet and kind young boy had died such a sudden and shocking death, but now the family was split apart. It all happened so fast. They got divorced, dropped out of the church, and went their separate ways. They never reconciled. I could not figure out how they could not draw close to God and to each other in their pain. And how no one could counsel them out of it. This great family—praying and believing people who had this horrible thing happen to them—could not rise above it. Their other two children lost not only their brother but their father as well as their home and church. It was unthinkable. It still makes me very sad every time I recall it.

Pray that this horrible kind of loss never happens to you or your husband (wife). It's worth whatever effort it takes in order to keep the horrendous plans of the enemy from succeeding. Even if we must pray this way every day for the rest of our lives, it will be worth the time.

Job Suffered Horrible Loss and Grief

Next to Jesus, probably no one in the Bible suffered more than Job. He literally lost it all—including his children and his health. Job believed his life was over after losing everything. "My spirit is broken, my days are extinguished, the grave is ready for me" (Job 17:1). "My eye has also grown dim because of sorrow, and all my members are like shadows" (Job 17:7). "My days are past, my purposes are broken off, even the thoughts of my heart" (Job 17:11).

Job was a good person. God called him "a blameless and upright man" (Job 1:8). In his misery Job said, "Have I not wept for him who was in trouble? Has not my soul grieved for the poor? But when I looked for good, evil came to me; and when I waited for light, then came darkness. My heart is in turmoil and cannot rest; days of affliction confront me. I go about mourning, but not in the sun; I stand up in the assembly and cry out for help" (Job 30:25-28). He did nothing to deserve what happened to him. He was always trying to do the right thing. His compassion toward other people who suffered was great.

Job lamented that no one could know the depth of his pain and loss. He said, "Oh, that my grief were fully weighed, and my calamity laid with it on the scales!" (Job 6:2). That is true of all of us. No one knows the depth of our suffering over loss. Even when Job talked about it with others, it didn't help. "Though I speak, my grief is not relieved; and if I remain silent, how am I eased? But now He has worn me out; You have made desolate all my company" (Job 16:6-7).

Job refused to "curse God and die" like his wife advised him to do (Job 2:9). He said, "Shall we indeed accept good from God, and shall we not accept adversity?" (verse 10). In all Job's suffering, he "did not sin with his lips" (verse 10). Job's affliction was the work of the enemy, but Job never turned away from the Lord. (He did have to repent of his attitude of hopelessness and unforgiveness toward his friends because they lacked compassion and understanding and did not speak what was right about God.)

In the end, the Lord blessed the latter days of Job more than his beginning—even giving him seven sons and three daughters just as he had before this disaster happened. Now, we know that if, God forbid, we ever lost a child, we would be grateful to have the new child, but we would still always miss our child who died. And in Job's case, the fact that it would take at least ten years to have ten children again is something to consider. But it is good to recognize that God restored all this to Job because he prayed and turned *to* God instead of *away* from Him.

Draw Near to the One Who Is Acquainted with Grief

Isaiah described the suffering and death of Christ, the coming Messiah, saying, "He is despised and rejected by men, a *Man of sorrows and acquainted with grief.* And we hid, as it were, our faces from Him; He was despised, and we did not esteem Him" (Isaiah 53:3). *He suffered to bear our grief and sorrow.* He gave His life so that we who open our hearts to receive Him will have life forever *with* Him. He suffered to give us His peace and healing.

Isaiah went on to say, "*Surely He has borne our griefs and carried our sorrows...* He was *wounded for our transgressions,* He was *bruised for our iniquities*; the chastisement for our peace was upon Him, and by His stripes we are healed" (Isaiah 53:4-5).

Isaiah prophesied that the coming Messiah would suffer through no fault of His own, but He would do it for us so we wouldn't have to. And that is exactly what Jesus did. We have to keep that in mind when we suffer loss and grief.

Isaiah also said, "All we like sheep have gone astray; we have turned, every one, to his own way; and the Lord has laid on Him the iniquity of us all. He was *oppressed* and He was *afflicted,* yet He opened not His mouth; He was *led as a lamb to the slaughter,* and as a sheep before its shearers is silent, so He opened not His mouth...for *He was cut off from the land of the living*; for the transgressions of My people *He was stricken.* And they made His grave with the wicked—but with the rich at His death, because *He had done no violence, nor was any deceit in His mouth*" (Isaiah 53:6-9).

We have to remember that Jesus bore our grief so we wouldn't have to be devastated by it. We must turn to Jesus in our grief and sorrow so *He* can comfort us.

Solomon Prays in Advance

In Solomon's prayer of dedication of the temple he built, he came with open hands before the Lord, in worship and humble submission to God, and asked this of God,

> When there is famine in the land, pestilence or blight or mildew, locusts or grasshoppers; when their enemies besiege them in the land of their cities; whatever plague or whatever sickness there is; whatever prayer, whatever supplication is made by anyone, or by all Your people Israel, *when each one knows his own burden and his own grief, and spreads out his hands to this temple:* then hear from heaven Your dwelling place, and forgive, and give to everyone according to all his ways, whose heart You know (for You alone know the hearts of the sons of men), that they may fear You, to walk in Your ways as long as they live in the land which You gave to our fathers (2 Chronicles 6:28-31).

"When Solomon had finished praying, fire came down from heaven and consumed the burnt offering and the sacrifices; and the glory of the LORD filled the temple" (2 Chronicles 7:1).

When famine or drought is in a land, there is severe loss and grief. It is frightening. When a plague is in the land and there is sickness and death, it is also frightening and causes grief. Solomon *prayed in advance* and asked God to hear their prayers and their expressions of grief. *God not only heard their prayer, He blessed them with His presence.*

What followed next was that God promised to Solomon a famous promise that still stands today:

> The LORD appeared to Solomon by night, and said to him: "I have heard your prayer, and have chosen this place for Myself as a house of sacrifice. When I shut up heaven and there is no rain, or command the locusts to devour the land, or send pestilence among My people, *if My people who are*

called by My name will humble themselves, and pray and seek My face, and turn from their wicked ways, then I will hear from heaven, and will forgive their sin and heal their land" (2 Chronicles 7:12-14).

God said, "Now My eyes will be open and My ears attentive to prayer made in this place. For now I have chosen and sanctified this house, that My name may be there forever; and My eyes and My heart will be there perpetually" (2 Chronicles 7:15-16). These words were given to Solomon by God when He appeared to Solomon, and the Lord's presence came to dwell with His people.

We can never ignore Solomon's prayer for God's protection in advance.

How We Should Respond in the Face of Loss and Grief?

Drawing near to God at the first sign of loss will make all the difference. If we worship and praise God for who He is and for His love and power on our behalf, He will walk with us through it, and He will restore us to wholeness. "By Him let us *continually offer the sacrifice of praise to God,* that is, the fruit of our lips, giving thanks to His name" (Hebrews 13:15). The word "continually" means even in the bad times.

In times of loss, we are capable of putting up a good front and learning how to laugh again but still hurt terribly in our heart. We may think that is the right thing to do because it is the only way we know how to cope. "Even in laughter the heart may sorrow, and the end of mirth may be grief. The backslider in heart will be filled with his own ways, but a good man will be satisfied from above" (Proverbs 14:13-14). We may think we can handle it on our own, but God wants us to run to Him and lean on His love and power to enable us to survive loss and grief.

God, Jesus, and the Holy Spirit Know Suffering and Grief

We don't know why bad things happen to good people. The Bible says, "In much wisdom is much grief, and he who increases knowledge increases sorrow" (Ecclesiastes 1:18). This is talking about *human* wisdom, and how the best that man can do alone can't cut it when it comes to surviving grief. The best we can do on our own to try and handle the pain and unbearable sense of loss is never enough. We must turn to God who truly understands our pain and knows grief.

God was grieved. "For forty years I was grieved with that generation, and said, 'It is a people who go astray in their hearts, and they do not know My ways.' So I swore in My wrath, 'They shall not enter My rest'" (Psalm 95:10-11).

The Holy Spirit was grieved. "In all their affliction He was afflicted, and the Angel of His Presence saved them; in His love and in His pity He redeemed them; and He bore them and carried them all the days of old. But *they rebelled and grieved His Holy Spirit*; so He turned Himself against them as an enemy, and He fought against them" (Isaiah 63:9-10). "Do not grieve the Holy Spirit of God, by whom you were sealed for the day of redemption. Let all bitterness, wrath, anger, clamor, and evil speaking be put away from you, with all malice. And be kind to one another, tenderhearted, forgiving one another, even as God in Christ forgave you" (Ephesians 4:30-32).

Jesus was grieved. "He entered the synagogue again, and a man was there who had a withered hand. So they watched Him closely, whether He would heal him on the Sabbath, so that they might accuse Him. And He said to the man who had the withered hand, 'Step forward.' Then He said to them, 'Is it lawful on the Sabbath to do good or to do evil, to save life or to kill?' But they kept silent. And when He had looked around at them with anger, *being grieved by the hardness of their hearts*, He said to the man, 'Stretch out your hand.' And he stretched it out, and his hand was restored as whole as the other. Then the Pharisees went out and immediately plotted with the Herodians against Him, how they might destroy Him" (Mark 3:1-6).

Jesus said that you are blessed by God when you mourn because you will be comforted by His presence (Matthew 5:4). That is a beautiful promise. He says that the loss you experienced that has caused you to mourn has a good side to it because the Lord is close to those who mourn, and His presence comforts you. If you have ever mourned for someone who has departed, and you turn to God for solace in that time, you will sense God's powerful presence comforting you. It is unmistakable. But too often people don't turn to the Lord for comfort. Too often they turn away from God because He did not prevent the loss from happening. When your heart is broken by sorrow, it breaks your very spirit. If you allow bitterness in, you become hard-hearted (Ecclesiastes 7:3-4).

If This Has Already Happened to You

If you or your husband already have a deep place of sorrow, grief, and sense of loss, turn to God and ask Him to remove the pain from your heart—and your husband's (wife's) heart as well. When your foundation is shaken and you are afraid for the future, fear melts your heart. "I am poured out like water, and all My bones are out of joint; My heart is like wax; it has melted within Me" (Psalm 22:14).

But the truth is, "*the LORD is near to those who have a broken heart, and saves such as have a contrite spirit*" (Psalm 34:18). It helps to know that so you can run to Him in prayer, expecting to sense His comfort, and you will have an unmistakable sense of God's presence. It is palpable. If you turn to the Lord, sorrow can be taken away eventually, and your heart made stronger. Pray that God will take away all the deep sorrow of loss from your life. You won't lose the memories. They just won't hurt so unbearably anymore, and you can live your life.

If you don't do that, you can end up with a *spirit of grief*. That is where grief takes over your being and seems to have a life all its own. I am not saying that will happen within a few months after what caused the grief has occurred. I am talking about after a couple years or even more of mourning. Don't let the enemy bind you up with grief so you cannot function or rise above it for even a moment. Because everyone is different and processes grief differently, have mercy on your spouse for how he (she) processes grief.

Blaming God for the loss that happened—or the protection that *didn't happen*—is more common than you might think. And many people don't even recognize it in themselves because people know that blaming God for anything is not the best position to take. But often we can hardly see it in ourselves. Things happen, and we can be angry at God because He didn't stop them.

If you say, "Lord, why did you allow that person I loved so much to die?" God understands those feelings, and He can take the honesty. You're not telling Him anything He doesn't already know. He is just waiting for you to pour your heart out to Him honestly and ask Him to set you free from feelings of grief that are keeping you captive. After you do that, the best way to keep any unforgiveness from creeping back in is to lift up praise to God and thank Him for everything He has done for you. Keep going until you feel that hardness break in your soul and transform your heart.

There Can Be an End to Grief

Just know that when you walk with God there will be a reasonable end to grief. That doesn't mean you will stop missing that which was lost, but you won't always feel the way you do in the beginning. It's hard to imagine not feeling the loss or grief, especially if the loss was sudden and devastating. The road back to recovery is traveled one step at a time. With God.

God wants you to take each of those steps with Him. *He* wants to bear the heaviest part of the burden. As He says, His burden is light when you walk with Him (Matthew 11:30). Take His hand in prayer, and He will keep you steady as He draws you closer to Him. Even if you cannot see the future, just know that *He* can and He will enable you to get there.

Even so, you don't have to rush grief. Be present in every stage of it, and allow your spouse to be able to grieve in his (her) way and in his (her) time. We all know how waves of grief come and go. Just when you think you are getting over it, you will see or hear something that triggers a memory, and you are suddenly in tears and feeling that pain again. That is normal. Welcome God into those moments, and let Him bring healing to the wound in your soul.

Always keep in mind that God is good and the enemy comes to kill and destroy. Too often people blame God for the painful things that happen to them. But God knows your suffering, and if you invite His comforting presence to walk with you through each day, He will take the endless pain away so you can recover and know joy again. It doesn't happen overnight, but it does happen. But if you don't draw near to God, it's possible you may never recover.

Although we all appreciate the sympathy others show us, no one can really know the depth of our sorrow. They don't know the loneliness of our suffering. Only God knows. Only God can lift us out of this dark, bottomless pit we seem to be falling deeper into every day. Only He can restore us to a livable degree of recovery. If we expect a person to help us fully recover from great loss and grief, we will always be disappointed. A person can help, but their words can't always make the deep pain of loss go away. Mere humans don't have the right words, and some of us are at a complete loss for words unless we have experienced the same loss. And even then we wonder what words can make it better anyway.

The only thing that makes the pain better is the healing love of God. God's love can shine through others, in whom the love of God is communicated. But God is the only one who can help us get through the pain of loss. Only He can help us survive it and recover. Only He can make us whole again after so terrible an explosion in our lives.

We can find comfort in the Lord, and we must. "This is my comfort in my affliction, for Your word has given me life" (Psalm 119:50). Perhaps we can't find the comfort we need in other people or in the things we used to enjoy, but we *can* find it in the Lord. And in His Word, where He promises that our mourning will one day end. It will become less painful and soul-crushing a little bit at a time.

PRAYERS *for* MY MARRIAGE

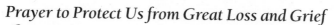

Prayer to Protect Us from Great Loss and Grief

Lord, I pray that You would protect my husband (wife) and me from suffering great loss and grief. Keep us and our loved ones safe. Keep us from accidents, plagues, or diseases. Keep us from losing our abilities, good health, finances, and home. Thank You, Lord, that if we do suffer loss, You will fill the empty places in us that are there because of the loss that we have suffered. Even though things change in our lives, You never change. You are never lost to us. You can always be found. Where we have suffered loss, help us to cast our burden of grief on You because it is too heavy for us to bear ourselves. Lead us through the process when we feel we cannot live through the pain of it. Help us to grieve and not deny ourselves that healing process, and enable us to heal and get beyond it so we can have a good and meaningful life again.

Lead us step-by-step each day so we can walk safely into the future You have for us. Thank You, Lord, that with You nothing is impossible. Thank You that with You, all things are possible. Thank You that You are acquainted with grief and You have compassion on us when we grieve. Help us to always turn to You together, as well as in our separate times with You. In Jesus' name I pray.

Prayer to Set Me Free from Loss and Grief

Lord, when I have experienced great loss and now still find myself suffering grief because of it, I pray You would walk with me through this. I need Your comfort and healing power to work in me. Help me to not blame or resent my husband (wife) for any reason and put a terrible burden on him (her) that our marriage can't survive. I know that no one person can heal so great a loss, but You can.

I pray I would never have any hard feelings toward You for anything bad that happens. If I do, show me and I will confess that as sin before You. You are the source of everything good in my life. I worship You as my Healer, Comforter, and Restorer—my peace and the source of everything good in my life. Take all heaviness from my heart and mind—and off my shoulders, which are not built to carry it. I know I can go nowhere to escape it except to You. I turn to You who are acquainted with grief and ask You to lift the burden of this grief off of me now. In Jesus' name I pray.

Prayer for My Husband (Wife) to Be Set Free from Loss and Grief

Lord, I pray for my husband (wife) that if he (she) is suffering from a great loss and the grief that goes along with it, I pray he (she) would turn to You for comfort. I pray that he (she) would not blame me or see me as the enemy. Enable him (her) to see who the real enemy is who causes disaster in our lives.

Help us to never blame each other, or You, for whatever loss we suffer. Teach us instead to blame the enemy of our soul, who comes to destroy. Help us to forgive people and events we feel contributed to any loss we experience so that we can be completely free of that burden too.

Lord, You have promised that those who mourn will be comforted (Matthew 5:4). Your Word says, "The days of your mourning shall be ended" (Isaiah 60:20). Enable my husband (wife) to turn to You in his (her) sorrow so that he (she) will know the comfort of Your presence coming alongside of him (her) to walk him (her) through this to the other side of devastating grief and mourning. In Jesus' name I pray.

TRUTH *to* STAND ON

I am troubled, I am bowed down greatly;
I go mourning all the day long.

PSALM 38:6

I will turn their mourning to joy, will comfort them,
and make them rejoice rather than sorrow.

JEREMIAH 31:13

Blessed are the poor in spirit, for theirs is the kingdom of heaven.
Blessed are those who mourn, for they shall be comforted.
Blessed are the meek, for they shall inherit the earth.

MATTHEW 5:3-5

A time to weep, and a time to laugh;
a time to mourn, and a time to dance.

ECCLESIASTES 3:4

The sun shall no longer be your light by day,
nor for brightness shall the moon give light to you;
but the LORD will be to you an everlasting light,
and your God your glory.
Your sun shall no longer go down,
nor shall your moon withdraw itself;
for the Lord will be your everlasting light,
and the days of your mourning shall be ended.

ISAIAH 60:19-20

PRACTICAL STEPS *to* GOING DEEPER

1. Read Matthew 5:3-5 in the "Truth to Stand On" section at the end of this chapter or in your Bible. What does God say He will do for you in times of sadness or mourning? Have you ever felt that comfort of God in your own times of loss? If so, write out a prayer of thanksgiving for that and ask Him to always provide that for you and your husband (wife).

2. Read Psalm 119:49-50 in your Bible. What can give us comfort in our times of loss? Have you found that kind of comfort in your own times of loss? Has your husband (wife) found that? Write out a prayer asking God to give you that kind of comfort in His Word whenever you ask Him for it. Ask the same for your husband (wife) too.

3. Read Isaiah 60:19-20 in the "Truth to Stand On" section at the end of this chapter or in your Bible. What do these verses speak to you about any dark time of grief that you have experienced? What will God do for you? And what will happen to your mourning? Write out a prayer thanking God for all that. Be specific with any grief you or your husband (wife) are still experiencing.

12

Pray to Keep Working Toward Agreement and Unity

Jesus promised that if two agree on earth "concerning anything that they ask, it will be done for them by My Father in heaven" (Matthew 18:19). He went on to say, "Where two or three are gathered together in My name, I am there in the midst of them" (Matthew 18:20). How powerful is that? It's as simple as two people—a husband and wife perhaps—agreeing in prayer to bring the presence of the Lord. It's like God saying, "Just two of you praying, and I'm there with you." That doesn't mean if you are praying alone that He is not with you. He is. But there is an exponential increase of the power of His presence when two or more pray together. That's why there is such great power in a husband and wife agreeing in prayer about anything.

First you must agree with each other as to *who* you are praying to and *what* His Word says. And also agreeing with each other as to what you are praying about. *As a married couple, you always need that boost of agreement and unity.* It's more powerful than you may think or know.

The Bible also talks about separation. God says, "What God has joined together, let not man separate" (Mark 10:9). Any kind of separation between a husband and wife begins in the mind. And then it can creep subtly and slowly into the heart. All this starts when communication breaks down in a marriage, and a husband and wife no longer understand what the other is thinking, feeling, going through, or planning. It may be reinforced by anger or negative emotions. It intensifies when serious arguments happen over such things as financial problems,

219

one person's destructive behavior, the raising of children, or an unaffectionate, unsatisfying, or nonexistent intimate life.

This separation of heart can grow wider if there is no true forgiveness flowing to keep them from developing a hardness of heart. Soon, they are no longer each other's top priority. Not long after that, ungodly attractions creep into the mind, love dies, and divorce begins to be thought of as a way out of the marriage. And then the separation process is nearly complete. All it will take is some action that brings great hurt, followed by an overwhelming sense of hopelessness about the relationship enough to push it over the edge. At that point, leaving the marriage can seem like a relief. And it all started with disagreement and disunity.

The good news is that this process can be *stopped* at any point and totally *reversed* if there is *repentance* of heart and *forgiveness* flowing from a husband and wife to one another. But that must be prayed about as soon as there is an awareness of the need for it. All it takes is one person saying, "I don't want to go on like this. I want to make some changes. I want to seek the Lord and have Him make changes in me and you and in us together as a couple. Let's talk about the things that are bothering each of us and get counseling if we need to. I am willing to confess before you, and before God, anything I have thought—or said, or done, or *not* done—that was wrong. I want to ask for your forgiveness for not praying more concerning us coming to an agreement about things. I am willing to do what it takes to turn things around and renew our marriage so it will last."

I guarantee that if a man or a woman would sincerely say those words to their spouse, and if their spouse would receive them and agree to say the same kind of words in return, they could not only save their marriage, but they would make it better than they ever thought it could be. Sadly, too many people don't recognize the signs until it's too late. They are oblivious as to what is happening in themselves and blind to all that is going on in their spouse. But none of this has to happen at all if you ask God to protect your marriage, in the ways I have suggested in this book, and help you both to always work toward agreement and unity.

How often have we heard about a husband who comes home to find that his wife has suddenly moved out? He is shocked and baffled, but this was not a quick decision for her. She had been contemplating it for a very long time. No caring woman decides to leave her home and marriage on a whim. And a woman with children will not leave her home without thinking long and hard about it. It's way too traumatic and difficult to uproot children, deprive them of a parent, and start all over—trying to find someone trustworthy to take care of them while she finds find a way to provide for them. There has to be an emotional separation happening long before any physical separation occurs. If the husband is surprised, it's probably because he has not been listening for a very long time. Once a woman finally makes that decision, she is not going to come back unless some major changes are made.

We've also heard countless stories of a wife who was suddenly left by her husband. There may have been signs of emotional separation of heart long before the physical separation occurred. Of course, there are men who can be easily seduced by another woman, and far too many women who have no second thoughts about going after a married man and breaking up his family. But a wife has home field advantage if she can make herself and their home a place he doesn't want to leave. The reason a man can "suddenly" leave a marriage and do something impulsive, as in go off with some woman at his workplace, may be because he doubts things will get any better at home. Or he may just have an ungodly, cheating heart, and no matter how good a wife he had, he believed he deserved a better offer.

The best time to start praying about not allowing the idea of disagreements and disunity settling into your mind is the day you are married. Or better yet, even before you say yes to the proposal. But many newlyweds don't think that this separation of heart will ever happen to them. Most of them are thinking, *Everything is perfect. There is nothing I need to pray about.* How many people have had stars in their eyes when they got married and were greatly disappointed to find out the person they married was not perfect?

Please know there are always many things to pray about in a marriage every day. And the sooner you start praying about them, the better. Pray that disagreements don't become division in your marriage.

Actually, Three Must Agree

God has a lot to say about unity and agreement. The Bible says, "Can two walk together, unless they are agreed?" (Amos 3:3). We can't move on well together if we don't agree and work to preserve unity in our marriage relationship. We are encouraged to "dwell together in unity" because it produces good things (Psalm 133:1). The apostle Paul said we should live endeavoring "to keep unity of the Spirit" because that would produce peace in our lives (Ephesians 4:3). Without unity, we won't have peace. That's why we must keep working toward that every day.

In order for a marriage to not only survive, but also to be fulfilling and successful, three parties need to be involved: the husband, the wife, and God. The reason marriages have problems in the first place is because every married couple is made up of two *imperfect people.* One imperfect human plus another imperfect human equals one *imperfect marriage.* However, if you add the presence of a *perfect God* into this imperfect mix of two imperfect people, you then have unlimited possibilities for growing closer to the perfection God intended for the marriage relationship. Whether that happens or not is determined by how frequently and fervently God is invited to reign in the hearts of both husband and wife. It has to do with being willing to have three agree.

You and your spouse can agree about something, but it can still be a problem if *God* doesn't agree with it. For example, if your spouse wants you to view something you don't want to see but you agree to it, knowing this is a compromise you *both* agree to, but it doesn't agree with *God's Word,* this won't work. The Bible says to not let your eyes see worthless things (Psalm 119:37). Therefore, *God doesn't agree* with it. The two of you may be fine with it, but it offends God and violates His laws. If it's a point of contention with God, it will always be a problem in your lives together. It will inhibit all that God wants to do in each of you and in your marriage. You may fully agree on something together, but if it doesn't agree with God's ways, it will open the door for problems that will undermine the strength of your marriage.

There are consequences for violating any law of God—whether ignorantly or knowingly. Some people think that God's laws don't apply to them, but that doesn't make the consequences for violating them any less destructive. They may believe they are innocent of any violation, but God doesn't see it that way. It's like the law of gravity. You can jump out a tenth-story window and deny the law of gravity all the way down, but the consequences are still going to be the same when you hit the ground. God's laws are for our benefit. Life works better for us when we live by them.

It Is Good to Appreciate Each Other's Gifts

God made man and woman in His image. God's image is expressed in *both* male and female. When you are married, God's plan for you is to serve the Lord together. That doesn't mean you must be attached at the hip. You don't have to go every place together and do everything together. You don't even have to serve God in exactly the same way. It's great to be able to do that, and in many cases it's required. But God will combine your talents to bring out the best in each of you. That's because God designed the two of you to *complete* each other, not *compete* with each other.

Your personality differences—especially if you are opposites—will either be the greatest blessing of your life or the greatest battle of your life, depending on whether you live in the Spirit or in the flesh. If you recognize that you are called together, it will help you appreciate each other's gifts, talents, abilities, and strengths. If you cannot see how you can work this out together, put it in God's hand. He has a way of fitting a husband and wife together perfectly.

If This Has Already Happened to You

Every marriage has times of negotiating and compromising that, if not handled carefully, can allow a wedge to get in between a husband and wife. If they are unable to come to an agreement, this division can grow with each new unresolved problem, and eventually this division can become a *great* divide. Problems that are allowed to grow deep can completely break a marriage apart. And it can happen so stealthily that you don't even see it coming until one day you wake up and wonder how you let it get this far. And then you may not know what to do to stop the divide from widening. You don't see how you can ever bring it all back together again because the damage seems irreparable and the divide keeps widening, as though it is on a set path. The great divide seems to have a life of its own.

However, again, you must always remember that with the Lord nothing is impossible. And keep in mind that every division can be evaporated. It takes understanding what the true problem is that you're dealing with. If you don't understand, ask God, and He will reveal it to you or give you insight as to what the real cause of the disagreement is. Being aware of the problems in advance and praying to prevent them is powerful and well worth the time and effort it takes to resolve them. But so is praying after the divide has already happened.

If the two of you are at variance over something, and it's causing you to enter into arguments, disagreements, or conflicts over it, that means you probably have constant strife between you, and that is not good. For example, if your husband (wife) does something from time to time and you don't think it's the right thing to do, and the two of you can't fully agree on this, you then have a difference of opinion and a point that needs to be decided. If you confront your husband (wife) about this and ask him (her) to stop, and he (she) continues to do it anyway, knowing that you don't approve of it, then this problem has not been decided in a way that is acceptable to both of you. It makes you feel that he (she) doesn't care enough about you to stop doing something that deeply bothers you. It can become a point of contention that will eventually turn into a deal breaker with regard to your marriage.

At that point, a wife can do one of four things:

- *She can resolve the issue with some kind of compromise.* But this compromise may not be enough to satisfy either spouse.

- *She can choose to be silent and not press the issue.*

However, she may become resentful over time, especially if what he does affects their lives in a serious and negative manner.

- ***She can enter into conflict with him.*** This means having unpleasant disagreements, arguments, or strife, especially if what he does affects her sense of emotional well-being, which can cause her to view their future as being threatened because of it.

- ***She can pray for him that his eyes will be opened to God's will.*** And that God will do whatever it takes to bring about necessary changes in their lives.

I'm not picking on the husband here. It's the same when the wife is doing something—or *not* doing something—and the husband objects. It doesn't matter what the problems are; they have to be resolved in a way that is acceptable to *both* husband and wife. If they are not, these disagreements will become deeper and deeper.

Agree to Be on the Same Side

Problems in a marriage must be confronted because they usually don't go away on their own without one or both people making a great effort. But there is a powerful way to *prevent* problems in a marriage— or to *heal* and *eliminate* the problems that are already there. And that is to understand your God-given authority in prayer and to pray powerfully about them every day. Don't let them just build up until hopelessness takes over.

How many people have thought at one time or another, *I don't know if this is going to work.* Or worse, *My husband needs a wake-up call in order to see what is happening here.*

On the other hand, it's never too late to start praying that you and your husband (wife) will come to a place of unity and agreement. You cannot change your husband's (wife's) heart, but you can pray that *God* will. And you can ask God to reveal what you can do—or stop doing— that would bless him (her). Ask God to reveal the truth about you and your husband (wife) and your relationship.

Of course, it's impossible to be perfect for each other all the time. There are no two people who can live up to one another's expectations every moment. At some point there are going to be disagreements until those things are worked out. Some things that one person does are going to get on the other's nerves. Each one is going to disappoint the other sometime. But it's what happens during those times that sets the marriage on one path or the other. One path with fresh air leads to growing deeper and better together; the other path of suffocation leads to a breaking down of the bond of love and commitment.

When offenses happen—and they will in even the best of circumstances because of the differences in perspectives—these things have to be talked out. When you try to come to a mutual understanding, and you never can because one of you *refuses* to work it out, you can become so discouraged and hopeless that you withdraw and stop trying. But don't give up. When you invite God to help the two of you be of one mind and one spirit, things *can* work out. You can grow through the difficult times when you walk through them together with God.

I used to know a couple who fought and bickered with each other every day. It was exhausting just to hear about it. They were two very nice, godly people who loved the Lord, but they were also strong willed and not the kind of individuals who compromised and worked things out. It depleted them and took a toll on their children as well. I say that I used to know that couple because I don't know *that* fighting couple anymore. They have changed dramatically from where they used to be. They don't fight anymore.

Some difficult things happened to them that convinced them they needed to be on the same side against the things that were opposing them. Their eyes were opened to see that the things they bickered over endlessly didn't matter to them anymore. They weren't important and never really did matter. They started praying seriously about being in agreement with each other while also being in agreement with God. As a result, God has opened up their worldwide ministry together in a wonderful way. They complement each other perfectly.

That is what God can do in every married couple if they have humble hearts that say, "Show us *Your* will, Lord, and we will do it." The peace is priceless.

PRAYERS *for* MY MARRIAGE

Prayer That We Will Seek Unity and Agreement Together

Lord, I pray You would protect my marriage from the misunderstandings and disagreements that can happen when two people stop communicating. Help us to always be in close contact and emotionally current with one another. Teach us to be kind when we could be stern, merciful when we could be judgmental, and forgiving when we could nurture an offense. Open our eyes whenever either of us is blind to what is going on inside the other.

Always show us where we are being preoccupied with other things and other people more than with each other. Your Word says that You allow calamity to happen in our lives because of sin when we forsake You and worship other gods (Jeremiah 1:16). I pray that my husband (wife) and I will never depart from Your ways and become so wrapped up in other things that we begin to serve those things instead of You. Keep us on track and on the path You have for us so that calamity never comes near us. One of the greatest calamities would be to lose our marriage. I pray that it will never happen to us in any way. Give us revelation so that we can clearly see the truth (Proverbs 29:18). Teach us to always be in agreement with each other and with You. Help us to continually pray and be watchful about this. If You are *for* us, who can be *against* us? (Romans 8:31). In Jesus' name I pray.

Prayer for Me to Work Toward Agreement with My Husband (Wife)

Lord, help me to always have a soft heart that is willing to talk things through with my husband (wife)—especially in areas where we disagree. I refuse to let myself become anxious about any sense of disunity

I feel between my husband (wife) and me. Instead, I come to You with thanksgiving for who You are and all that You have done for us, and I let my requests be made known to You. Thank You that Your peace, which passes all understanding, will guard my heart and mind in Christ Jesus (Philippians 4:6-7). I will not let my heart be troubled, but I will trust in You instead (John 14:1). I know that Your grace is sufficient for me, and Your strength is made perfect in my weakness. I can trust that when I am weak You will be made strong in me, because I depend on You (2 Corinthians 12:9-10). Your Word says how good it is for us to dwell together in unity (Psalm 133:1). Enable us to do that. Show me what I can do to help facilitate that. In Jesus' name I pray.

Prayer for My Husband (Wife) to Work Toward Agreement

Lord, where my husband (wife) and I have disagreements that are causing problems, I pray You would help him (her) to be willing to talk things through with me and seek You for what we are supposed to do. Teach us not to fight for our rights, but instead enable us to draw closer to You and closer to each other. Help us sense the love we have for each other and know that it is far stronger and more important than anything we disagree on. Just as no one can "separate us from the love of Christ," I pray that nothing will be able to separate us from our love for each other (Romans 8:35).

Even when I feel that we cannot come to an agreement on important issues, I know that You are here for us, and we can be in unity with You. Help us to work things out. Make changes in each of us in whatever ways are needed. Your Word says that we should endeavor "to keep the unity of the Spirit in the bond of peace" (Ephesians 4:3). Help us to do that. In Jesus' name I pray.

TRUTH *to* STAND ON

How good and how pleasant it is
for brethren to dwell together in unity!

PSALM 133:1

Two are better than one, because they have a good
reward for their labor. For if they fall,
one will lift up his companion.
But woe to him who is alone when he falls,
for he has no one to help him up.

ECCLESIASTES 4:9-10

Teach me Your way, O Lord; I will walk in Your truth;
unite my heart to fear Your name.
I will praise You, O Lord my God, with all my heart,
and I will glorify Your name forevermore.

PSALM 86:11-12

The Lord will perfect that which concerns me.

PSALM 138:8

Count it all joy when you fall into various trials,
knowing that the testing of your faith produces patience.
But let patience have its perfect work,
that you may be perfect and complete, lacking nothing.

JAMES 1:2-4

PRACTICAL STEPS *to* GOING DEEPER

1. Read Amos 3:3 in your Bible. Is there anything specific about which
you and your husband (wife) do not have total agreement? Do you ever
feel it keeps you from walking together in unity? How so?

Read Psalm 133:1-3 in your Bible. What is it like when you can live in unity with your spouse? Do you feel you need to work on that together? If so, write out a prayer asking God to help you do that. If your answer is no, write out a prayer thanking God for that, and ask Him to help you always stay in agreement with one another.

2. Can you see how you and your husband (wife) could talk about any disagreement you are having so that you can compromise in some way to work it out? Write out a prayer asking God to soften your hearts toward one another so that you can always work out disagreements in a way that is acceptable to you both. If you have no disunity between you, write out a prayer praising God for that and pray that this will never be a problem for the two of you.

3. Read Romans 8:38-39 in your Bible. How strong is the love of God toward you and your husband (wife)? If nothing can separate you from God's love, and God's love is always in you and there for you, and your marriage is sacred in the eyes of God, do you believe that His love in you both can be a big factor in working things out between you? Write out a prayer thanking God for His unfailing love for you both, and ask that it will help you to always have unfailing love for one another.

13

Pray to Keep the "D" Word from Ever Becoming an Option

Most people get married with the intention of staying married in a wonderful relationship for the rest of their lives. You're in love with each other, and you both have an idea of what you think life together is going to be like. But it is impossible to know exactly what you are getting into before you're married, no matter how long you have dated or known each other. The truth is, we don't even know *ourselves* completely before we're married, let alone the person we are marrying.

Marriage reveals everything we are because there is no place to hide—not even from ourselves. The marriage contract changes things. The relationship is now *really* up close and personal, and the ways we may have formerly disguised ourselves no longer work. The truth comes out. That's why a marriage requires commitment and work. A fifty-fifty partnership doesn't cut it. That's what you do when you're just living together—one foot in and one foot out. But when you are married, each person has to be all in the relationship. And that's not easy to do when we are all selfish enough to want to hold back as much as we can so we don't get crushed in case it all falls apart. We can do that without even realizing it.

A marriage—just like the people in it—is either growing deeper and more solid, or it is breaking down and becoming more vulnerable. It never stays in just one place, although it may feel as though it does sometimes. Marriage actually has a life of its own and can move forward or backward. It can breathe deeply when given fresh air, or it can suffocate if it is deprived of spiritual oxygen. Each of you has a great influence on which direction your marriage will go by the words you speak, the way you act, how you listen, and the fervency of your prayers. Fresh air or suffocation; it's a choice you make. That's why it is important to pray that your marriage will always grow better and stronger and divorce will not become an option for either of you. It is, of course, best to pray this even *before* you walk down the aisle. Or at least as soon as you realize how important prayer is to maintaining a good marriage.

Marriage needs to be worked on all the time so it can grow stronger and deeper. If it doesn't grow, it is stagnating. It may feel as though it is being maintained, but in unseen places it is breaking down. It's like putting a pin in an egg and letting the contents inside slowly drain out. You don't see that happening. The egg looks the same. But then one day pressure is put on the egg, and it cracks. When a marriage cracks, divorce can seem like the only way to save your own life in an impossible situation. Didn't we all learn that Humpty Dumpty could never be put back together again? But with God, all things are possible—even complete renewal and restoration.

The idea of marriage revealing who we really are is not always a bad thing. At least, it doesn't have to be. It can be a *good* thing. It's good when what baggage we have on the inside is brought to the surface so we can bring it to God and be *free* of it. God allows it to surface in us for the very purpose of facing it and surrendering it to Him in order to get rid of it. Marriage is supposed to be a safe place where we can face our imperfections and, with the loving support of our spouse, do what we need to do to overcome them. Keep that in mind if you see something you don't like in yourself, or your spouse, showing its ugly self. God wants you both to be liberated from whatever is not good for your marriage.

Every marriage has two hearts that need to be changed and two completely different perspectives that need to be molded gently in order for two different individuals to truly become one. They don't become clones of one another; they will fit well together as they align themselves with God.

Of course, one person can be so wrapped up in themselves or their work that they are completely unaware that their spouse is feeling neglected and lonely. *They* believe that everything is great, but their *spouse* is miserable. The point is, if just *one* person in a marriage doesn't think everything is great, then the marriage is not great, no matter what the other person thinks.

The good news in all this is that even when one of you, or both, have made mistakes in your marriage and should have done things differently, God is a God of second chances. But a second chance is something not all couples are willing to give each other. God always gives us another opportunity to make things right. That means even if your marriage seems headed in the wrong direction, it's never too late to turn it around. But it takes *two* to do it. Or should I say *three*? We cannot underestimate how important our prayers are to God when He is invited to be a not so silent partner in our marriage.

How God Sees Divorce

Before I tell you this, if you are already divorced, or have been divorced for years and you and/or your husband (wife) are remarried to other people, do not beat yourself up for that. There are plenty of people who will do that for you. Instead, take it to the Lord, if you have not already done that, and confess it to Him and tell Him you are sorry for your part in it. If you don't see that you had any part in that divorce, then ask God to show how you could have done things differently. If He shows you something, ask for His forgiveness and tell Him humbly that you intend to never allow that to happen again. Above all, thank and praise God that He forgives, heals, and restores.

What God thinks about divorce is no secret. He hates divorce, "for it covers one's garment with violence" (Malachi 2:16). He uses the words "hate" and "violence" to describe His perspective on divorce. He said it to His people because they had violated His laws in every way, including breaking the covenant they had made with their wives. After He said this at the end of the Old Testament, He didn't speak to them again for about 400 years. That's an even longer silence than what can happen between warring couples. I believe He means it.

Jesus said it was because of people's hard-heartedness that divorce came about, but God never intended for it to be that way (Matthew 19:7-8). Divorce was never supposed to happen. But hard hearts made room for it, even knowing full well that God hates it.

God thinks of divorce as treachery. "The LORD has been witness between you and the wife of your youth, with whom you have dealt treacherously; yet she is your companion and your wife by covenant. But did He not make them one, having a remnant of the Spirit? And why one? He seeks godly offspring. Therefore take heed to your spirit, and let none deal treacherously with the wife of his youth" (Malachi 2:14-15). God wants us to have a strong commitment to loving and taking care of each other. He likes unconditional love because He invented it. That's who *He is.* If you deal treacherously with each other by divorcing, it grieves God's Spirit.

I by no means want to bring condemnation on anyone who has been divorced in the past. I myself am a member of that group, but there is healing from the effects of it—the restoration of your heart and a new beginning given to you by the Lord. God either makes all things new or He doesn't. If you choose to believe the Bible, then you are a candidate for complete renewal. But it is a mistake to remarry until you have found that place of complete restoration and wholeness God has for you. You also need understanding and knowledge of why your marriage didn't work the first time, and why you think it will work this time. Seek good counsel and much prayer through this process. Ask God to lead you.

One of the reasons that the divorce rate is so high is because divorce is considered an *option* in the minds of many people. It is spoken of as a *solution.* It appears to be the *only way out* of a miserable situation. But if you have the mind-set that you don't want that option, that solution, or that way out, it forces you to have to find a way *through* a seemingly impossible situation. But you can't do it alone.

God is a witness to your marriage, viewing it as a covenant. That means having an *enduring commitment of faithfulness and devotion to one another.* So when two people get divorced, it is a violent shattering of that covenant and of God's order for their lives. But when you keep your marriage vows, God stands behind your marriage. That's why your prayers for the preservation and strengthening of your marriage relationship bond have such power. They are already God's will before you even speak them. Praying puts God's will into action. It means God's power will stand against any enemy you face—whether the enemy comes from the outside or it is actually one or both of you.

Below are good ways to pray to prevent a divorce.

Pray That You Both Will Do the Right Thing

God says He wants you to have the kind of love for one another that is patient—not arrogant or prideful, not rude or selfish, and not easily provoked. He wants you to be the kind of people who don't think about evil things and don't enjoy lawlessness. He wants you both to be patient with imperfections in each other and to believe for the best in each other. He wants you to have the kind of love that never loses hope and believes that if you live God's way—and pray without ceasing—everything will turn out right. He wants you to have the kind of love that embraces the truth and is willing to endure whatever is necessary in order to do the right thing (1 Corinthians 13:4-7). God says that kind of love never fails (1 Corinthians 13:8). That kind of love comes from God and can only be developed by spending time with Him. That's because being in the presence of God changes us.

Transformation is found in the presence of God.

God can transform us from people who don't really know how to love into people who love the way He does. We have to sincerely ask Him to work that in us and then do what He says. We have to be *willing* to do what's right even if we don't always do it perfectly.

Pray That You Both Will Treat Each Other in a Way That Pleases God.

Marriage is supposed to be a manifestation of the relationship between Christ and the church. Christ doesn't walk out on, get fed up with, leave, desert, or divorce the church. He also doesn't get rude, abusive, mean, inconsiderate, selfish, unaffectionate, arrogant, or angry with the church, either. So many problems in a marriage could be solved if each person were to become more Christlike, especially with one another. A relationship disintegrates slowly with each careless word or insensitive action and every opportunity missed to comfort and support the other. It breaks down gradually with every criticism or complaint voiced to the other without any affirmation and love. If one person treats the other with disregard, abuse, or dishonor, it can shut off blessings God has for the marriage.

There has to be something to look forward to in your marriage. If you're married to someone who is getting meaner and more inconsiderate with each passing year and seems to enjoy being that way, all you will see for your future is being alone with someone like that. You can either become resigned to that joyless life or choose to not lose the dream in your heart for the future. Ask God for a miracle. I have seen Him do a miracle in our marriage. It took years of praying, but I am glad I didn't give up.

Nine GOOD REASONS TO *Stay Married*

1. You will please God.
2. You will be healthier.
3. You will live longer.
4. You don't have to divide up your income.
5. You don't have to divide up your children.
6. You don't have to lose friends.
7. You can build something together.
8. You won't leave a legacy of divorce for your family.
9. You can lift up one another when you fall.

No one knows what really goes on in a marriage except the two people who are in it. Every marriage can be vulnerable. Every husband-and-wife relationship takes work. Even in the best of situations, a marriage can still deteriorate and fall apart. I have seen what appeared to be the greatest of relationships disintegrate. Nothing surprises me in that regard anymore.

You have to do whatever it takes to turn your marriage in the right direction and away from divorce. That means guarding your heart and not allowing into it what God says is evil (Proverbs 4:23). You have to say, "I will not let divorce be an option for me. I will not seek divorce as the solution to my marriage problems."

It pleases God when you and your husband (wife) take a strong stand against divorce. Declare that you are building your marriage on the Word of God, and therefore you will not allow the enemy to break apart what God has joined together. Declare that your marriage is under God's covering, and you will not put other things or people before God or your husband (wife). Ask God to help you both see where work or activities have taken over one or both of your lives.

Be brave and ask your spouse to share how *he (she)* feels about your marriage. He (she) will surely be more than happy to tell you. But the thing is, you have to *listen* to what he (she) says and *not ignore* it. You have to *show interest* in his (her) *perspective*. Ask God to help you get rid of any anger, resentment, unforgiveness, and bitterness *before* you come together to talk. These emotions have no place in a marriage that lasts.

Pray That You Both Will Never Settle for an Emotional Divorce

What happens in your mind and emotions affects your relationship. The truth is that the enemy of your soul, your purpose, and your marriage relationship wants to influence your mind. Any exposure to outside influences that threaten the purity of thought you need to have toward each other, and any worldly and self-centered attitudes that destroy your trust in each another, will always cause your life together to become less than what it was intended to be.

Even though a couple may be committed to staying married, their minds and hearts can still be divorced from one another. When that happens, it sucks the oxygen out of a marriage, and it becomes lifeless. The Lord does not like that. And neither do we. Living in a dead and miserable marriage is hell on earth. And it doesn't glorify God in the least.

Whenever one spouse starts to feel *unloved*, and the other spouse is *unloving*, they can become strangers living in the same house but never making contact. And this is far more common than most people care to admit. If one or both of them then become involved in the activities of life and never include the other, they are allowing emotional divorce. They will grow completely apart if they don't take immediate steps to stop it. They have to start saying no to everything and everyone else and yes to each other. They have to decide if those activities and people are going to be that important to them if their marriage fails.

Don't settle for an emotional divorce. Don't settle for less than what God has for you in your marriage. And what He has for you cannot come about if you have a big "D" branded on your heart that represents the divorce you are always considering and leaving open as an option. Once that gets into your heart, it will start to burn an imprint. If you let it stay there long enough, your relationship will stop growing because you now have a clear way out.

We sometimes believe our heart is a private domain, and we can think and feel whatever we want, but it's not true. Whenever you entertain a thought that isn't of the Lord, you are inviting trouble. If you are struggling with thoughts of divorce, draw near to God and ask Him to fight the battle for you. "Do not be afraid. Stand still, and see the salvation of the LORD, which He will accomplish for you today...The LORD will fight for you, and you shall hold your peace" (Exodus 14:13-14). Put a protective guard over your heart, and don't let the "D" word in. You will be glad you stood your ground in the battle. If it still does not work out, you will have peace in knowing you did the right thing to the best of your ability.

Pray That You Both Will Consider the Need for Intimacy

Regarding your sexual relationship, the Bible says, "The wife does not have authority over her own body, but the husband does. And likewise the husband does not have authority over his own body, but the wife does" (1 Corinthians 7:4). That doesn't mean that you allow your husband (wife) to abuse you. Nor does it mean your spouse can force you to do something you don't want to do. And neither of you should require the other to practice abstinence far more than he (she) wants to. It means that if your spouse needs intimacy with you, you should provide it or have a really good reason why you can't. You have to consider your spouse's needs ahead of your own preoccupation.

Outside of the Lord's ways, sex is all about "*me* first." It's something that will make *me* feel better about *me*. But in the Lord, you always have to put one another first. So if you don't want to be intimate because you have been so hurt or disappointed by your spouse that you don't even want to be touched, then say so. Not saying anything and trying to force intimacy will surely make it go badly and do more damage than not doing anything at all. Tell him (her) you need to talk first and get things off your chest. On the other hand, just "not feeling like it" isn't a good enough excuse. Part of finding success in anything you do is doing what you need to do when you need to do it, whether you totally feel like it at the moment or not. Of course, there are times when you feel sick, are in pain, or are extremely exhausted, but that should not become the norm unless you are disabled for some reason.

Putting each other first in your sexual relationship will protect you both from temptations that arise. Whenever you refuse to have sex with your husband (wife), there is always the possibility that the enemy will place a snare right in front of him (her) the very next day. It may not be an actual person, but the sexual images that are everywhere could have a greater impact.

The stresses of life, such as building a career, establishing a home, raising children, coping with sickness or injuries, financial struggles, disagreements, and arguments, can all affect your sex life. But if each of you puts the other first, an active sex life will keep your relationship alive. It will also clear your mind and keep you feeling younger. It will balance things out between you. Forget about the bills, the disagreements, the kids, the problems at work, and concentrate on each other. If you always think in terms of *What can I do to make this good for him (her)?* instead of *What can I get out of this for me?*, then this will be a good thing.

As a helpful suggestion, it is important to bring any sexual encounter you had before marriage to the Lord and repent of it so that it won't affect your marriage now. Even if you never had sex before you got married, if there was anything you did with someone that you suspect was not God's will for your life, or if something was perpetrated upon you, ask God to cleanse you of the consequences and memory of that. If you don't do this, the recollections of these encounters will come up like specters every time you are intimate with your husband (wife). Ask God to bring all those incidents to mind so you can confess them before Him and be free. If you were a virgin before marriage, thank God that you don't have to go through this graveyard of past memories and kick out each ghost one by one.

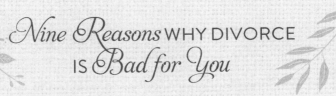

Nine Reasons WHY DIVORCE IS Bad for You

1. It destroys what was once your dream.
2. Many friends will desert you.
3. You have to divide up your children between you.
4. Your children will suffer more than you know.
5. You may lose your home.
6. There will be loss of income.
7. It takes a big toll on your health.
8. You have to divide up your belongings.
9. You may always have a sense of failure about it.

Pray That You Both Will Seek Godly Counseling When Needed

There may be times in your marriage when it seems as though your prayers are not being heard. Or you feel so upset that you can't pray. Or you are at an impasse and unable to get beyond the great disconnect between you and your spouse. Or there is so much hurt and strife between you that you can't even talk. That's when you need the help of a good, godly marriage counselor. And you may need more than one in a lifetime of being married because "in a multitude of counselors there is safety" (Proverbs 24:6). Especially if your husband (wife) won't sit down and work things out with you, then find a good Christian marriage counselor. Often it takes a wise third party who knows what they're doing to wake up people who are drifting apart.

Keep in mind that any problem can threaten a marriage seriously enough to cause a divorce. That's why I strongly suggest that if anything is negatively affecting your marriage to the point where you or your spouse are miserable or are contemplating divorce because of it, find a godly and wise counselor who is willing to work with you both in order to save the marriage. And I say "godly" because not all "Christian counselors" necessarily give godly advice.

My husband and I once sent a Christian couple who were close friends of ours to a Christian counselor we had seen ourselves. This counselor had given us godly counsel at an impasse in our marriage, and it helped us tremendously. However, when we sent this couple to him years later, he told them that their problem was so serious that they should get divorced. When the couple told us what happened, we were shocked and greatly disappointed.

Fortunately, this couple was committed to staying married and didn't take this counselor's advice. They ended up going to our pastor instead, and he helped them recover. They stayed married for more than 30 more years until one of them died of cancer in their sixties. There are many great Christian counselors out there. Ask God to lead you to the right one and keep praying the prayers in this book.

I am aware that the expense of counseling can make you think about it very carefully, but the cost of divorce is far greater in the long run and in so many ways. If you absolutely cannot afford even two or three sessions with a professional counselor, ask at your church if there is a person or a couple who is gifted in Christian marriage counseling— knowledgeable, mature, trustworthy believers who would be willing to help you save and enrich your relationship. There are many good individuals who will meet together with you regularly for free and help you talk through problems and work things out together. There are also great marriage classes, retreats, and seminars available for little or no money. Just make sure they are given by highly reputable people. Pray for God to lead you to the best people to help you.

Pray That You Both Will Resist the Idea of Divorce

Ideally, this idea of divorce is best decided once and for all *before* you get married. But whether you are recently married or you've been married a long time, you can still decide today to not let the word "divorce" become an option in your words or thoughts. Even if you and your spouse have talked about divorce in the past, you can still agree today to no longer think of it as an option. Decide to never speak of it as a threat to each other again. Instead, agree to talk things out and listen to each other's feelings and thoughts. Find a way to compromise and make it work. Agree that you will do whatever it takes to get beyond every impasse or problem that arises, because above all you don't want this relationship to fail. You don't want to divide up the property, the children, the income, and start all over again. You definitely don't want the things that have been bothering you for a long time to continue, but you *do* want to find a way to make some changes and work it out.

You have to remember that your words always have power. When you say the word "divorce" as a solution or a threat, there is a spirit of divorce that gets into your mind and heart—or your husband's (wife's) mind and heart—and the enemy waits at the door you have just opened to use it against you. You may have merely used the word as an idle threat, perhaps to bring about an awakening as to the seriousness of the situation, but not meaning to actually follow through on it. But now that thought has been planted in your husband's (wife's) mind too. You have put it out there in your relationship, and the enemy will feed the idea so it can grow like a cancer. Because our words have power, take the power of the word "divorce" away by confessing to God that you said it—or thought it—and ask for God's forgiveness so you can be released from the consequences of that.

Pray That You Both Stand Strong Against Infidelity

Keep in mind that the enemy despises your oneness with each other, and he will do all he can to undermine it. That's why everywhere you look there are sexual enticements to get you off track—if not in deed then at least in thought. Promiscuity is glorified. Temptation is justified. Sex *outside* of marriage is exalted far above sex within marriage. You can see sexual images on something as innocuous as a billboard while you're driving down the street, or even in regular news magazines, popular TV shows, or what is supposed to be a decent film. These images can water down the impact of your sex life with your spouse by making it seem less than what it should be. Or even worse, *more* than what it was ever intended to be.

Sex can be exalted to the point that if you are not experiencing romantic, fulfilling, amazing sex every time you are with your husband (wife), something must be wrong with you or him (her). Because of the way our society is crazed over sex, our minds can be so completely messed up about it that we can end up with anxiety or uncertainty. Something that God meant to be deeply meaningful and pleasurable can become another added pressure, giving you doubts about yourself or your mate. Sex was never intended to be an idol that we worship, but it has become that in our culture.

Sex was God's idea, and He had a specific plan for the way it should be so that our greatest fulfillment could be achieved. Adultery violates that plan, and the consequences for it are severe. In fact, God is so grieved by infidelity in marriage that, as much as He hates divorce, He allows infidelity to be grounds enough to justify it. That's why infidelity is one of the leading causes of divorce. If your husband (wife) committed adultery, you could get a divorce if you wanted to—no questions asked and you are free to go—because God understands the devastation of infidelity in our souls.

Infidelity does the greatest damage of all sins, besides murder, because its consequences are so far reaching. It not only violates a trust and a covenant made before God, but it hurts your heart and soul irreparably. Every other sin a person does is outside the body, but sexual immorality is a sin against your own body (1 Corinthians 6:18). Our bodies belong to God, and they are the dwelling place for His Spirit. Whatever we do with our body, we are doing with the temple of God's Holy Spirit (1 Corinthians 3:16-17).

Do you realize, *husbands,* that every time you are rude, critical, demeaning, verbally abusive, cruel, neglectful, or abandoning of your wife that you create in her a fertile ground into which seeds of unfaithfulness can be planted? Unless she is extremely strong in the Lord, deep longings and thoughts will come to her heart and mind, and she can become ripe for an affair of the heart, if not the body. It's amazing how attractive someone else can look to you when the person who is supposed to love you no longer acts as though he does (2 Timothy 2:22). If you have set your wife up for that kind of fall, then you are partly to blame for what happens.

Do you realize, *wives,* that every time you criticize your husband in a demeaning way, put him down in front of others, neglect to compliment him and let him know that he is valuable to you, or refuse to have sex with him for no good reason, that you make it much more difficult for him to resist the temptations that are everywhere around him? You can set him up for infidelity. He is more susceptible to flattery and unholy attention than he would have been otherwise.

Of course, there are certain husbands and wives who have already determined in their heart that they are open to the slightest advance from someone and will welcome any opportunity to commit adultery. There is nothing you can do with these people because they have a "self-sickness" and are wired for sin. They will not change without a professional counselor in their face confronting them, and even then that may not work. So don't blame yourself if you feel you have done your best to be a good husband or wife and your spouse still cheats. It is not your fault, and there is nothing you could have done to stop it. Tell him (her) "Goodbye and good luck!" and move on to a better life.

The more you give place to divorce as an option, the deeper the imprint burns, the greater the distance that grows between you, and the more disconnected you will feel from one another until you have a spirit of divorce setting up a stronghold in your life. Then it becomes a tearing of the heart. It becomes not about *if* you will divorce, but *when*. Once the "D" word takes hold in your mind and heart, the spirit of divorce takes over and gets the process rolling. It's as though a divorce demon says, "I'll take it from here." Then you stop making plans for a future together and you only make plans for a future alone. Things will get worse between you, and one day when you have strife, arguments, and discord, divorce will seem like a pleasant relief.

If you find yourself in a dead marriage relationship where there is no joy, no pleasure, no communication, no common interests or goals, nothing to look forward to, and no hope for the future—in other words, no fresh air—then you must do something immediately. Get before the Lord and confess every thought you have had of divorce so a spirit of divorce won't establish a stronghold in your heart. Pray for God to renew a right spirit in your spouse as well, and take away any spirit of divorce in him (her).

If This Has Already Happened to You

If divorce is already being considered at your house, just know that no marriage is too far gone to save if *both* partners want to save it. Even if you are married to someone who is determined to get a divorce, there are still things you can do and ways you can pray that can cause things to turn around. I've even seen marriages that have gone through divorce court and the divorce has been granted when either the wife or husband started to pray fervently for it to be reversed. And it was. However, if you have done all you can do and your spouse is still determined to leave, then release him (her) into God's hands. Let God deal with him (her), and you get on with doing what God has called you to do.

As I mentioned earlier, I was married before I became a believer to someone who also was not a believer. That marriage was doomed from the start because I went into it knowing it wouldn't last. I just wanted to have a home and some kind of security and companionship, even if those things were only temporary. Divorce was always at the back of my mind. We each had our own expectations for our spouse, and neither of us could ever live up to them. I didn't expect my marriage to last two years, and we never even made it to the second anniversary. As miserable as that marriage was—and *I* was the one who left *him*—the divorce was awful. It felt as though my life were ripping apart. I didn't know about covenants and God's ways, but even so I felt the violence God speaks of with regard to divorce. I can't imagine how painful a divorce is when you don't want it and your spouse does. I decided then that I would never do anything so stupid again. If I were to ever get married a second time, I would never go into it planning divorce as an option.

I am not saying there are no grounds for divorce. Some marriages are a disaster. Allowing yourself to be destroyed in a marriage is not glorifying to God, either. When I was married the first time, I told someone I would rather be dead than stay married, and I meant it. I didn't want to live another day in the hell I was in. I know many people have that same feeling, and my heart goes out to them. The person they are married to may be too mean, abusive, angry, frightening, godless, or evil to ever want to work things out. And people must do what they have to do in order to survive. Marriage was never designed by God to destroy you. He has a better life for you than that.

If your husband (wife) has already acted on his (her) attraction to someone else, keep in mind that anyone can feel an attraction to someone else. It's what they do with that attraction that matters most. The person feeling the attraction must shut it down immediately and completely. If you sense temptation happening in you, run as fast as you can to God, get on your face before Him, confess any obsessive attraction as sin, ask Him to take it away completely, and stay there until it is gone.

The good news is that God will still bless *your* life, even if your spouse has to go through some hard things until he (she) gets it. The problem is that what happens to your spouse happens to you. Everything he (she) does affects you in some way. But when you pray, God can rescue you from any situation—even your spouse's mistakes or sins. You can even be rescued from any negative aspect of your marriage while God works through your prayers to restore it.

I have talked with more people whose marriages were devastated by infidelity than for any other reason. It's epidemic because of our culture. You may not realize how prevalent it is because few people let it be known to others. It's embarrassing for everyone involved, and not many want to disclose it. The way I see it, if your spouse commits adultery, you have three choices:

- **Choice 1.** God says you can leave, and He does not blame you for doing that. He has given you a way out. He understands that the pain of a husband's (wife's) adultery can be too hard to bear. He doesn't require you to endure it.

- **Choice 2.** You can stay and make his (her) life as miserable as he (she) has made yours by letting your anger, unforgiveness, and bitterness make him (her) pay for what happened for the rest of his (her) life. The problem with that is *you* will pay for it for the rest of your life too. Forgiveness is a must because the alternative will kill you. Don't even think of trying to pay your spouse back for all the pain he (she) has caused you. That never works, and it will always hurt you more than it hurts him (her). Plus, it makes you look bad, and then he (she) feels justified in finding someone else.

- **Choice 3.** You can stay and do whatever it takes to find healing and restoration for both of you and your marriage. If you choose to stay and work it out, and choose to hear what God says to you about how to proceed, He can work a miracle. This is definitely not easy—and everyone understands if you don't want to do that—but I have seen it done successfully.

Pray That You Both Will Consider What a Legacy of Divorce Means

Children always suffer in a divorce. If that isn't true, then why are there so many books for the hurting adult children of divorced parents? And why are they selling so well? It's because people who are products of divorce struggle terribly. They know what it's like to have their worst fears come upon them. They have seen their prayers that Mom and Dad won't get divorced not be answered by God. (That is, if they were not made to understand that their prayers weren't answered because of the strong will of one or both of their parents.) They blame themselves for the divorce. They have trouble in school because they are hurt, depressed, anxious, confused, and unable to concentrate. They frequently seek alcohol, drugs, and promiscuity as a way out of their pain.

For your children, divorce is like experiencing a death, only without the sympathy one receives from others when there is a real death. In a physical death there is a mourning period, a period of recovery, and then you eventually grieve less. With a divorce, however, they are not afforded a mourning period with sympathy cards. There is no period of recovery. And they never seem to grieve less. They may *appear* as though they do, but they carry the ramifications of the divorce into their own relationships. They have fear and insecurity in their own marriage later on. There may be exceptions to that, but they are not in the majority. The majority are hurting. Keeping your children from all that pain is worth whatever effort it takes to stay peacefully married.

If you have children and you are already divorced, pray they won't blame themselves. Ask God to heal them of any guilt they carry for thinking that if they had been a better child, then this divorce wouldn't have happened. And pray they won't blame you or your spouse either. Everything that goes wrong in their life after the divorce might be seen as their parents' fault. They will have a harder time honoring you if they are blaming you for their miserable life. Pray that they will forgive you and your husband (wife) so they can be free of anger, and so they won't grow up and take their anger out on the person they marry.

Pray That You Both Will Be Strong and Resist Temptation

No matter how much you try to live a sinless life, there will always come some kind of temptation. And you have to remember that when it comes, it is not God helping you to find greater fulfillment; it is the enemy trying to destroy you. But God will give you a way out. He says to *submit* to *Him* and *resist* the *devil,* and when you do, the enemy has to leave (James 4:7). If you ever find yourself being tempted, resist all inclination to act on it, humble yourself before God, and pray until the enemy is forced to exit.

The important thing in marriage is to guard your heart from any stray thoughts (Proverbs 4:23). If you are ever with other people and find a particular person attractive, force yourself to resist those thoughts. Ask God to help you and your spouse keep your eyes on each other. The Bible warns us about being enraptured by immorality, saying that the adulterer "did not know it would cost his life" (Proverbs 7:20,22-23). Lust seduces us away from the life God has for us and into the pit the enemy has set as a snare.

An adulterous spirit is everywhere in our society. It's in the workplace, in the neighborhood, sadly in some churches—nearly every place you go. It is impossible to avoid some kind of contact with it completely. You have to be clear in your understanding of what it *is*— which is a trap to ensnare and destroy your marriage. And what it is *not*—a means of achieving true happiness and fulfillment.

Remember that no matter how strong the temptation is, God will not allow you to be tempted beyond what you are able to resist. He will show you a way out and give you the strength and ability to successfully resist it (1 Corinthians 10:13). Cling to God and embrace Him as your way out of all temptation.

I just heard on the news that more and more married couples are choosing to continue living together after they divorce and lead separate lives. Their reason is that "it's cheaper that way." But I have an idea. Why not do what it takes to stay together and actually learn to love and enjoy one another? It can be done with hearts that are *repentant enough* to be *willing* to let God *change them.* Even if you are the only one with a willing heart, your humble prayers can pave the way for God to do miracles in you, and your husband (wife), and in your marriage relationship. It's worth trying for.

PRAYERS *for* MY MARRIAGE

Prayer to Keep Us from Seeing Divorce as an Option

Lord, I pray You would help my husband (wife) and me to always be able to rise above any thoughts of divorce as a solution to problems in our marriage. Keep our hearts so close to You and to each other that we never even speak the word "divorce" in regard to each other. Help us to always be affectionate to one another, "in honor giving preference to one another" (Romans 12:10). Show us where we are doing things that are breaking down our marriage instead of building it up. Teach us both to grow stronger in You so we treat each other in a way that pleases You.

Enable us to stand strong together through every situation. Keep us from falling into denial about what is going on in our relationship so that we are never blinded to what the enemy is doing.

Take away any ungodly attraction from our hearts and replace it with Your love. Show us what we can do to build each other up and be what we need to be for each other. Keep us from all pride, and give us repentant hearts before You if ever we are even tempted in our thoughts. Help us to be cleansed to become "a vessel for honor" for Your glory prepared for every good work (2 Timothy 2:20-22). Keep us far from anyone who would try to lead us into anything ungodly. Help us to always live in integrity before You and each other so that we will walk securely (Proverbs 10:9). In Jesus' name I pray.

Prayer to Keep Me from Any Temptation to Consider Divorce

Lord, I pray I will not allow divorce to be a part of my thoughts at any time. If I have ever considered divorce in my mind or have seriously uttered that word to my husband (wife), family members, or friends in regard to my marriage, I confess that before You and ask You to forgive me. I know it displeases You and You hate divorce. I do not want to grieve Your Spirit, so I pray You would help me to never do that from this day forward.

I smash down any dream I have entertained of being loved by someone else. Help me to see this as a false god I have set up to worship in place of You. Show me anything in me that has given place to infidelity in my heart. If ever I have thought of another man (woman) and how it would be like to be married to him (her) instead of my husband (wife), I confess that as sin. Take all sinful and lustful thoughts out of my heart. I refuse to listen to the lies of the enemy telling me that anything would be better for me than what I have in my husband (wife).

I reject any spirit of divorce that I have invited into my heart and our marriage by the careless words I have spoken or thoughts I have had. I recognize these thoughts as evil, and I repent of them before You. I turn to You for solutions to any problems in my marriage. Give me wisdom to do things Your way. In Jesus' name I pray.

Prayer to Keep My Husband (Wife) from Any Temptation to Consider Divorce

Lord, I ask that You would keep any thoughts of divorce out of my husband's (wife's) mind and heart. If he (she) ever entertains those kinds of thoughts, I ask that You would open his (her) eyes to see how far away that is from Your best for his (her) life and our lives together. For any time he (she) has ever thought of the word "divorce" as a way out of our problems, I come before You on my husband's (wife's) behalf and ask for Your forgiveness. Forgive him (her) so that a spirit of divorce cannot find a home in his (her) heart. If it already has, I ask that You would break that stronghold by the power of Your Spirit.

I pray that my husband (wife) will never be lured into any trap or enticement by the enemy. Open his (her) eyes to see that if You are for us, no one can be against us and succeed (Romans 8:31). Enable him (her) to "taste and see" that You are a good God and that he (she) will find the greatest blessings by following You and trusting in Your ways. (Psalm 34:8). Show him (her) a better way, which is Your way for our lives. Let there be no divorce in our future. In Jesus' name I pray.

TRUTH *to* STAND ON

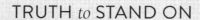

The Lord God of Israel says that He hates divorce,
for it covers one's garment with violence.

MALACHI 2:16

If any brother has a wife who does not believe,
and she is willing to live with him, let him not divorce her.

1 CORINTHIANS 7:12

A woman who has a husband who does not believe,
if he is willing to live with her, let her not divorce him.

1 CORINTHIANS 7:13

Watch and pray, lest you enter into temptation.
The spirit indeed is willing, but the flesh is weak.

MATTHEW 26:41

If two lie down together,
they will keep warm;
but how can one be warm alone?

ECCLESIASTES 4:11

PRACTICAL STEPS *to* GOING DEEPER

1. Read Colossians 3:13, Ephesians 4:32, and Proverbs 4:23-27 in your Bible. In light of these Scriptures and with regard to your spouse, what should you both do? Write your answer out as a prayer for you and your

husband (wife). (For example, "Lord, help my husband (wife) and me to always be forgiving of one another and _____.") Be specific if you recognize places where either of you fall short in that respect.

2. Read Psalm 62:5-7 in your Bible. Write this section of Scripture out as a prayer, telling God that you want to always run to Him when things become difficult rather than away from Him toward thoughts of divorce. Pray for the same thing for your husband (wife). Ask Him to help you both trust in His ability to protect and transform your marriage relationship.

3. Read 1 Corinthians 13:4-7 in your Bible. This description of how true love behaves is fantastic. Write out a prayer asking God to enable you and your spouse to be able to *do*, and *not* do, the things listed here for each other. Specifically mention what you each already do that demonstrates love for each other. List also the areas where you feel you both need improvement.

14

Pray to Keep Hope and Faith in the God of Miracles

*T*here are different seasons in every marriage, just as there are different seasons in the life of every man or woman. In marriage there is first the *romantic-exciting-passionate-fun-getting-to-know-each-other* period. This is when love is so heady you can't see clearly, which means you can't always see exactly what you've gotten into. Love is blind, so you focus on the good things and may think the questionable things are cute. The intensity of that period will fade no matter how hard you try to keep it from happening, and although that feeling is great, it is also exhausting.

The next stage is the *busy-making-a-home-establishing-a-career-getting-to-really-know-each-other* time. When children come along, there is the *too-little-sleep-never-a-moment-when-something-doesn't-need-to-be-done-and-there-is-not-enough-time-in-a-day* season. Later comes the *children-are-gone-and-you-have-to-remember-why-you-got-married-and-get-to-know-each-other-and-fall-in-love-all-over-again* period.

Then it's the *I'm-too-old-to-put-up-with-this-anymore-and-I-don't-want-to-spend-what-time-I-have-left-with-this-kind-of-upset-so-some-changes-have-to-be-made* season. And, unfortunately, that is where a lot of marriages end. But think how good it could be if you can both work hard through each season of life, and be willing to make changes and adjustments as needed. You would then have the *I-hope-we-grow-old-together-because-I-don't-want-to-start-over-with-anyone-else-and-*

I-know-we-will-take-care-of-each-other-until-the-end season to look forward to.

Things can go wrong in a marriage in any one of these seasons, but if you know these times are coming, and you also know they will end as you move into another season, it makes getting through them a lot easier. It gives you hope in each season. It gives you faith to believe for a miracle in the difficult times.

You may feel full of hope about your marriage today, and if so, I pray that it will always be that way for you. May you both be prisoners of hope no matter what happens in your lives together (Zechariah 9:12). However, if you ever do start to feel hopeless about any particular aspect of your marriage or your life, let this chapter be an encouragement to you. And if you ever get to the point where you feel that all hope is lost for your marriage and it would take nothing less than a miracle to save it, then I have good news for you. God is in the miracle business. That means even if it got so bad that you were in divorce proceedings, and the divorce papers had already been signed and the ink is completely dry, there is still hope because you can run to the God of the impossible and ask Him to work a miracle.

Over the years I have heard from countless couples who had come to that point in the divorce proceedings, and one of them started to pray for the other and things turned around to the point of total reconciliation. They canceled their plans to be divorced and got completely back together. Some had to get remarried because the divorce was final. How can that be anything less than a miracle?

One particular couple I talked to is especially precious to me because their story is extremely touching and miraculous. They waited for more than two hours after I spoke at a couples' event while I signed books. I saw them waiting, and at the end of the line they came up to me. They told me that at one point they had experienced great strife in their marriage and had separated. While they were separated, he was put in prison for a year, and she eventually filed for divorce. He received the Lord while in prison, and the day before he was to be released, someone gave him a copy of my book *The Power of a Praying Husband.* He read the entire book the day and night before he was to be freed from prison, and he said he knew in those moments as he was reading that his life would never be the same. He called his wife when he got out and told her what had happened and that God had revealed to him what kind of husband he was supposed to be and how he needed to be praying for her every day. He asked her to forgive him for not being a good husband and to take him back. And he promised to do whatever it took to be the husband she needed.

His part of the story was amazing enough, but then his wife went on to tell her half of the story. She said that she too had been given one of my books just a few days before her soon-to-be ex-husband was to be released. It was called *The Power of a Praying Wife*. When she read it, she said her eyes were opened as to how she needed to be praying for her husband.

As they were relating this story to me, their eyes filled with tears, and they struggled to get out the words without choking up. They told me that they had driven hundreds of miles just to tell me their story and to thank me in person for writing those books and saving their marriage. I told them *God* saved their marriage because they were willing to humbly pray and do what He asked them to do.

At the point I met them they had canceled their divorce and were back together, and their marriage was strong and their lives had been set on a totally different path than they had ever been on before. They showed me their worn-out books and asked if I would sign a special message to them, which I felt honored to do. I told them that meeting them and hearing their story was one of the best gifts I have ever received, and I will always remember them and keep them in my prayers. They were in a hopeless situation, but when they started to pray for one another the way God wanted them to, and learned to live His way, God did a miracle.

Our God is a God of hope. He is the all-powerful God of the universe, and nothing is too hard for Him. He wants us to have faith in Him to work miracles in our lives. What He did for them, He can do for you if you will commit to pray for your husband (wife). God will be with *you* to guide and help you every step of the way. God's will is to save, restore, and preserve your marriage, and if you seek Him for that, He will give you everything you need to do it.

What to Do When You Need a Miracle

You may not feel hopeless about your marriage, but perhaps you are concerned about one important aspect of it. Or maybe your *spouse* has a habit or reoccurring problem that drives you crazy. Or it could be *you* who has developed a habit that your spouse has no patience with, and without his (her) support, you feel you cannot overcome it. Or it could happen that you feel hopeless because you can't see how your situation can ever be any different. But take comfort in knowing that no matter what your particular situation is, as long as you walk close to God, there is always hope.

The Bible says, "Weeping may endure for a night, but joy comes in the morning" (Psalm 30:5). Your sorrow has an end. Even though there are no guarantees that your spouse will change, it is certain *you* will. And if *you* do, there is a greater possibility that *he (she)* eventually will too. But still, he (she) has a will, and if he (she) *will not* listen to God speaking to his (her) heart—exactly the way you have been praying that he (she) would—then keep in mind only God can make changes in us that last. You have to pray that God will make those changes and cause your husband (wife) to have an open heart to hear God. We have to maintain our unwavering faith in God in the process.

Remember that God is a God of miracles. He can bring back what has been lost, and He can resurrect what has died. When you turn to God as your only hope for a miracle, you are in the best position to receive one. But you must come to the point where you give up—not on the marriage, but on trying to make a miracle happen yourself. Just humble yourself before God like a child and tell Him you can't do this without Him (Matthew 18:4). Tell Him you have come to the point where your hope is entirely in Him, and you trust that you will never be disappointed because of His great love for you. The hope that is in you reflects the faith you have in God and His Word, which says that all things are possible to him who believes (Mark 9:23).

Put your hope in the Lord. Know that anything can happen because He is the God of the impossible. God is in charge, and He can turn anything around in an instant. You can be in despair one moment, and after you seek God for help, suddenly you can have a change of heart and be headed in the direction of joy. One of the greatest things you can do while waiting for your miracle is to invite the joy of the Lord to rise in your heart.

Keep making happy plans for the future. One of the things that having hope allows you to do is to keep making plans for your future. Hopelessness, on the other hand, keeps you from seeing a future at all. Jesus said, "By your patience possess your souls" (Luke 21:19). At first glance this verse seems as if you almost have to be passive and wait around for things to happen and someday maybe they will get under control. But the word "patience" can be active as well as passive. Being patient can mean bearing up under pressure. Sometimes victory comes simply because we are patient enough to not give up hope that we *have* a future—even if we have to fight one battle after another to get there.

Refuse to give up. Too many people give up way too early. I could have given up in my marriage a long time before I started to see changes in my husband—and in me. But both of us have truly changed over the years. And I believe these changes are lasting because God did a miracle in our lives. I feel Michael and I communicate far better now, and he doesn't let anger control him as before. It took a lot of prayer, and bearing up under pressure, but it happened. We made it, and we are in that last stage now, with more than 48 years of marriage. We know we will always be together, and whatever happens we will work through it. There is great peace in that.

Seek the peace God has for you. You can't view losing hope as the end of the world. It is actually a setup for God to do a miracle. We win by standing strong to the end. We say, "God, help me to be at peace where I am right now in the situation I am in, knowing You won't leave me there forever. Help me to say as Paul did that " 'I have learned in whatever state I am, to be content' " (Philippians 4:11).

Ten Things TO REMEMBER
ABOUT *God's Peace*

1. ***Knowing God brings strength and peace.*** "The LORD will give strength to His people; the LORD will bless His people with peace" (Psalm 29:11).

2. ***Seeing the Lord fight for you brings peace.*** "The LORD will fight for you, and you shall hold your peace" (Exodus 14:14).

3. ***Humility brings peace.*** "The meek shall inherit the earth, and shall delight themselves in the abundance of peace" (Psalm 37:11).

4. ***Obedience brings peace.*** "Oh, that you had heeded My commandments! Then your peace would have been like a river" (Isaiah 48:18).

5. ***Faith brings peace.*** "Your faith has saved you. Go in peace" (Luke 7:50).

6. ***Following Jesus brings us His peace.*** "Peace I leave with you, My peace I give to you; not as the world gives do I give to you. Let not your heart be troubled, neither let it be afraid" (John 14:27).

7. ***Life in the Spirit brings peace.*** "To be carnally minded is death, but to be spiritually minded is life and peace" (Romans 8:6).

8. ***Living God's way brings peace.*** "The work of righteousness will be peace, and the effect of righteousness, quietness and assurance forever" (Isaiah 32:17).

9. ***Loving God's laws brings peace.*** "Great peace have those who love Your law, and nothing causes them to stumble" (Psalm 119:165).

> **10.** *Pursuing peace with others brings peace.* "Pursue peace with all people, and holiness, without which no one will see the Lord" (Hebrews 12:14).

As long as you are walking with God, and you have not turned your back on the Holy Spirit, then you are going from glory to glory and strength to strength, whether it feels like it or not. "We all, with unveiled face, beholding as in a mirror the glory of the Lord, are being transformed into the same image from glory to glory, just as by the Spirit of the Lord" (2 Corinthians 3:18). When you walk with the Lord, you are always becoming more like Him.

So once you pray, believe that God has heard and move into the peace that He has for you. It's not the kind of peace you can get from anything in the world, because there is no earthly reason for it (John 14:27). But His peace will help you to bear up under pressure. And that sounds like a good future to me.

If This Has Already Happened to You

Even if you or your husband (wife) has lost hope in your marriage, if just *one of you* wants your marriage to succeed—and *God* wants your marriage transformed—that's two out of three. And that is a powerful enough majority to be able to sway the last third of the equation. So pray that God will give you and your husband (wife) the ability to see your situation from the Lord's perspective. Pray that you both will be able to lift your eyes up to where your help comes from (Psalm 121:1-2).

If you are truly wanting to see your marriage enriched and made to be all it's supposed to be—which I know you do or you wouldn't be reading this book—then don't be around people who tell you that you are crazy to even consider staying together. Pray that any pain, disappointment, or discouragement you or your spouse experience will drive you closer to God and not farther away. Find people who are supportive of what you are trying to do, and believe for, in your marriage. (Unless, of course, you are in an abusive situation and people are trying to convince you to get out for your own safety. Read chapter 2.) Be around people who will pray with you and for you. Spend time with people who are full of hope and faith and will stand with you in prayer.

If you've been married long enough to experience more than a few trials, know that prayer to the almighty God of the universe, who created marriage in the first place, will unleash His power to restore it. God says, "When you pass through the waters, I will be with you; and through the rivers, they shall not overflow you. When you walk through the fire, you shall not be burned, nor shall the flame scorch you. For I am the LORD your God, the Holy One of Israel, your Savior" (Isaiah 43:2-3).

Remember that hopelessness doesn't happen overnight, although things can happen suddenly that thrust you into a hopeless state. Hopelessness usually happens little by little, as each offense, each disappointment, each hurt builds up until discouragement sets in and covers those things like cement, solidifying the wall that has been built between you. Hopelessness usually happens when your prayers have not yet been answered and you don't believe they ever will be.

You may even be at a point where you feel as though you and your marriage are in a free fall and only the hand of God can reach out and save you before you crash at the bottom, but your prayers for your marriage can influence the hand of God at any moment. That's why you always have hope. When you have given up hope that *anything* will ever be any different, know that God's will is to change *everything* in the two of you and your situation. Know that you can reject hopelessness and put your hope in a miracle-working God.

When you put your hope in God, *you will not be disappointed* (Isaiah 49:23 NCV). *Good things will happen to you* (Lamentations 3:25), *you will please God* (Psalm 147:11), *you won't need to be sad* (Psalm 42:11), and *you will find rest* (Psalm 62:5 NCV).

Ten Good REASONS TO NOT LOSE *Hope*

1. ***God's plan is to give you hope.*** "I know the thoughts that I think toward you, says the LORD, thoughts of peace and not of evil, to give you a future and a hope" (Jeremiah 29:11).

2. ***God's Word gives you hope.*** "Whatever things were written before were written for our learning, that we through the patience and comfort of the Scriptures might have hope" (Romans 15:4).

3. ***God is pleased when you put your hope in Him.*** "The LORD takes pleasure in those who fear Him, in those who hope in His mercy" (Psalm 147:11).

4. ***When you put your hope in God, He keeps His eye on you.*** "The eyes of the LORD are on those who fear him, on those whose hope is in his unfailing love" (Psalm 33:18 NIV).

5. ***You have hope because of Jesus.*** "Blessed be the God and Father of our Lord Jesus Christ, who according to His abundant mercy has begotten us again to a living hope through the resurrection of Jesus Christ from the dead" (1 Peter 1:3).

6. ***There is always hope for your future.*** "There is surely a future hope for you, and your hope will not be cut off" (Proverbs 23:18 NIV).

7. ***God fills you with hope as you put your trust in Him.*** "May the God of hope fill you with all joy and peace as you trust in him, so that you may overflow with hope by the power of the Holy Spirit" (Romans 15:13 NIV).

8. ***You always have hope that God will deliver you.*** "He has delivered us from such a deadly peril, and he will deliver us again. On him we have set our hope that He will continue to deliver us" (2 Corinthians 1:10 NIV).

9. ***We have hope because God is faithful to keep His promise.*** "Let us hold fast the confession of our hope without wavering, for He who promised is faithful" (Hebrews 10:23).

10. ***True hope is when you don't give up, even when you see every reason to.*** "We were saved in this hope, but hope that is seen is not hope; for why does one still hope for what he sees?" (Romans 8:24).

The love and respect that is commanded in the Bible between a husband and wife is not based on "if you feel like it" or "if your spouse deserves it." *It's based on doing what God says to do because He has poured His love into you.* God loves us even when we do something wrong and disappoint Him. He loves us even when we neglect to spend time with Him and forget to show that we love Him back. He says we are to love others even when they don't seem to love us. "If you love those who love you, what reward have you?" (Matthew 5:46). The reason we can love at all times is because of the unconditional love of God poured into us. That's why you can keep loving your spouse even when you lose hope, and even when love seems to have died.

So don't allow negative thoughts about yourself, your spouse, or your marriage to dominate your mind. Demand of your thoughts that they be positive and good. Cast down every argument that "exalts itself against the knowledge of God, bringing every thought into captivity to the obedience of Christ" (2 Corinthians 10:5). *Require of yourself to be loving to others the way the Lord is toward you.* Set your heart as Daniel did to understand the Lord and His ways, and humble yourself before Him. The angel said to Daniel, "Do not fear, Daniel, for from the first day that you set your heart to understand, and to humble yourself before your God, your words were heard; and I have come because of your words" (Daniel 10:12). That means your prayers are being heard, too, whether it seems like it or not. And there will come a day when you will say, "I am so glad I put my hope and faith in the Lord, because He did not disappoint me." The Lord will bring change when you cry out to Him with a pure heart and ask Him to move in power in your life and in the life of your husband or wife. Refuse to give up hope! Stand in faith in the God of miracles for whom nothing is impossible!

Find God's Rest While You Wait on Him to Work

With God, things can change. People can change. But they have to at least *want* to. They have to at least have some degree of love and appreciation for their spouse and want to see that fire rekindled and the marriage restored and enriched. But if you don't give up praying and you keep doing what God is telling you to do, He will bring you to a place of rest.

Ten Things TO REMEMBER ABOUT *Finding God's Rest*

1. ***God has promised you rest.*** "Therefore, since a promise remains of entering His rest, let us fear lest any of you seem to have come short of it" (Hebrews 4:1).

2. ***You will find rest in God's presence.*** "He said, 'My Presence will go with you, and I will give you rest'" (Exodus 33:14).

3. ***God is with you to give you rest in every situation.*** "Is not the LORD your God with you? And has He not given you rest on every side?" (1 Chronicles 22:18).

4. *God has rest and refreshing for you if you will listen to Him.* "He said, 'This is the rest with which You may cause the weary to rest,' and, 'This is the refreshing'; yet they would not hear" (Isaiah 28:12).

5. *God's rest is complete and all-encompassing.* "Now the LORD my God has given me rest on every side; there is neither adversary nor evil occurrence" (1 Kings 5:4).

6. *Because you are God's child, He has rest for your soul.* "There remains therefore a rest for the people of God" (Hebrews 4:9).

7. *When you are burdened, God will give you rest.* "Come to Me, all you who labor and are heavy laden, and I will give you rest" (Matthew 11:28).

8. *When you turn to God, you will find rest.* "In returning and rest you shall be saved; in quietness and confidence shall be your strength" (Isaiah 30:15).

9. *When you obey God, you will find rest.* "To whom did He swear that they would not enter His rest, but to those who did not obey?" (Hebrews 3:18).

10. *When you yoke up with God, He will give your soul rest.* "Take My yoke upon you and learn from Me, for I am gentle and lowly in heart, and you will find rest for your souls" (Matthew 11:29).

Deepening your relationship with God is one of the best things you can do for your marriage. Get close to God and ask Him to show you the truth about yourself, about your spouse, about your marriage, and about His ways. God asks you to come to Him in your struggle and lay your problems at His feet, and He will give you a place of rest from them. Do that and you will have peace in your heart, no matter what is going on in your marriage.

Plan to Be a Success Story

Just last week I heard of another couple close to us who are getting a divorce. They are Christian parents of two and are well known in our community. They always seemed like the perfect family, so talented and funny. Everyone loves them. But their family is being *ripped apart* now, and all the people around them are *deeply saddened.*

Today I talked with a single mom who was married for twenty-five years but has been divorced for five, and she is still hurting over the divorce. She works very hard to support herself and her two children, and she always struggles with guilt over the time she has to be away from them in order to do that. Her entire extended family has been *negatively impacted* by this.

Recently a well-respected pastor divorced his wife because she resumed an unholy relationship with an old boyfriend. There had been tremendous loneliness in their marriage for some time. The congregation and the community are *shaken,* as well as their children.

Days ago a wonderful young married couple severed their relationship completely because of a terrible misunderstanding on both their parts. Their families are *devastated and grieved,* and the *fallout* seems to be without end.

I know all of these fine people personally, and it breaks my heart to see their *sadness and pain*—especially when I know that it all could have been avoided because God has a better way. I don't judge them. I know how hard it is to make a marriage work. But I also know that it is worth every effort to rise above the problems and hurt and see that your marriage not only survives, but becomes good and solid. That's what happened in my marriage, and it was worth the years it took of praying and learning to live God's way, even in the face of hopelessness. It was worth having my heart reconstructed by God until repentance, forgiveness, and love flowed through it every day no matter what. This is something God did because I was willing to do what it takes. That's why my prayer for you is that you too will find the strength, faith, and courage to do whatever it takes to see your marriage become one of the success stories.

It is never too soon to start praying for God to *enrich* your marriage. And it is never too late to start praying that God will *restore* your marriage. And I will be pulling for you all the way.

PRAYERS *for* MY MARRIAGE

Prayer to Keep Hope and Faith Alive in Our Marriage

Lord, I commit my marriage to You. May it become all You want it to be. Even in times where we may experience hurt or misunderstanding, I believe You are well able to keep all I have committed to You (2 Timothy 1:12). I pray You would help my husband (wife) and me to never fall into hopelessness, especially with regard to our relationship. Teach us to grow strong in faith in You, and help us to always put our hope in You, for You are our helper and protector (Psalm 33:20). May Your unfailing love and favor rest on us (Psalm 33:22). Enable us to inherit all You have for us because we continually have hope in our hearts (Psalm 37:9).

Lord, I pray we will always have patience to wait for You to work in our lives and our marriage. Thank You that because You were crucified and resurrected from the dead, we can have hope that You can resurrect anything in our lives no matter how dead and hopeless it may seem (1 Peter 1:3). Teach us to not give up on each other, but rather to "let patience have its perfect work" in us so that we "may be perfect and complete, lacking nothing" (James 1:4). Help us to "lay aside every weight, and the sin which so easily ensnares us, and let us run with endurance the race that is set before us, looking unto Jesus, the author and finisher of our faith, who for the joy that was set before Him endured the cross" (Hebrews 12:1-2). Enable us to keep our eyes on You. In Jesus' name I pray.

Prayer for Me to Have Strong Hope and Faith in the God of Miracles

Lord, I come before You and cast all my cares at Your feet, knowing that You care for me (1 Peter 5:7). I thank You that Your plans for me are for a good future filled with peace and hope (Jeremiah 29:11). Help me to remember that no matter what is happening in my life and in my marriage, You will never leave me or forsake me.

I confess as sin any time I have felt discouraged about my situation and especially about important aspects of my marriage. Your Word says that "hope deferred makes the heart sick, but when desire comes, it is a tree of life" (Proverbs 13:12). When time passes for so long and I see no change, help me not to feel heartsick and hopeless. You have said that whatever doesn't come from faith is sin, so I confess any hopelessness I have to You (Romans 14:23). I know it reveals that my faith in Your power to change things is weak. Help me to not hesitate having hope again out of fear that I will be disappointed. I commit to trusting You at all times. I pour out my heart before You, knowing You are my God of refuge (Psalm 62:8).

Teach me to become like a child—entirely dependent upon You, for I know that this is the safest place I can be. "Search me, O God, and know my heart; try me, and know my anxieties; and see if there is any wicked way in me, and lead me in the way everlasting" (Psalm 139:23-24). Enable me to become all I need to be. In the midst of challenges in my marriage I say, "Be merciful to me, O God, be merciful to me! For my soul trusts in You; and in the shadow of Your wings I will make my refuge, until these calamities have passed by" (Psalm 57:1).

Even though we may be hurt at times in our marriage because of things one or the other of us has said or done, or not said and not done, I know You are "able to do exceedingly abundantly above all that we ask or think, according to the power that works in us" (Ephesians 3:20-21). I declare that I will be strong and take heart because my hope is in You (Psalm 31:24). I pray that You, Holy Spirit, would give me "beauty for ashes, the oil of joy for mourning, and the garment of praise for the spirit of heaviness" (Isaiah 61:3). I have hope and faith that You can change everything in my life (1 Thessalonians 1:3). In Jesus' name I pray.

Prayer for My Husband (Wife) to Have Strong Hope and Faith in the God of Miracles

Lord, I release my husband (wife) into Your hands. I pray that any hopelessness he (she) has felt about himself (herself) will be taken out of his (her) heart. Make him (her) all You created him (her) to be. Break down any strongholds in his (her) mind where hopelessness has been allowed to reign. Help him (her) to put his (her) hope in You and understand that it is not by our might or power, but by Your Spirit that our relationship can be transformed to become all it was made to be.

Take away any hopelessness he (she) feels about me, our marriage, and our life together. Thank You that You are the God of hope, and You are "the same yesterday, today, and forever" (Hebrews 13:8). Help my husband (wife) to understand that because of Your power in our lives, our situation is never hopeless (John 14:26).

We may be "hard-pressed on every side, yet not crushed; we are perplexed, but not in despair" (2 Corinthians 4:8). That is because *You* sustain us. And we don't have to live with despair because our hope is in *You.* I pray that the eyes of his (her) understanding will be opened so that he (she) will come to understand "what is the exceeding greatness" of Your power toward those who believe (Ephesians 1:18-19). Make him (her) to be a pillar of righteousness for Your glory. Help him (her) to not cease his (her) "work of faith, labor of love, and patience of hope in our Lord Jesus Christ" (1 Thessalonians 1:3). I pray now that You, the God of all hope, will fill my husband (wife) with faith and hope in You, by the power of Your Holy Spirit (Romans 15:13). I pray You would lift up Your countenance upon him (her) and give him (her) Your peace (Numbers 6:26). In Jesus' name I pray.

TRUTH *to* STAND ON

Those who wait on the LORD shall renew their strength;
they shall mount up with wings like eagles,
they shall run and not be weary,
they shall walk and not faint.

ISAIAH 40:31

For everyone who asks receives, and he who seeks finds,
and to him who knocks it will be opened.

MATTHEW 7:8

The righteous cry out, and the LORD hears,
and delivers them out of all their troubles.

PSALM 34:17

O Israel, put your hope in the LORD,
for with the LORD is unfailing love and
with him is full redemption.

PSALM 130:7 NIV

Being confident of this very thing,
that He who has begun a good work in you
will complete it until the day of Jesus Christ.

PHILIPPIANS 1:6

PRACTICAL STEPS *to* GOING DEEPER

1. Read Hebrews 10:23 in your Bible. In light of this verse, why can you have hope that doesn't waver? What do you hope for with regard to your marriage?

Read Hebrews 11:1. What is the ingredient you need in your life in order to not lose hope?

2. Read Deuteronomy 20:3 in your Bible. When you see that your marriage is under attack, what should you not do? Write out a prayer to God telling Him that because His power is greater than anything the enemy tries to do to you and your husband (wife) and your marriage, and because His Word is in your heart, you will not be afraid of what lies ahead. Ask God to protect you and your spouse and teach you both to always put your hope and faith in Him without wavering.

3. Read 1 Corinthians 13:13 in your Bible. What is even greater than faith and hope? Write out a prayer asking God to help you and your husband (wife) to be so filled with God's love in your heart that it overflows to one another and gives you the hope and faith in the God of miracles that you need for a marriage that lasts a lifetime.